Noel, Tallulah, Cole, and Me

Noel, Tallulah, Cole, and Me

A Memoir of Broadway's Golden Age

John C. Wilson
with
Thomas S. Hischak and Jack Macauley

ROWMAN & LITTLEFIELD
Lanham • Boulder • New York • London

Published by Rowman & Littlefield
A wholly owned subsidiary of The Rowman & Littlefield Publishing Group, Inc.
4501 Forbes Boulevard, Suite 200, Lanham, Maryland 20706
www.rowman.com

Unit A, Whitacre Mews, 26-34 Stannary Street, London SE11 4AB

British Library Cataloguing in Publication Information Available

Library of Congress Cataloging-in-Publication Data

Wilson, John C., approximately 1899–1961.
  Noel, Tallulah, Cole, and me : a memoir of Broadway's golden age / John C. Wilson ;
with Thomas S. Hischak and Jack Macauley.
    pages cm
  Includes bibliographical references and index.
  ISBN 978-1-4422-5572-2 (hardback : alk. paper) — ISBN 978-1-4422-5573-9
(ebook) 1. Wilson, John C., approximately 1899–1961. 2. Theatrical producers and
directors—New York (State)—New York—Biography. I. Hischak, Thomas S., editor.
II. Macauley, Jack. III. Title.
  PN2287.W485A3 2015
  792.02'32092—dc23
  [B]
                                                                    2015018414

∞™ The paper used in this publication meets the minimum requirements of
American National Standard for Information Sciences—Permanence of Paper
for Printed Library Materials, ANSI/NISO Z39.48-1992.

Printed in the United States of America

To my wife
and
to Noel Coward,
who not only instigated, but also shaped and guided
my theatrical career for many years

~

Contents

~

Preface

We were *always* in the first or second row, peering down at the orchestra, close enough to smell the greasepaint. There were such hits as *Camelot*, *Gypsy*, and *Bye, Bye Birdie*, and they were tough tickets to get—but not for us. It was as if we knew Robert Goulet or Ethel Merman personally. That's what I remember about attending my first Broadway shows in the late 1950s and early 1960s with my parents.

The reason we had those great seats was because Mom's uncle—my great-uncle—was Broadway producer and director John C. "Jack" Wilson. Neither *Gypsy* nor *Camelot* were his shows, but that didn't matter. Landing front-row seats from Uncle Jack was never an issue. It seemed he knew everyone who had anything to do with Broadway and that everyone knew him. For me, that experience proved short-lived. Uncle Jack died in 1961, at the age of sixty-two. I was nine.

Thanks to his long-standing business and personal relationship with Noel Coward and Uncle Jack's major hits, including *Kiss Me, Kate* and *Gentlemen Prefer Blondes*, he really did know just about every famous actor, producer, director, playwright, composer, lyricist, and set and costume designer during Broadway's golden age. The modern-day equivalent—in 2015—of a typical weekend gathering at Jack and Aunt Natasha's Connecticut estate would be an invitation to join George Clooney, Taylor Swift, Bradley Cooper, Tory Burch, and Lady Gaga for cocktails—and having them all actually show up (refer to appendix B and you'll see what I mean). And did I mention that

Jack's wife Natasha was first cousin to the last czar of Russia—a bona fide Romanov—and a *Vogue* model?

The original manuscript for this book was an autobiography completed by Jack Wilson in 1958, near the end of his career. For nearly fifty years, it sat gathering dust in my mother's closet, along with other amazing memorabilia from his career, and then it arrived at my house after my mother passed away a few years ago. The question for me was whether to bring this work to life. I knew next to nothing about publishing a book and little about theater. We had heard the family stories about him for years—most of them more than once—but would anyone else be interested?

As I thought about this, I recalled one evening in the mid-1990s, when my wife Molly and I met Carol Channing at Radio City Music Hall in New York. We were attending a Liza Minnelli concert, and there was Miss Channing seated a couple of rows away. At intermission I approached her and introduced myself as Jack Wilson's great-nephew. Amazingly, she knew everyone on the Wilson side of my family by name and credited Uncle Jack with having launched her career when she was cast in *Gentlemen Prefer Blondes*.

I was also aware of Uncle Jack's influence at the Westport Country Playhouse, still active today in Connecticut. Wilson had been a pioneer at Westport, bringing big-name stars to summer stock and running a highly successful internship program, which provided its own launchpad for hundreds of teenagers interested in theatrical careers. But despite his professional accomplishments, the public record on Uncle Jack's influence was limited.

Throughout the years there have been numerous books, films, and television programs about Jack Wilson's close friends Noel Coward and Cole Porter, their star power and lifestyles. Most of these only mention Wilson in passing—sometimes with inaccuracy. Yet, I know from Jack's original correspondence, scrapbooks, and documents, which few have seen, he had an important, positive impact on the lives of such figures as Coward and Porter, as well as the lives of so many others. Why this discrepancy? Because Jack Wilson wasn't around for authors or screenwriters to interview. He never got to tell his story. The story was sitting in Mom's closet.

My colleague in this effort, Professor Thomas S. Hischak, explains in his introduction how we decided to respect Wilson's original draft and approach this fascinating project. I hope you enjoy reading it as much as we were excited to work on it.

In addition to Tom Hischak, who is an unbelievable resource on the history of theater and a joy to work with, I would like to thank the individuals who inspired and supported me during the early days of this project, especially Amber Edwards, Hank Scherer, David Charles Abell, Phil Furia, Robert Kimball, and, at Yale, Suzanne Lovejoy and Melissa Barton. For providing additional family facts and memories of their Uncle Jack, special thanks go to Theodore W. Cart and Jim Wilson. At home, thank you Molly for your love and never-ending support. I dedicate having this work come alive to the life of Jack Wilson and the memory of my mother, Barbara Cart Macauley.

—Jack Macauley

~

Acknowledgments

Unless otherwise noted, photographs appearing in this book are part of the John C. Wilson Archive, the entirety of which has remained in John C. Wilson's family since the death of Natalie Paley Wilson in December 1981. The family reserves all rights for any further use of these photographs. The editors wish to thank Photographic Solutions, LLC, in Norwalk, Connecticut, for its highly professional restoration and copying of these photos, some of which were more than 100 years old at the time of publication.

~

Introduction

John C. Wilson is . . . a man with his head in the clouds and his feet planted squarely in the box office.

—Noel Coward

I was aware of John C. Wilson as just a name in a lot of theater books, the producer and/or director of many plays by Noel Coward and others, and the man who staged the original Broadway productions of *Kiss Me, Kate* and *Gentlemen Prefer Blondes*. Aside from the fact that he worked with most of the top playwrights, performers, and other artists during a golden era of the American and British theater, I knew little else about him. In the summer of 2013, Wilson's grand-nephew, Jack Macauley (no relation to the hoofer Jack McCauley who appeared as Gus the Button King in the original *Gentlemen Prefer Blondes*), contacted me and said that he had inherited some family memorabilia, including an unpublished autobiography by Wilson, and was wondering if I would be interested in reading it. I immediately thought to myself, "A memoir by a man who was the business manager and romantic partner of Noel Coward? A man who frequently worked with Katharine Cornell, Alfred Lunt, Lynn Fontanne, Gertrude Lawrence, and others? A man who married a Russian princess and was part of Cole Porter's international set? Certainly I would be interested in reading it!"

John Chapman Wilson (1899–1961) was active during some of the most exciting years of the American theater, roughly 1925 to 1955. He had worn many hats during his lifetime, but by the late 1950s, he was winding down his career as director and producer, and looking back on his life and the many fascinating people he had known. Wilson was only in his late fifties himself, but he must have been in a nostalgic mood or maybe he had a premonition that his time was limited, because he embarked on writing it all down in an autobiography. We don't know exactly when he started the project, but the final draft dates to 1958. He died three years later, at the age of sixty-two. Whether Wilson made any attempt to get the autobiography published is not known, nor is it known to whom he showed the manuscript, if anyone. For half a century, the memoir, accompanied by photos, scrapbooks of clippings, playbills, and other Wilson memorabilia, was safely kept by the family. The time has certainly come for Wilson's memories and observations to be shared.

While the writing in the manuscript is polished and intelligent, it has some shortcomings, which an editor would have suggested fixing in 1958, and one might hope to address now. Wilson assumes that the reader knows the people he writes about. Fifty years ago, more Americans would have immediately recognized such names as the Lunts, Beatrice Lillie, Cecil Beaton, Clifton Webb, Katharine Cornell, Anita Loos, and others. These theater giants were not only still alive in the late 1950s, but also still working. Wilson writes about them in the present tense, which is touching yet odd for the contemporary reader. He also assumes that many of the famous plays he mentions are known to everyone interested in theater. Unfortunately, this is not the case today. Thus, we have attempted to "fill out" Wilson's autobiography and make it more accessible, while at the same time minimally altering his prose. Boxes have been added to describe people and titles that are important to know in understanding Wilson's text. If the reader is familiar with American and British theater history, these added descriptions may not be necessary and can easily be ignored. We have also corrected Wilson's occasional errors or inaccuracies, as any editor would. Throughout the autobiography, additions or explanations are clearly placed within [brackets] or in a separate box. In this way we hope to preserve Wilson's genial prose style, while making his autobiography more thorough and satisfying.

In this task I must acknowledge the assistance of Jack Macauley, who provided many family stories about Wilson, as well as photographs and scrapbooks for this project and the manuscript itself. Thanks must also be extended to Stephen Ryan at Rowman & Littlefield and Cathy Hischak for her careful proofing of the manuscript.

—Thomas S. Hischak

~

Prologue

Looking for Lorelei Lee

[In the spring of 1949, Wilson was hired by producers Herman Levin and Oliver Smith to direct the Broadway musical version of Anita Loos's best-selling comic novel *Gentleman Prefer Blondes*.]

In the theater I cannot recall ever having worked with a more coopera-tive author than Anita Loos, and we actually survived the trials of *Gentle-men Prefer Blondes* without one word of disagreement. There were the usual theatrical problems, however, starting, as always, with casting.

As the world must know, the character of Lorelei Lee was a dainty blonde, not overloaded with intelligence, but solidly and thoroughly kept. We auditioned at least fifty blondes, some of them famous and all of them dainty—although I cannot vouch for the other requisite of being natural blondes. The trouble was they weren't funny; the more *right* they looked, the less amusing they became. I was adamant during this period and insisted to Anita, Herman, and Oliver that we should not go into rehearsals until we found someone who could make us laugh. It was, after all, a comedy, and all we had got in the auditions to date was a wispy and slightly false sincerity.

Then one of us went for perhaps the second or third time to see a current revue called *Lend an Ear* and hit upon the idea of auditioning a girl in the cast called Carol Channing. She was tall, buxom, and by no standards dainty, the antithesis of everything we had been searching for, and the next day she came to read on the Ziegfeld stage and, for the first time, we all laughed. She was promptly hired, and a star was born.

Carol was a dream to work with. She had relatively little theatrical experience and knew it but decided to put her trust in me, and we worked together in perfect harmony throughout the entire production. She was particularly exciting to direct. If you came up with a bit of business, zany or otherwise, she would immediately seize upon it and proceed to embellish it. Nothing ruffled her, not even the troubles we were having with the authors at the time.

Herman Levin had bought Anita's book but was unsure of her ability to dramatize it, so he engaged Joe Fields, a well-known comedy playwright, as her coauthor. [Joseph Fields (1895–1966) was coauthor of such musicals as *Wonderful Town* (1953) and *Flower Drum Song* (1958), and such hit plays as *My Sister Eileen* (1940), *Junior Miss* (1941), and *Tunnel of Love* (1957).] After a number of weeks they unfortunately fell out, to the extent that during rehearsals Anita would sit on one side of that vast theater and Joe very definitely on the other. There came moments, however, when I needed additional dialogue or perhaps even an additional scene, whereupon they would each write their ideas on separate pieces of paper, which were solemnly handed to me over the footlights. It was then my job not so much to choose one scene or the other, but to select the best bits from their separate suggestions and weld them together for what usually turned out to be a darn good scene.

Carol accepted the changes without a murmur. She never complained and frequently just giggled. It suited her to play dumb, but it was obvious that underneath she was as shrewd and aware of what she was doing as [gossip columnist] Elsa Maxwell.

At the time Carol was married to a man called Axe, who must have led an interesting life. He played professional football for the Ottawa Rough Riders and was a private detective on the side. What with all this, plus being married to Carol, there couldn't have been a dull moment. But later in some scrimmage, which I presume was on the football field, he damaged his back, forcing him to retire and devote all his time to his wife. Fortunately by then Carol had been elevated to stardom and was well able to support his damaged coccyx, so he toured with her, brewed her morning coffee, but the atmosphere must have been contagious because he became wildly stage struck. The next thing we knew he was running a summer theater and subsequently Carol's career with mixed results. In any case, they were later divorced, and Carol married her business manager in California, Charles Lowe, who apparently has no trouble with his back. [Channing has been married four times. Her first husband was writer Theodore Naidish. Alexander "Axe" Carson was her second husband. Her third husband, Lowe, was her manager and publicist. After forty-two years of marriage, they separated, and he died in 1998, while divorce proceedings were pending. At the age of eighty-two, Channing married Harry Kullijian, her junior high school sweetheart, whom she had not seen in six decades. The marriage lasted eight years, terminated by his death in 2011.]

Anyway, *Gentlemen Prefer Blondes* was a smash hit, and Carol became the talk of the town overnight.

~

Chronology

1899 Born in Trenton, New Jersey

1913–1917 Attends Phillips Academy Andover

1917–1922 Attends Yale

1922 Tours Europe during the summer following graduation; works for brokerage firm in New York; acts at the Amateur Comedy Club

1923 Cast as an actor in *Polly Preferred* in San Francisco

1924 Works as assistant at Astoria film studio on Long Island

1924–1925 Travels in Europe

1925 First meets Noel Coward in London; returns to brokerage firm in New York; reunites with Coward in New York and they become lovers

1926 Becomes Coward's business manager; moves to London

1931 General manager for *Private Lives* on Broadway

1932 Forms Transatlantic Productions, Ltd., with Noel Coward, Alfred Lunt, and Lynn Fontanne

1933 Buys the Connecticut country estate and names it Pebbles

1934 Produces *The Shining Hour* in London; produces *Theatre Royal* in London; meets Natalie Paley in London

1935   Produces *Point Valaine* on Broadway; coproduces *The Taming of the Shrew* revival on Broadway

1936   Produces *Tonight at 8:30* in London; produces *Mademoiselle* in London

1937   Weds Natalie Paley at Pebbles; produces *You Can't Take It with You* in London; produces *Excursion* on Broadway; produces *George and Margaret* on Broadway

1939   Produces *Dear Octopus* on Broadway; produces *Operette* in London; produces *Set to Music* on Broadway

1941   Coproduces *Blithe Spirit* in London; produces and directs *Blithe Spirit* on Broadway; begins tenure as general manager, coproducer, and director at Westport Country Playhouse in Connecticut; produces and directs U.S. tour of *Blithe Spirit*

1942   Codirects *The Pirate* on Broadway

1942–1945   Operations at Westport Country Playhouse cancelled due to World War II

1942–1943   Coproduces U.K. tour of *Present Laughter*

1943   Directs *A Connecticut Yankee* revival on Broadway; coproduces *Lovers and Friends* on Broadway; coproduces *Present Laughter* in London; coproduces *This Happy Breed* in London; coproduces *There Shall Be No Night* in London

1944   Produces *Bloomer Girl* on Broadway; produces and directs *In Bed We Cry* on Broadway; produces *The Streets Are Guarded* on Broadway; coproduces *Private Lives* revival in London; coproduces *Love in Idleness* in London

1945   Directs *Foolish Notion* on Broadway; coproduces *Sigh No More* in London; produces and directs *The Day Before Spring* on Broadway

1946   Produces *O Mistress Mine* on Broadway; returns to Westport Country Playhouse as a coproducer and director; produces and directs *Present Laughter* on Broadway

1947   Produces *Ruth Draper* on Broadway; coproduces *The Importance of Being Earnest* revival on Broadway; produces and directs *The Eagle Has Two Heads* on Broadway; coproduces *Love for Love* revival on Broadway; coproduces *Present Laughter* revival in London; coproduces *Peace in Our Time* in London; coproduces *The Winslow Boy* on Broadway

1948   Coproduces *Power without Glory* on Broadway; produces *Private Lives* revival on Broadway; directs *Kiss Me, Kate* on Broadway

1949   Coproduces *I Know My Love* on Broadway; directs U.S. tour of *Kiss Me, Kate*; directs *Gentlemen Prefer Blondes* on Broadway

1950   Coproduces *The Lady's Not for Burning* on Broadway; directs *Bless You All* on Broadway

1951   Directs *Make a Wish* on Broadway; coproduces *Nina* on Broadway; coproduces *Relative Values* in London

1952   Produces and directs *The Deep Blue Sea* on Broadway; coproduces *Quadrille* in London

1952–1953   Produces U.S. television program *The Buick Circus Hour* on NBC

1953   Coproduces *The Little Hut* on Broadway; directs *Late Love* on Broadway

1954   Produces and directs *The Starcross Story* on Broadway; coproduces *The Burning Glass* on Broadway; coproduces *Quadrille* on Broadway

1955   Directs *Seventh Heaven* on Broadway

1957   Ends his tenure at Westport Country Playhouse; produces *Eugenia* on Broadway; sells Pebbles; moves to New York City

1958   Coproduces *Garden District* Off Broadway; completes his autobiography

1961   Dies in New York and is buried in Ewing, New Jersey

1981   Natalie Paley Wilson dies in New York; Wilson's archives (including his autobiography) go to niece Barbara Cart Macauley

2010   Barbara Cart Macauley dies; autobiography inherited by her son, Jack Macauley

2015   Autobiography published

CHAPTER ONE

~

Andover and Yale

This book is not about me. It is about the people with whom I have had the privilege of working, producing, and associating. If I intrude into the pages, as I shall, it will only be as a rack on which to hang their famous hats and coats, and to provide some context for my happy life and incredibly good fortune.

Even under the age of ten, my interest in the theater began to emerge. I would spend hours in my room, cutting mannequins and backgrounds for scenery from magazines and meticulously implanting them in shoeboxes with a sort of peephole at one end. As there was no taint of theatrical blood in my family on either side, these activities were looked upon with indulgent amusement, as if one were playing with a toy train or teddy bear. My parents even went so far as to give me several of those garish toy theaters that were so popular at the time. I'm certain that in their beneficent ignorance, they had no idea of what they were letting themselves in for down the road.

My father, James J. Wilson, owned and managed Wilson & Stokes, a local lumber company in Trenton, New Jersey, and served for several years as director of the local bank, Broad Street National. He was a stocky, dour gentleman whose only vices, as far as I knew, were coffee and cigars. He was a complete teetotaler, and it wasn't until his death that my mother ventured toward an occasional glass of sherry—preferably at her favorite resort, Pinehurst, North Carolina. Mother was a stout, grey-haired little lady, raised in a social Philadelphia family, which may have accounted for her lack of ability to run a household. She did have three children, however, and I am the

1

oldest of the lot. [He was born John Chapman Wilson on August 19, 1899, in Trenton, New Jersey. James J. Wilson was a prominent Trenton business-man, and the family lived an upper-class lifestyle that afforded servants, private schools, and other luxuries.]

Sister Dorothy came next. We have always been very close and in later years became even closer. She is comfortably married to a prominent luggage manufacturer, Theodore S. Cart, and she manages with miraculous efficiency a large household in New Jersey, a weekend cottage at a hunting and fishing lodge in Pennsylvania, and a winter home in Bermuda. Her husband and chil-dren, Barbara and Theodore W., have always been her main preoccupations. I know of no family more sedulously cared for. My younger brother, James Taylor Wilson, whom we have always called Bus, was the one I expected would take over our father's business interests, as my career path very definitely gleamed elsewhere. But a few years after father's death in 1937, Bus moved to Virginia, where he bought a farm with cows and horses, and set himself up as a country gentleman with his wife Jane and son James. Wilson & Stokes was eventually sold, and the bank was turned over to the board of directors. [Wilson neglects to mention that younger brother "Bus" Wilson did, in fact, become president of their father's lumber business, commuting from his Virginia farm to New Jersey for several years during the 1940s to run the company.]

As children we lived on a tree-shaded street in Trenton, appropriately called Chestnut Avenue. The house was large and comfortable but, in retro-spect, rather ugly. It had an over-furnished parlor that was never occupied and a cozy sitting room that always was. There was a large backyard, a gravel drive, a porte cochere, two hired girls, and more than plenty to eat. On Sundays, we cooked dinner ourselves, and I was allowed to dry the dishes, with the sullen assistance of brother Bus and the eager enthusiasm of sister Dorothy. Ours was a very happy childhood, and although I have since experienced a great number of varied milieu, I still look back on those early years with nostalgic affection.

I attended a private middle school in Trenton, rather ambitiously called the "Model School." In addition to the usual courses, they had a manual training department, where one was encouraged to demonstrate tactile skills and whimsies. Naturally, the first thing I built was a miniature theater that was rather unique. It featured a glass stage lit from below, and when I eventu-ally added a Victrola for musical accompaniment, it was a twelve-year-old's version of Dillingham and Ziegfeld combined! [Charles Dillingham (1868–1934) and Florenz Ziegfeld (1867–1932) were colorful Broadway producers known for their lavish productions.] The performers were again magazine cutouts, manipulated rather clumsily by me through what must have been appalling plots of my own concoction. But with the addition of the Victrola and the lights under the stage, I figured I was giving a helluva show. These performances were eventually witnessed by indulgent parents and a few carefully selected, and more than probably highly bored, neighbors.

At fourteen, I was off to Andover in Massachusetts. This was, and still is, one of the finest schools in the country, but I don't recall ever being happy there. [Phillips Academy Andover, founded in 1778, boasts famous writers, statesmen, judges, scientists, and U.S. presidents among its alumni.] I never liked getting up at 6:30 in the morning and don't like it to this day. Somehow I adjusted in a somewhat befuddled way, running on the track team and playing in the Mandolin Club. But my real love was the Dramatic Association, where I played anything that they would give me.

In addition to these amateur efforts, I was able at an early age to indulge in professional theater. On alternate Saturdays, we were allowed an afternoon in Boston. I don't know where my fellow students spent their time, but for me it was the theater. At that early and formative age, there were Vernon and Irene Castle, Billie Burke, Julia Sanderson, and Ina Claire (all of whom I was to know later) on the stages of the Colonial, the Wilbur, and the Shubert theaters, where I was to eventually sweat and struggle. [The Castles were celebrated ballroom dancers who appeared in Broadway musicals during the first two decades of the twentieth century. Burke, Sanderson, and Claire were popular on the New York stage, and Burke had a significant film career as well.] On one Saturday afternoon, I actually saw Sarah Bernhardt. I am sure she was magnificent, but being so young and not understanding a word she said, I'm afraid I didn't properly appreciate her. [Sarah Bernhardt (1844–1923), who always performed in French, toured the United States for the last time in 1915, so Wilson was about sixteen years old when he saw her in Boston.] In all my theatergoing experience, these were the most exciting days. It was pure glamour, make-believe, and excitement. It would be a long while before I learned of the toil and trouble that was behind the magic of those performances.

I attended Andover graduation in 1917 but did not earn a diploma, having proven desperately incapable of passing German. It was humiliating and, I expect, equally so for my family, but the college board examinations were passed and I moved to Yale for the next phase. The choice of Yale was a little offbeat, as several members of my family had been Princeton graduates, but by this time the Chestnut Avenue house had been sold and the family was ensconced in a charming new residence in Lawrenceville, only six miles from Princeton. Knowing my mother to be a pillow puncher, an organizer, and only too eager to look after her little boy, it seemed wise to put a comfortable distance between us.

During the summer, World War I crept up on those of us who had insensitively passed the age of eighteen. Some power in the government with an exaggerated view of our possible IQs decided that incoming Yale students should enroll in on-campus officer training instead of a regular academic class schedule. The college was divided into half Army and half Navy, and I ended up in the Navy lot. We were summoned at dawn by bugle calls, went through all sorts of drills, and on the whole were as thoroughly uncomfortable as anyone in a proper training camp should be. Most unhappy were the established Yale professors of great importance who were forced to instruct us on subjects about which they knew absolutely nothing. I recall one distinguished Greek scholar trying to explain the difference between port and starboard, and knowing less about it than we did.

In the end, everyone went through the motions. I had some special uniforms made by a New York tailor and admired myself very much. The naval corps also formed a band and sought out people of rumored musical leanings to participate. Not being very good in brass, I ended up playing the bass drum and can still recall with pleasant embarrassment marching up and down Chapel Street in New Haven, thumping away with the undisguised enjoyment of a Salvation Army bandsman. The nearest any of us ever came to the sea was the view from the Yale campus of Long Island Sound. This came to an end in November 1918, with the Armistice, which we celebrated with a vigor and excitement that should only have gone to people who had actually contributed to its achievement. The Armistice led to a holiday, the discarding of our uniforms, and the reopening of Yale after New Year's Day.

Again, I became the eager beaver anxious to prove himself in every possible field of endeavor: running the mile on the track team, singing in the Glee Club, writing rather undistinguished poems for the literary magazine, and even trying out for manager of the swim team. My heart, again and of course, was with the theater, and all primary extracurricular activities were devoted to the Yale Dramatic Association. At that time, Professor George Pierce Baker and his School of Drama were comfortably ensconced at Harvard, so our only theatrical outlet lay in the student organizations. We had no school of the theater but somehow managed productions two or three times per year. There was one great advantage at Yale in that our director was a sharp-tongued, highly intelligent, polished gentleman named Edgar Montillion "Monty" Woolley. I only wish that I had been sufficiently sophisticated to appreciate his wit and humor. In any case, he seemed willing to train my immature talents, and under his direction I "trod the boards" of the Shubert Theatre in New Haven, where I have since had a great many experiences—perhaps more adult, but certainly not as exciting.

Monty Woolley (1888–1963) was a celebrated educator who, later in his life, found fame as an actor and director. He was born Edgar Montillion Woolley in New York, to a prosperous family in the hotel business, and educated at both Yale and Harvard. He spent seventeen years teaching and directing drama at Yale (among Woolley's other students of note were Stephen Vincent Benét, Cole Porter, and Thornton Wilder), before becoming a professional director and actor. He staged several classic revivals and then turned to the musical theater to direct such shows as *Fifty Million Frenchmen* (1929), *The New Yorkers* (1930), *Walk a Little Faster* (1933), and *Jubilee* (1935). In 1939, he won applause after appearing in the musical *On Your Toes* but, with his pointed beard and sour hauteur, is best recalled as Sheridan Whiteside, the bellowing, cantankerous celebrity in *The Man Who Came to Dinner* on Broadway in 1939, and on screen in 1942. Woolley's other notable screen credits include *Arsene Lupin Returns* (1938), *Man About Town* (1939), *Since You Went Away* (1944), *The Bishop's Wife* (1947), and *Kismet* (1955), as well as the Cole Porter biopic *Night and Day* (1946), in which he played himself. Woolley was also popular on the radio as an actor and raconteur.

Many years later, my name appeared on the marquee of that same theater as producer, and across the street at a movie house was Monty's, in—naturally—larger letters. With a Brownie camera, I managed to focus our two billings in one picture and later mailed the snapshot to him in Hollywood in memory of our earlier days. When I first knew him, the traditional Woolley beard had not yet blossomed. He was short and rotund, with a tendency to overanimate his wasp-like wit. His method of directing was always constructive but delivered with a caustic sarcasm that he later brought to his own performances. Some years after our Shubert experiences, when both of us were no longer at the university, the Baker School of Drama was moved (thanks to Standard Oil millions) from Harvard to Yale; however, Monty was not asked to be on the staff, and letters from infuriated ex-members of the old "Dramat" began to flood the new organization, but to no avail. So Monty decided to go to Hollywood to seek his future.

By this time his beard was profusely evident and his waistline considerably expanded, although his financial prospects had not. Then one night George Kaufman—the producer, director, and, in this case, coauthor of *The Man Who Came to Dinner*—phoned Monty from New York to offer him the leading role in that same play. Monty thought it was a practical joke being played by one of his friends, and it took several more long-distance calls to convince

George S. Kaufman (1889–1961) was one of the most successful playwrights and directors of the American theater, with a four-decade career filled with hits. He was born in Pittsburgh and served on the staffs of newspapers in Washington, D.C., and New York, before joining with Marc Connelly to write his first successful play, the comedy *Dulcy* (1921), followed by such successes as *To the Ladies* (1922), *Merton of the Movies* (1922), and *Beggar on Horseback* (1924). Throughout his career, Kaufman was known as the "Great Collaborator," because all of his works (with the exception of the 1925 solo effort *The Butter and Egg Man*) were written with others. With Edna Ferber, he penned *Minick* (1924), *The Royal Family* (1927), *Dinner at Eight* (1932), and *Stage Door* (1936). With Morrie Ryskind, he wrote the musical librettos for *Animal Crackers* (1928), *Strike Up the Band* (1930), *Of Thee I Sing* (1931), and *Let 'Em Eat Cake* (1933). But it was with Moss Hart that Kaufman wrote his most interesting (and often successful) shows: *Once in a Lifetime* (1930), *Merrily We Roll Along* (1934), *You Can't Take It with You* (1936), *I'd Rather Be Right* (1937), *The Man Who Came to Dinner* (1939), *George Washington Slept Here* (1940), and others. Other works with other collaborators included *The Cocoanuts* (1925), *June Moon* (1929), *The Band Wagon* (1931), *The Late George Apley* (1944), *The Solid Gold Cadillac* (1953), and *Silk Stockings* (1955). Most of his stage works were filmed, and he contributed to such original screenplays as *Roman Scandals* (1933), *A Night at the Opera* (1935), *A Day at the Races* (1937), *Nothing Sacred* (1937), and *Star Spangled Rhythm* (1942). Kaufman was also a highly sought-after director. Aside from staging many of his own plays, he directed such hits as *The Front Page* (1928), *My Sister Eileen* (1940), and *Guys and Dolls* (1950). To the public, Kaufman was a master of the barbed riposte in newspaper columns, on radio, and on television, but his professional associates also admired his ability as a play doctor and impeccable sense of timing both in his writing and direction.

him that it was really Kaufman and the offer was bona fide. He returned to New York, took over the part of Sheridan Whiteside, and was an enormous success. His acting career blossomed. Hollywood, having ignored him in the beginning, raised its eyebrows, and at the close of the play, Monty found himself a star at Twentieth-Century Fox.

Monty's and my paths were to cross frequently in Venice at Cole Porter's palazzo and again later in Hollywood, where he led a rather solitary existence. After a day at the studio, he would appear in the smartest restaurants alone with a book, whereupon he would solemnly imbibe a considerable number of cocktails. Having reached the boiling point, he would put the book aside and cavort among the tables, visiting his innumerable friends. Owing to ill health, he eventually abandoned California altogether and put himself out to pasture at Saratoga Springs, New York.

One of my few intellectual successes at Yale was an election to the Elizabethan Club. [The Elizabethan Club at Yale was founded in 1911, as a place for informal yet serious discussion of literature, in particular of Shakespeare and others from the Elizabethan era. The club still exists today and houses rare manuscripts and folios from that period.] One went there for tea, and important professors of literature would drop in, as well as important (at least potentially) members of the student body. Conversationally, the bars were down, and one was stimulated by such exciting people as professors Skinner, Berdan, and Phelps. William Lyon Phelps was a particularly sympathetic man who worshipped the theater and did not hesitate to encourage young people's interest in it. As a result of his enthusiasm, no play ever played the Shubert without my presence, and under his insistence I also made many trips to New York to see everything from *Hamlet* to *The Ziegfeld Follies*.

One of the observations that Professor Phelps was very keen in making was that the best test of boredom in the theater was when your bottom began to ache. I have since learned that he was fundamentally and—to coin a phrase—"basically right." It was Professor Phelps who insisted that we see a new young actress named Katharine Cornell in an exciting new play called *A Bill of Divorcement*, then playing at the George M. Cohan Theatre in New York. A great many of us heeded his suggestion and were richly rewarded for our pains. Miss Cornell's performance was as exciting as the play, but as she was then a slip of an ingénue, she had not yet achieved the dignity and elegance that have since singled her out as one of theater's leading personalities.

Naturally, as a college undergraduate watching her performance, I hardly conceived that twenty-two years later, in 1943, we would be coproducing together. Our venture was called *Lovers and Friends* by Dodie Smith. It was a pseudo-intellectual drama about a well-bred English woman amorously involved with two men, one of them fortunately her husband. Kit not only coproduced, but also starred in it, and, of course, her husband, Guthrie McClintic, directed. With Motley doing the setting and costumes, we achieved a truly impressive production. [Motley was the name of three British theater designers who did scenery and costumes on Broadway and the West End.] Raymond Massey, whom I had known since my early London days, was costar, and we also had Henry Daniell, Carol Goodner, and Anne Burr in other important roles. Rehearsals progressed smoothly, as it is impossible, when working with Kit, for things to progress any other way. She is patient

Katharine Cornell (1893–1974) was an acclaimed actress and manager in the American theater. The daughter of a onetime theater manager, she was born in Berlin, where her father had gone to study medicine, and made her stage debut with the Washington Square Players in Manhattan in 1916. Afterward she continued her apprenticeship in stock companies before calling attention to herself as the determined flapper Eileen Baxter-Jones in *Nice People* (1921). Further accolades came when she portrayed Sydney Fairfield, the daughter who stands by her mentally disturbed father, in *A Bill of Divorcement* (1921); the lively Mary Fitton in *Will Shakespeare* (1923); and the shy, homely Laura Pennington in *The Enchanted Cottage* (1923). Cornell's performance in *Candida* in 1924 consolidated her reputation and was followed by two of her most sensational roles: the carnal, doomed Iris March in *The Green Hat* (1925) and Leslie Crosbie, who kills her lover, in *The Letter* (1927). Other successes at that time included *The Age of Innocence* (1928) and *Dishonored Lady* (1930). With producer-director Guthrie McClintic, whom she married in 1921, Cornell embarked on a career as actress and manager, and scored her greatest triumph in her first offering, when she played Elizabeth Barrett in *The Barretts of Wimpole Street* (1931). In 1934, she reprised her role as Elizabeth on tour, playing in seventy-seven cities in seven months. Among her subsequent achievements were leading roles in George Bernard Shaw's *Saint Joan* (1936), *Wingless Victory* (1936), *No Time for Comedy* (1939), *The Doctor's Dilemma* (1941), and *The Three Sisters* (1942). She then spent much of the war years playing Candida and Elizabeth Barrett for soldiers, followed by notable performances in *Antigone* (1946), *Antony and Cleopatra* (1947), *The Constant Wife* (1951), and *The Dark Is Light Enough* (1955). Her last appearance was as Mrs. Patrick Campbell in *Dear Liar* (1960). Although Cornell seemed tall and regal on stage, she was not quite five feet, seven inches, with dark hair, a dark complexion, and broad features that were called exotic and even Asian. She was unique in that she refused all offers from Hollywood, her only film being a cameo in the fund-raising movie *Stage Door Canteen* (1943).

and cooperative, and consequently makes fairly poor copy for the tabloids. Kit's love for the theater is unquestionably sincere, as she is by no means financially dependent on it, having inherited a large amount of money from her family in Buffalo. Her father had been blessed with the ingenuity and good sense to invent windshield wipers.

Guthrie, who has been her husband for a good twenty years, must have accumulated a fairly tidy sum himself, as throughout their alliance he has staged almost all of her plays and a great many others as well. They have a house in

Guthrie McClintic (1893–1961) was a notable director and producer most remembered for the productions he did with his actress-wife, Katharine Cornell. He was born in Seattle and studied at the University of Washington and the American Academy of Dramatic Arts, before making his acting debut in 1913. His directing career began when he became producer Winthrop Ames's assistant. McClintic embarked on his own when he produced and directed *The Dover Road* (1921). He subsequently directed, and frequently produced, such popular plays as *The Shanghai Gesture* (1926), *Saturday's Children* (1927), *Brief Moment* (1931), *Winterset* (1935), *Ethan Frome* (1936), John Gielgud's *Hamlet* (1936), *High Tor* (1937), *The Star Wagon* (1937), *Mamba's Daughters* (1939), and *Key Largo* (1939). McClintic first directed Cornell in *The Green Hat* (1925) and *Dishonored Lady* (1930), and beginning with *The Barretts of Wimpole Street* (1931), he both directed her in and coproduced with her all her later plays. Although he was a sensitive, knowing director, he was a prissy, volatile man who was deftly parodied as Carleton Fitzgerald in Moss Hart's hit comedy *Light Up the Sky* (1948).

Beekman Place in New York, a virtual mansion on the cliffs overlooking the Hudson, and another, less pretentious house at Martha's Vineyard, a favorite summer resort for the rich who enjoy playing at simplicity. A few years ago, they were featured on the cover of the Easter issue of a *New York Sunday* supplement as the most happily married theatrical couple—something that naturally annoyed the Lunts, who had been married considerably longer and felt that the citation should have been awarded to them.

Kit's performance in *Lovers and Friends* was as impeccable as always, but we were only decorously received by the critics and public, and settled down to a snug, if not sensational, success. [The 1943 play ran twenty-one weeks on Broadway on the strength of Cornell's popularity and enthusiastic notices.]

Among the group that sat around the fire at the Elizabethan Club at Yale drinking rather indifferent tea were Thornton Wilder, Henry Luce, and Stephen Vincent Benét. These men had yet to make their mark in the world, but it was clear even then, from the stimulus of their individual personalities, that they would. [Luce (1898–1967) was the most powerful and successful magazine publisher of his era, founding *Time, Life, Sports Illustrated,* and *Fortune* magazines. Benét (1898–1943) was an outstanding American poet and author, perhaps best known for his short story *The Devil and Daniel Webster* (1936).]

I was to work with Thornton years later at the Westport Country Playhouse and continued my acquaintance with Henry, mostly through his irrepressible

Thornton Wilder (1897–1975) was a celebrated novelist and playwright known for his diverse and sometimes offbeat subject matter and writing style. He was born in Madison, Wisconsin, the son of a newspaper editor, and spent some of his childhood in China with family missionaries. Wilder was educated at Yale and Princeton, where he began writing plays and stories, and then taught French at the Lawrenceville School (across the street from Wilson's parents' house) in New Jersey and the University of Chicago. His first novel, *The Cabala*, was published in 1926, followed by such noteworthy works as the popular *The Bridge of San Luis Rey* (1927), *Heaven's My Destination* (1935), *Ides of March* (1948), *The Eighth Day* (1967), and *Theophilus North* (1973).

Wilder's playwriting career began with the notable 1931 one-act plays *The Long Christmas Dinner*, *Pullman Car Hiawatha*, and *The Happy Journey to Trenton and Camden*. Three of his full-length plays are among the most interesting in the modern American theater: the small-town drama *Our Town* (1938); the expressionistic *The Skin of Our Teeth* (1942); and the merry farce *The Matchmaker* (1954), a rewriting of his earlier *The Merchant of Yonkers* (1938) and the source for the musical *Hello, Dolly!* (1964). Despite the diversity of themes and forms, his best plays offer thoughtful, perceptive views of essentially ordinary people and seem to grow richer throughout time.

wife, Clare Boothe Luce. Her highly publicized career is fascinating, I think, having determinedly progressed from a secretary at a publishing house in Greenwich, Connecticut, to U.S. ambassador to Rome. I first knew Clare after she had given up her first marriage to a New York millionaire, George Tuttle Brokaw—one of the innumerable Brokaws—and become an editor at *Vanity Fair*. Under the aegis of Frank Crowninshield, the magazine's editor in chief, her position solidified, and she embarked on altering some of its policies. For all its wit and humor, the magazine had been kindly disposed to publishing a series of laudations under the title *We Nominate for the Hall of Fame*, extolling, among others, such celebrities as playwright Lillian Hellman, choreographer Agnes de Mille, and theater producer Max Gordon. Rather intriguingly, Clare instituted another series called *We Nominate for the Hall of Oblivion* and nominated names like Adolf Hitler, writer Michael Gold, and publisher Samuel Roth. Apparently all of them achieved exactly that, although one went about it more flamboyantly than the others.

Clare eventually took up the theater and wrote several plays, including *The Women* and *Kiss the Boys Goodbye*. Due to our personal friendship, she offered me an opportunity to produce *The Women*, which I turned down on

Clare Boothe Luce (1903–1987) was a noted playwright, editor, politician, and diplomat in a time when many of those jobs were denied to women. She was born Ann Clare Boothe in New York City, the product of a common-law marriage, and grew up in various towns in Illinois, New Jersey, and Tennessee. Her mother had acting ambitions for her daughter, and Clare was on the stage and in silent movies by the time she was ten years old. As an adult she worked as a journalist and was managing editor at *Vanity Fair*, before turning to playwriting and writing books. Boothe first won success with *The Women* (1936), a witty, slashing comedy of female manners. *Kiss the Boys Goodbye* (1938), a spoof of Hollywood's celebrated search for a Scarlett O'Hara, and *Margin for Error* (1939), in which a Jewish policeman is assigned to guard a Nazi diplomat, also won favor. Boothe's fiction and nonfiction works include *Stuffed Shirts* (1931) and *Europe in the Spring* (1940).

In 1935, after divorcing her alcoholic husband, George Tuttle Brokaw, she married publisher tycoon Henry Luce and aided him in his journalistic pursuits. She also became active in conservative politics, serving in the U.S. House of Representatives and delivering the keynote speech at the 1944 Republican National Convention. She served a stint as U.S. ambassador to Italy, the first woman appointed to a major diplomatic post abroad, and later as ambassador to Brazil.

the grounds that an assortment of females residing in Reno for marital extradition was not in the best possible taste. Max Gordon, however, didn't agree. He picked up the option, gave it a first-rate production, and made a fortune. Needless to say, I was never offered a Boothe play again. [*The Women* ran two years on Broadway, was a hit movie in 1939, and has been revived on Broadway and regionally many times throughout the years.]

Clare's theatrical aspirations even embraced a stint at acting. Gus Schirmer—an offspring of the Schirmer music publishing firm—persuaded her to play Candida in a summer-stock production in Stamford, Connecticut. The opening-night performance was preceded, rather unprofessionally, by a dinner party for about thirty people at the Luce residence, to which my wife Natasha and I were invited. Clare graciously presided over the dinner, and the other guests included such "theatrical personalities" as celebrity wives Mrs. William Randolph Hearst and Mrs. George F. Baker, and distinguished financier Bernard Baruch. It was pouring rain that night, but we managed to plunge through the deluge and arrive at the theater—a converted movie house—to find a star-studded audience of social friends and theatrical cynics, some of them having journeyed from as far away as Long Island, Bucks County, and even Maine.

Clare, of course, looked lovely. She was, and still is, a seemingly frail blonde, which somehow belies her inner determination. I regret to report, however, that as Candida, she wasn't any good. At the end of the performance, and with the rain still pouring down, Natasha and I splattered our way around to the stage door to pay our respects, only to be confronted by a burly policeman who refused us admittance. I explained that we were friends of Mrs. Luce and that we were there at her personal invitation, but he was adamant and reiterated that his orders were to allow no one backstage. As we were both soaking wet and in no mood for dressing room devoirs anyway, we paddled off to our car greatly relieved.

Back at Yale, I continued running the mile for varsity track, singing in the Yale Glee Club, and acting my heart out in the school "Dramat." But this time I graduated with a diploma, which I keep framed in my bathroom as concrete evidence against potential disbelievers. As a reward for this scholastic achievement, the family provided a trip to Europe, where I relentlessly visited every palace, cathedral, and museum from Liverpool to Venice, from John o'Groat's to Cannes. It was an experience that was to prove of immeasurable value in years to come, for when I eventually lived there, it was unnecessary to visit such places again.

In the fall of 1922, facing the necessity of the facts of life, I was most willingly inducted into an important Wall Street brokerage firm, C. D. Barney & Company, just as my father expected after springing for Andover and Yale. There was to be the usual routine—errand boy, office clerk, bookkeeping assistant—until one could expect to emerge into some junior capacity in the front office. Certainly a warm and friendly place! I have to say that I disliked almost every minute of it.

Again, of course, theater took me by the hand. I joined a famous New York organization called the Amateur Comedy Club, and most of my evenings were spent rehearsing and preparing for various shows. I also got on the debutante list of eligible and/or acceptable young men, and on the nights that we were not in rehearsal, I was whirling around the ballrooms of Manhattan with such enjoyment that I was generally the last to leave. How I made it to the office on the subway the next morning is still a mystery. [The Amateur Comedy Club (ACC) is perhaps the oldest existing theater organization in the United States. It was founded in 1884, as a venue for nonprofessional theater in New York City. It is still in operation, presenting theater productions and stand-up comedy in its original location in a mews off of East 36th Street in the Murray Hill neighborhood.] The "Club" was an interesting organization. One of its firm rules was that no professionals were permitted to be members, and so, of course, I eventually had to resign. Dur-

Hope Williams (1897–1990) was a gifted comic actress who excelled at sophisticated comedy on Broadway in the 1920s and 1930s. The peppy blonde with bobbed hair and a bouncy walk was born in Manhattan, the daughter of a prosperous lawyer, and trained in the theater at the ACC and in Junior League charity productions. Williams made an auspicious debut in the supporting role of Fanny in Philip Barry's comedy *Paris Bound* (1927), so Barry wrote his character of the free-thinking Linda Seaton in *Holiday* (1928) with the young actress in mind. The role made her a Broadway star. Her understudy was Katharine Hepburn, who later admitted she borrowed heavily from Williams's performance when she made the 1938 screen version of *Holiday*. Williams's other plays and revues included *Rebound* (1930), *The New Yorkers* (1930), *Too True to Be Good* (1932), *Strike Me Pink* (1933), and *The Importance of Being Earnest* (1939). Her only film was the drama *The Scoundrel* (1935), with Noel Coward. Williams left the theater during World War II to run her drafted manager's ranch in Wyoming and never returned to the stage.

ing that early period, however, I did everything from one-act melodramas on their own private stage to full-length musicals at the Heckscher Memorial on upper Fifth Avenue, invariably as the leading man. I particularly remember a sensitive and frail young lady who usually played the maid. Her name was Hope Williams. Starting from what could be called "slightly below scratch," she would later become a star on Broadway.

In vogue during this period were boyish ingénues—forthright, spunky females—and Williams filled that bill. Such playwrights as Philip Barry and Donald Ogden Stewart created starring roles for her, and for a decade she played them to the hilt. The plots were invariably the same, no matter who wrote the play: a rich, pampered daughter with rebellious ideas who never failed in the third act to run off with some enchanting, although impecunious, young man. It was sentimentalism, of course, but at a time when women were just beginning to become more assertive, the audiences were naturally intrigued. Having retired from the stage, Williams, who has always been independently wealthy, divides her time between her New York apartment and her ranch in Wyoming, but she's still the same: forthright, rebellious, and full of spunky ideas.

While I was still involved with the "Comedy Club," Miss Genevieve Tobin crossed my path. She is now the wife of the Hollywood director William Keighley, but at the time she was the shining star of Arthur Hopkins's stable and was playing in the highly successful *Polly Preferred*. She was a petite, ultra-feminine young lady, invariably dressed by Boué Soeurs, Paris couturiers famous for their frills and lace. In consequence, she was covered with rose buds, on stage and off. Her brother had been at Yale with me, and through him I managed an introduction and even to frequently take Genevieve to tea at the Plaza. I sometimes thought she was under the erroneous impression that the teas were purely social, but I tried during our many pleasant moments together to inculcate the idea that I wanted to go on the stage. That she disapproved of this was patently obvious. She had even forbidden her brother from embracing the profession (which he later did anyway), but after sufficient polite badgering on my part, she offered to help get me a job. Her run in the New York production of *Polly Preferred* was nearing its close, and she had been invited to play a limited engagement of the play in San Francisco. With great kindness and, I suspect, considerable effort on her part, I was included in the company. I say "effort" because the other members of the troupe were local San Francisco actors, and although it was obvious that she, as the star, should be transported 3,000 miles, it must have been through her good offices that I, as a minor member of the cast, was also sent.

Meanwhile the powers at C. D. Barney had been less than impressed by my theatrical defections, and when the San Francisco opportunity arose, it was clearly time to leave my desk at the brokerage firm. Many years later,

Genevieve Tobin (1899–1995) was a sprightly actress and singer on Broadway and the screen. The native New Yorker began her career as a child actress in 1912, and within a few seasons she was being touted by many critics as a successor to Maude Adams for her sparkling, youthful performances. Although her career never lived up to its early promises, she won praise as immigrant Patricia O'Day in *Little Old New York* (1920), chorine-turned-star Polly Brown in *Polly Preferred* (1923), Cordelia in *King Lear* (1923), the assertive Nancy Blake in *The Youngest* (1924), and American tourist Looloo Carroll in *Fifty Million Frenchmen* (1929). She made her screen debut as Little Eva in a 1910 short of *Uncle Tom's Cabin* but was not busy in movies until the 1930s, when she was frequently cast in supporting but noticeable roles. Tobin made nearly forty films during the decade, including such titles as *One Hour with You* (1932), *Pleasure Cruise* (1933), *Easy to Love* (1934), *The Woman in Red* (1935), *Broadway Hostess* (1935), *The Petrified Forest* (1936), *Zaza* (1938), *Yes, My Darling Daughter* (1939), and *No Time for Comedy* (1940). Tobin married film director William Keighley in 1938, and two years later she retired from acting and happily led a high-society life for the next fifty-five years.

the daughter of the firm's senior partner, Charles Harding, would marry a man named Tom King. During his college years, Tom worked for me in the internship program at Westport; he then became a Broadway stage manager and eventually a prominent Dartmouth professor. Who knows? Perhaps in later years the partners at Barney altered their view of the theater. My father, who was equally, if not more, unimpressed, actually pretended to friends and family that I was going to California to work for a bank. [Although Wilson jokes about his father's disapproval, their adult relationship was never a warm one. James J. Wilson was not supportive of his elder son's career path and made those feelings known on multiple occasions. After his father died in 1937, Wilson and his sister Dorothy Wilson Cart purchased their own future gravesite in a different cemetery so that they could be buried together, separately from their parents.] In any case, it was "farewell Wall Street" and off to San Francisco with Genevieve, her ebullient mama, and her sister Vivian. We arrived at the Fairmont Hotel, a hostelry that I have faithfully patronized ever since, although in later years my accommodations have been a little more commodious.

The company was indeed a local one, with the exception of me and our imported star. We had to provide our own wardrobe, and I found myself lending clothes to some of the other actors. I have a suspicion that I wasn't very good in my part—merely amiable, eager, and nice looking—but one night Mrs. Tobin praised me by admiring the shape of the back of my head. I think that's about as near as I ever got to a good notice. [Wilson's description of himself as "nice looking" is an understatement. He was actually very handsome and attractive to both men and women. His ambitions to be on the stage must have been fueled by his self-awareness that he was so physically appealing. Wilson managed to retain his good looks until a few years before his death, when the effects of heavy smoking and alcohol use, and his commitment to a hard-charging, high-society lifestyle, finally took their toll.] My presence in the company was looked upon by the other actors with mild suspicion. I am certain they were convinced that Genevieve and I were having a love affair. This was, unfortunately, only half true, because although I was unmistakably in love with her, her interest in me was clearly limited to friendship.

At the end of our San Francisco engagement, a shrewdly limited one, Edward Everett Horton invited me to join his repertory company in Los Angeles. [Edward Everett Horton (1886–1970) was one of Hollywood's most distinct and beloved character actors, playing the quintessential nervous, bubbling, frustrated sidekick in 120 movies. He was mostly active on the stage when he offered Wilson a job.] I gratefully but firmly refused, as by now it was Broadway and Broadway alone that I saw as my future oyster. I was, however, gravely mistaken. Despite numerous letters that Genevieve kindly wrote to many managers back in New York, they were scarcely impressed with my experience in a San Francisco stock company. Courteous as they were, they were obviously indifferent to my possibilities. Meanwhile, a liaison was arranged with the agents Chamberlain and Lyman Brown, who courageously sent me out day after day after day for every available part in town, from school boys to elderly character roles. It was certainly not their fault that I never landed even one of those jobs. They tried, and I shall always be grateful. The agency's waiting room wall was adorned with photographs of the great actors they had represented, from George M. Cohan to Bert Lahr. It is a slightly ironic twist that, after all these years, my photograph now hangs there as well . . . and at their request.

Striking out at every turn was not helping my confidence. I recall weeks of inactivity, frustration, and bad moments of real despair. The family was losing patience, and helpful and considerate as they were, it was fairly clear to them that I was at a standstill. At this crucial point, I ran into a friend, a prominent Fifth Avenue art dealer whom I had met on the boat on my first transatlantic crossing just after Yale. He would later be a brokerage client, and I would handle his considerable bond investments. It seemed an appropriate time to explain my new ambitions to him. Fortunately, he mentioned that his brother was an important director at Paramount's East Coast studios, which, at that time, were operating elaborately at Astoria, Long Island.

I quickly wrote and mailed a letter to his brother, landed an interview, and was hired in the smallest possible role as assistant assistant assistant assistant director. No problem! It was the time of the glamor of silent films, and I was suddenly in the middle of it all. Elsie Ferguson, a tall, regal beauty, was supposed to be filming *The Swan* on the adjoining set, but the cameras were not rolling because she had posted a notice on her dressing room: "Please, no one will speak to Miss Ferguson, including the director!" In the end, she reached a satisfactory, mutual agreement with the producers and departed from the film. [Elsie Ferguson (1885–1961) was a beautiful and beloved stage star active on Broadway between 1901 and 1943. She made two dozen silent films and one talkie before returning to the theater. A great favorite with theatergoers, Ferguson was usually applauded more for her gorgeous looks than her acting talents.] After frantic delays, Miss Ferguson was followed by a young, unknown Broadway actress, dug up in what was virtually a panic, named Frances Howard. She would become better known in later years as Mrs. Samuel Goldwyn. [Samuel Goldwyn (1879–1974), the pioneering Hollywood filmmaker, was an independent film producer by the time Wilson met him. Frances Howard (1903–1976) was a stage actress with many New York credits before making her first movie in 1925, the same year she married Goldwyn. After four movies she retired from acting and remained married to Goldwyn until his death nearly fifty years later.]

Frances was a slim brunette, not a beauty, but so charming that you never noticed it. She and Goldwyn, a balding, rotund, perfectly cast Hollywood mogul, were married soon after the completion of *The Swan* and returned to California. Their marriage was a huge success, and Frances became of immeasurable value to Sam throughout the years. He was a perfectionist but inclined to be cantankerous, if not downright rude, to actors, designers, writers, and just about everyone on the lot. It was always Frances who would rush about calming the troubled waters and persuading the bruised victims to return to their jobs.

During my various trips to California, I was invited to dine at the Goldwyn's impressive house, as well as at Jack Warner's miniature of Versailles and Louis B. Mayer's abode. Mayer also lived extremely well, but somewhat less pretentiously. At these gatherings it was customary that dinner be followed by a preview of the latest Hollywood film. Guests were herded into a drawing room and comfortably seated with a drink, at which point a portable screen would ascend from the floor. Your everyday Matisse or Picasso would be slid to the side, exposing the projection booth. And rather than conversing with one another, everything would go deathly quiet and the evening's entertainment would begin. The films were often lent by rival producers, and I was always amazed by the fact that I never heard one studio head say a kind word about another's product.

The film I was assigned to during my early days at the Paramount lot on Long Island had a more peaceful, although perhaps less glamorous, working situation than *The Swan*. In fact, the movie was so relatively unimportant that I can't even remember its name. It starred Richard Dix, a husky, handsome leading man of the period. His vitality was equaled only by his virility. Richard's costar was an attractive, dark-haired young actress named Jacqueline Logan, with whom I promptly fell in love. I never told her that, however. She wisely ended up marrying an extremely wealthy man with whom she lived in luxury near Katonah, New York. [The movie was *A Man Must Live* (1925), an adventure film that is believed to be lost. Richard Dix (1893–1949) had a prodigious career in more than one hundred silents and talkies. Jacqueline Logan (1901–1983) was a former *Ziegfeld Follies* girl who was featured in sixty silents and talkies before retiring in 1931.]

One of my fellow assistant assistants at Paramount was poet E. E. Cummings. He had apparently been in need of a job at that moment, and Frank

E. E. Cummings (1894–1962) was a distinctive poet whose unconventional verses are now considered masterworks of American literature. He was born Edward Estlin Cummings in Cambridge, Massachusetts, to parents who were Unitarians and inspired the author's transcendentalist philosophy. He began writing poetry as a boy and continued during his studies at Harvard and early career as a book dealer. After being imprisoned by the French during World War I on suspicion of espionage, Cummings wrote about the ordeal in his first novel, *The Enormous Room* (1922). His poetry, in which lowercase words are placed in unusual patterns, started to gain notice in the 1920s. By the time of his death at the age of sixty-seven, e. e. cummings (as he signed his work) had left more than 2,500 poems, two novels, many essays, and four plays.

Crowninshield had arranged to make a place for him at the studio. Both of us felt like visitors from Mars but became great friends, inhaling smoke and exhaling opinions on long lunch-hour walks over bridges spanning the Long Island railway yards. We actually wrote a scenario together of which I am still somewhat ashamed and I expect E. E.—great literary figure that he is—has sedulously forgotten. It was never bought and never produced; anyway, we enjoyed our walks!

So now I was a writer. Admittedly, the scenario had not been sold, but the virus of creative imagination was surging through immature veins. I decided to sublet my tiny apartment in New York and, thanks to more patience and financial support from the family, managed another trip to Europe on an inexpensive cargo ship. The budget for this trip was limited, so this time my excursion was a matter of *pensiones*, third-class train cars, and general economy. The plan was simple: Once the allotted amount ran out, the party was over.

I did, however, manage to cover considerable ground: Paris to Naples to Sicily, where I was put up by a kind old gentleman, a friend of the family from New Jersey named Commendatore Wood. His hospitality reduced my expenses considerably and advanced my social position even more. It was through him that I met the elegant society of Taormina, Sicily, which mostly consisted of elderly English ladies with authentic but somewhat remote titles, presided over by another very elderly Englishman, the Duke of Bronte. His lands and peerage had come to him as a nephew and heir of Admiral Lord Nelson, to whom a grant had been made by a grateful government for his services in winning the Battle of Trafalgar. It was at the Duke's villa that I met my first royalty, when King George V and Queen Mary arrived one morning on the royal yacht and stayed for lunch. The Duke had been Her Majesty's personal secretary in London, and I learned at a relatively early age how to complete my first royal bow, which, considering my Trenton background, I think I managed quite well.

Meanwhile, residing in the sun-drenched atmosphere of Commendatore Wood's converted monastery, I persevered with my writing. But I was becoming slowly and appallingly aware that my talents did not really lie in that direction. So after two unproductive, although pleasant, months, the journey north began. First to Rome; again a cheap *pensione* and seeing the sights. Then Paris, where I stayed in a fleabag hotel, which I later learned was a brothel, but I was stupid enough not to notice at the time. It was in Paris that I ran into the Crossetts, whom I had first met in Taormina. They were a delightful family from Chicago who were palpably very rich. Their party included four family members, governesses, maids, and even their own courier to deliver messages. Mr. Crossett suggested that I fly with him to London in one of the somewhat sketchy planes of that time, as he did not wish to trust his family to a mode of transportation that he had not first experienced himself. Nevertheless, we arrived safely, and that night he invited me to dine with him at the Berkeley Hotel, having by now decided to bring his family within the next forty-eight hours.

And this is where the story really begins . . .

CHAPTER TWO

~

Noel

The coincidence of my meeting Noel Coward was a fluke, the sort of freakish circumstance that just happens and suddenly alters the future. The reigning hit show of London in 1925 was the American musical *No, No Nanette*, and Mr. Crossett ordered the hotel to get tickets for it at once and invited me to join him; however, the concierge told us that it had been impossible and they had obtained seats at another show, *The Vortex*, starring Noel Coward. This was dismal news for both of us, as we had never heard of Noel Coward nor his play. Nevertheless, we went and found ourselves seated in the middle of the front row. I can't speak for Mr. Crossett, but I found myself overwhelmed by the play, as well as the cast, particularly Lilian Braithwaite, and most particularly by Mr. Coward himself. It seemed one of the most exciting performances I had ever seen, and at the end, in seats so close that our chins were practically in the footlights, I applauded with an enthusiasm and zeal that could only be justified by its genuine honesty. [Lilian Braithwaite (1873–1948) was a lovely actress on the British stage and screen in the first two decades of the twentieth century. By 1924, she was playing character parts in dramas and comedies. Her alcoholic mother in *The Vortex* was considered the finest performance of her career.]

I had several letters from friends in New York to their friends in London, and as the rest of the Crossett family and staff had now arrived en masse, I had time to deliver some of them. One was to a young man named Sholto Bailie, a most hospitable London dilettante, living on an allowance from his mother. In the course of a dinner, I casually mentioned my enthusiasm

Noel Coward (1899–1973) was a multitalented British performer, playwright, songwriter, and director who was popular on both sides of the Atlantic for more than half a century. Although the very name Noel Coward conjures up images of sophistication, wit, and high living, he was born in the working-class neighborhood of Teddington, a suburb of London, the son of a piano salesman, and raised in Surrey, where he went on the variety stage as a boy. He first received acclaim as a songwriter and playwright, before becoming a familiar and much-loved figure performing on the stage. His disturbing drama *The Vortex* (1924) brought him his first recognition, although it was atypical of his later work. Coward's comedies include *Fallen Angels* (1925), *Hay Fever* (1925), *Private Lives* (1930), *Design for Living* (1933), *Present Laughter* (1939), *Blithe Spirit* (1941), *Quadrille* (1952), *Nude with Violin* (1956), and *Waiting in the Wings* (1960), and his most accomplished dramas were *Easy Virtue* (1925), *Cavalcade* (1931), *This Happy Breed* (1939), and *Suite in Three Keys* (1966). He wrote the book, music, and lyrics for several musicals and revues, among them *This Year of Grace* (1927), *Bitter Sweet* (1928), *Words and Music* (1932), *Conversation Piece* (1933), *Tonight at 8:30* (1935), *Sail Away* (1959), and *The Girl Who Came to Supper* (1963).

Coward also had a distinguished movie career. Most of his plays and musicals were filmed, and he wrote and/or acted in such films as *Tonight Is Ours* (1933), *The Scoundrel* (1935), *In Which We Serve* (1942), *Brief Encounter* (1945), *Our Man in Havana* (1959), and *Bunny Lake Is Missing* (1965). Coward often appeared in his stage and screen works, as well as acted in movies that he didn't write, and late in his career he performed in nightclubs and on television. He was a small, excessively suave man with a studiously clipped enunciation. Despite such a British demeanor, he was very successful in the United States. Many of his plays and musicals appeared on Broadway, and he wrote some just for American audiences. Coward's life and works were celebrated in such revues as *Oh, Coward!* (1972), *Cowardly Custard* (1972), and *If Love Were All* (1999). When Wilson first met him in 1925, Coward was just beginning his meteoric rise to fame.

for Noel Coward's performance, and Sholto said that if I cared to meet him, he could make arrangements, as he knew Noel well. My answer was obvious, and a few days later Sholto generously arranged for a complete Coward evening. We went to the London Pavilion, where Charles Cochran was presenting the Coward revue *On with the Dance*, starring Alice Delysia and incorporating, among other hits, Noel's famous "Dance Little Lady." [Alice Delysia (1889–1979) was a French singer-actress who appeared in several

The Vortex was a controversial 1924 play by Noel Coward that brought him his first recognition in the London theater. Coward himself played Nicky Lancaster, who returns from Paris with his fiancée, Bunty Mainwarring (Molly Kerr), to introduce her to his mother, Florence (Lilian Braithwaite), a woman who desperately clings to her youth by having affairs with younger men. When Florence's latest paramour, Tom Veryan (Alan Hollis), steals Bunty from Nicky, both mother and son are miserable, Nicky confessing his cocaine addiction and Florence her self-deluded sex life. The blatant use of drugs and depiction of sex among the upper classes shocked and intrigued audiences when the play opened in Britain in 1924, and it ran for a year. There was less fuss when Coward and Braithwaite reprised their roles on Broadway in 1925, and the production lasted only four months. But *The Vortex* introduced Coward to New York audiences and launched his American theater career. The 1928 silent film version of *The Vortex* stars Ivor Novello and Florence Lancaster. The play also showed up on British television in 1960, 1964, and 1969.

British musical revues and operettas.] After this stimulating dose of Cowardiana, Sholto took me back to the theater where *The Vortex* was playing, and we went backstage to the star's dressing room.

Noel was absolutely charming, as I've seen him be to so many people throughout the years, even when meeting someone for the first time. To my amazed delight, he remembered me as the enthusiastic, wide-eyed, overapplauding young man in the front row three nights before. He took me to meet Lilian Braithwaite and several other members of the cast. My appreciation of the performance had apparently been so violent that it was noticed by everyone concerned. Lilian Braithwaite was an austere, elegant old pro who was later to be made a Dame of the British Empire. She was a great friend of Queen Mary (the one who wore the tocques), but she avoided the social aspects of English life and, until her death, sedulously devoted herself to the theater. She left a daughter, Joyce Carey, who, for years, has been a firmly ensconced member of Noel's entourage and a popular favorite on both the London and New York stages. [Joyce Carey (1898–1993) was a British character actress of stage, screen, and television who is most remembered for her many roles in Noel Coward works. Her acting career spanned seven decades and included everything from Shakespeare roles to British sitcoms.]

I don't remember the other members of *The Vortex* cast whom I met that night, but I do recall being slightly shocked during the introductions as Noel walked around his dressing room clad only in a pair of silk drawers. I had yet to learn that such theatric behavior was not only average, but normal—at least for him. In any event, as I was leaving, Noel asked me to look him up again that autumn when he was scheduled to arrive in New York with the same play. With hindsight, I suspect the invitation was perfunctory and merely a courtesy. He didn't know what he was in for.

[When Coward wrote his first autobiography in 1937, he expressed his first impression of Wilson. "One night in May," he recalls, "a young man in the front of the stalls caught our attention early in the first act. His rapt absorption in the play inspired Lilian and me to renewed efforts, and at the final curtain we both conceded him a gracious bow all for himself. . . . The young man responded nobly to our bow by applauding even more loudly. I remember remarking to Lilian that he must be an American because he was wearing a turn-down collar with his dinner jacket." When the two men first met a few days later, the encounter was far from love at first sight, at least not on Coward's side. As he later wrote, "Jack Wilson walked nervously, and with a slightly overdone truculence, into my life. Gladys Calthrop was in my dressing room, and we both considered him amiable enough but rather uppish. He left after a drink and a little commonplace conversation, having asked me to lunch with him in New York when I came over with the play. We promptly forgot all about him, no clairvoyant being present to tell us that my trio of closest, most intimate friends, Gladys, Jeffrey (Amherst), and Lorn (Lorraine), was fated, in those few minutes, to become a quartette. We should, I think, have laughed at the idea that that almost defiantly American stockbroker would become so much a part of our lives that scarcely any decision could be made without him. That, however, is what ultimately happened."]

Upon my return from London, I went back to my post on Wall Street. The theater seemed like a closed door, and I reluctantly decided it would be wise to lock it. C. D. Barney was more gracious than I expected, considering my previous backsliding. In short order, I was once again peddling stocks and bonds, and my theatrical ambitions were presumably renounced forever.

"But came autumn," as the silent movies used to say, and Noel arrived in New York. Both he and his play were instantly successful, and he was the pet of the Broadway season of 1925. He shared this adulation with Michael Arlen (or "Dikran," as he preferred to be called by his friends), whose *The Green Hat*, starring Katharine Cornell, had opened the night before *The Vortex*. It naturally suited the Broadway critics to assume these two Englishmen were rivals—perhaps even enemies—but Arlen and Noel made frequent appearances together in the best New York nightclubs to prove that this was not the case. In fact, it was indeed not the case, since Michael had been an important original investor in *The Vortex* in London and owned a considerable share of the New York production as well. [Michael Arlen (1895–1956) was an Armenian-born writer of plays, fiction, essays, and screenplays who was a popular literary figure in Great Britain in the 1920s.]

It was a breakthrough season for Noel on Broadway. In addition to *The Vortex*, he had *Easy Virtue*, starring Jane Cowl, and Laura Hope Crews in another of his comedies, *Hay Fever*. It had played the full 1925 season in London and is still kicking around both England and the United States in repertory and summer theater. To me, *Hay Fever* is not as good a play as Noel's *Blithe Spirit* or *Private Lives*, but it is apparently indestructible.

I followed up on Noel's invitation and looked him up. Surprisingly, he actually remembered me, and we began seeing one another often for lunch or dinner out. At one of these meetings, he mentioned that the three plays were bringing him around $18,000 per week, including his salary and royalties, and asked if he could open a New York–based account with me at the brokerage. This went forward, and the partners at C. D. Barney were pleased to have such a prestigious client. [Wilson does not, or could not, mention at

Hay Fever is a 1925 farce by Noel Coward and his first of many hit comedies in the theater. The Bliss household in the English countryside is always in chaos. Temperamental, flighty actress Judith Bliss (Marie Tempest) wavers from weariness of the stage and missing it when she is away. Her grown children, Simon (Robert Andrews) and Sorrel (Helen Spencer), are playful, demanding, spoiled, and plenty of fun. Her mild husband David (W. Graham Browne) enjoys a peaceful existence by ignoring everyone and everything around him. Each member of the family has invited a guest for the same weekend, someone they are interested in romantically or to feed their ego, but once the guests arrive they are pretty much neglected by the family, who is really only content with one another.

Although there is little plot or character development, the comedy is delightfully daffy and has remained an audience favorite throughout the decades. The original London production ran a year, so the Shuberts put together an American cast headed by Laura Hope Crews as Judith, and it opened on Broadway in the fall of 1925. Either because the cast was lacking or the production failed to work, the comedy was not well received by the New York press and lasted only six weeks, even though *Hay Fever* would go on to become one of Coward's most-produced and enjoyed comedies. Curiously, a movie version of *Hay Fever* was never made, but there were television productions in 1938, 1939, 1946, 1960, 1968, and 1984.

this point that he and Coward had become lovers. The relationship started off awkwardly. When Coward received a letter from Wilson asking to meet for lunch, Coward dictated a letter of acceptance. In his memoir, Coward recalls that he "waited, in a mounting rage, for three quarters of an hour on the day specified, and finally was forced to lunch alone in a cafeteria. It later transpired that my secretary had never posted the letter." Wilson was equally enraged that Coward did not reply to his invitation. According to Coward, after several drinks at a cocktail party, Wilson worked up the courage to come to the Henry Miller Theatre and "attack me for not having answered his invitation to lunch. Fortunately I remembered his face and, after a moment's scurried thinking, his name, which mollified him somewhat . . . I took him back to dine at the studio. . . . From then onwards we became close friends." Wilson may not have been Coward's first lover, but this would become his first long-lasting romantic relationship.]

It was during this period that I first met Gertrude Lawrence. Many years later, after her tragic death, I was asked to deliver a radio tribute. I decided to recall the story of our first meeting, and the reaction it inspired in me:

Just about twenty-eight years ago, I walked onto a darkened stage of a 42nd Street theater and met and fell in love with Miss Gertrude Lawrence. She had just come over to do *Charlot's Revue*, and she was nervous and shy and utterly unaware of the place that she was to take in the hearts of the American public.

She was doing two numbers by Noel Coward, and as he was in town, she had asked him to come and stage them. It was he who took me there on that occasion. I had never before met a glamorous, lovely star such as she. I do not know what I would have said if anyone had told me that in the years to come, I would be privileged to know the joy of her personal friendship, that I would be associated with and/or present her in several of her most outstanding hits and even be given the pleasure of actually directing her. Cooperation and generosity characterized not only her personal life, but also her behavior during the innumerable crises and chores that dominate all theatrical productions.

I have been on many darkened rehearsal stages since and peered into many empty auditoriums. That thrill has become a little jaded and considerably less interesting. But the excitement of meeting her has never gone and never will. I know that I can never see her on the stage again, but as on that first occasion so many years ago, I am still in love with Miss Gertrude Lawrence.

My friendship with Noel had lasted for several months, until one day he asked me if I could recommend someone to be his business manager. He wanted to devote more of his time to writing and acting. And Noel had no particular flair for business, particularly American business, about which he

Gertrude Lawrence (1898–1952) was a British actress who was equally beloved by London and New York audiences during a career spanning three decades. Although she could not dance well and sometimes sang off-key, this graceful, haughty beauty was one of the great stars of the musical stage, as well as nonmusical comedy. She was born in London and began her theatrical career as a child performer with the young Noel Coward; the two remained friends for the rest of their lives. Lawrence first made a name for herself in revues, in particular *Charlot's Revue*, which was a hit in London in 1924, and in New York the next year. Broadway audiences immediately embraced the comic actress, and she returned to New York often throughout her career.

Lawrence starred in *Oh, Kay!* (1926), followed by leading roles in *Treasure Girl* (1928), *Candle-Light* (1929), and *The International Revue* (1930). She then scored a major success as Amanda Prynne, playing opposite Coward in his comedy hit *Private Lives* (1930 in London, 1931 in New York). She played opposite Coward again in his *Tonight at 8:30*, a bill of one-act plays, in 1936, in London and then New York. Successes followed as Susan Trexel in *Susan and God* (1937), and as neglected wife Lydia Kenyon in *Skylark* (1939). Lawrence returned to musicals to play fashion magazine editor Liza Elliott in *Lady in the Dark* (1941). After the war, she appeared as Eliza Doolittle in a revival of *Pygmalion* (1945). Her last appearance on stage was perhaps her most beloved, as English teacher Anna Leonowens in Rodgers and Hammerstein's original production of *The King and I* (1951). Lawrence's screen career was sporadic and not very memorable. She appeared in only nine films, most memorably in *The Glass Menagerie* (1950). Julie Andrews played the stage favorite in the musical biopic *Star!* (1968).

was naturally unfamiliar. That did it, of course. I immediately proposed myself for the job. He thought it over for twenty-four hours and then accepted me for the post. I walked out of Wall Street for the third time, this time forever. I took an office in the Henry Miller Theatre, where *The Vortex* was playing, and proceeded to devote my time to looking after Noel's business affairs.

Then a further development occurred. Gladys Calthrop, whom Noel had brought to New York as his scenic designer and who was also his inseparable companion, became intrigued by Eva Le Gallienne and her work in the theater. Noel had no objection to their relationship—in fact, he was delighted—until Gladys announced that she was leaving him and his commercial attitudes toward the stage to go to work on an ambitious season at Eva's

Gladys Calthrop (1894–1980) was a leading set and costume designer in the British and Broadway theater and is most known for her many designs for Noel Coward plays and musicals in both venues. She studied at the Slade School of Fine Art in London and began her professional theater career designing Coward's first play, *The Vortex*, in 1924. Two years later, Calthrop was also designing scenery and costumes in New York, first for Eva Le Gallienne's Civic Repertory Theatre and later for Broadway commercial productions. She continued to work on both sides of the Atlantic into the 1960s.

Eva Le Gallienne (1899–1991) was a pioneering theater manager and director, as well as an accomplished actress. Daughter of famous novelist and poet Richard Le Gallienne, she was born in London and trained at the Royal Academy of Dramatic Art, acting briefly in England before making her American debut in *Mrs. Boltay's Daughters* (1915). Le Gallienne scored her first major success as Julie who loves the ne'er-do-well hero in Ferenc Molnar's *Liliom* (1921), and she consolidated her newfound fame when she played Princess Alexandra in a second Molnar play, *The Swan* (1923). In the 1925–1926 season, she mounted and acted in her own productions of *The Master Builder* and *John Gabriel Borkman*. In 1926, Le Gallienne established her Civic Repertory Theatre in an attempt to offer low-priced productions of classics. She directed and appeared in many of its productions throughout the next six years, including *The Three Sisters*, *Twelfth Night*, *The Cradle Song*, *Alison's House*, *Alice in Wonderland*, and the title roles of *Hedda Gabler* and *Peter Pan*.

In 1942, Le Gallienne won applause as the spiteful sister Lettie in *Uncle Harry*. With Cheryl Crawford and Margaret Webster, she made another attempt at forming a permanent ensemble in 1946, calling it the American Repertory Company, but its life was short. Many of Le Gallienne's subsequent appearances were in short-lived failures, but years later she scored a major success as the theatrical dowager Fanny Cavendish in a 1975 revival of *The Royal Family*. Her last appearances were in *To Grandmother's House We Go* (1981) and *Alice in Wonderland* (1982), which she also directed. A small woman, with a tiny, tight-featured face but a regal persona, her acting struck some as too studiously mannered, but she brought an exceptional intelligence and dedication to her work.

new 14th Street Repertory Theatre. Gladys moved out of Noel's apartment and joined Eva in hers so that they could work more closely on their mutual project downtown. This served to bring Noel and me closer. He was, and still is, one who likes a steady companion around when he is in the mood.

Noel's household in New York that year was quite famous. He had a large duplex apartment, which he described as "early Metro Goldwyn," in the Hotel Des Artistes, sublet from movie actress Mae Murray. There were two large gates of impressive stature leading into the dining room. The only catch was that when you touched them, you found that they were made of plywood and sprang back and forth like a rubber band. In any case, it was in this elaborate setting that Noel had ensconced both his mother and Gladys—before her defection—and where he entertained privately and with several large parties. He also bought himself a large, if rather antiquated, Rolls Royce and drove around Central Park in a sort of early Newport grandeur, back and forth from the theater or to and from various appointments. In fact, it was his first taste of really big money, and he was fully enjoying it.

As for the plays, the debut run of *Hay Fever* was a disappointment, and the play had to close. [The comedy ran only forty-nine performances, as opposed to 337 performances in London.] *Easy Virtue* continued in New York, and when *The Vortex* went even slightly under capacity, Noel decided to take it on tour to Chicago and Cleveland. The play's failure in the former city was as grave a shock as the buildup had been immense, and the reception was anything but brilliant. Mary Garden, the reigning queen of the Chicago Opera, had written a personal advertisement in the newspapers, which roughly ran: "My divine, windy city—you have four words that spell 'genius' in Chicago: Noel Coward, *The Vortex*!" But somehow even her enthusiasm failed to stimulate ticket sales. There is still written on a dressing room wall in Chicago's Selwyn Theatre the phrase "Noel Coward Died Here." And it is written in Noel's handwriting.

There were some amusing compensations in Chicago, however, because Max Reinhardt's *The Miracle*, starring Lady Diana Cooper and featuring Miss Iris Tree, was playing there at the time. Diana was accompanied by her mother, the always amusing but somewhat unpredictable Duchess of Rutland. [Diana Cooper (1892–1986) was one of the most famous socialites in London and Paris in the 1910s and 1920s. She was married to statesman Duff Cooper and in her three memoirs vividly describes the high society of her day. Her mother (1856–1937) was born Violet Manners but became the Duchess of Rutland in 1906. Iris Tree (1897–1968) was the daughter of famed British actor Herbert Beerbohn Tree but was not known so much as an actress as an eccentric bohemian, model, and poet.] The Duchess could be seen almost any morning on Michigan Avenue with a string bag on her way to the Stop & Shop to collect the day's victuals, which she took home to cook herself. Another of her idiosyncrasies was that she always wore a bandeau, and the fringe of bright red hair peeping out from under it had been carefully selected at the local five and dime. Diana, Iris, and the Duchess stayed together in a rather modest room in the Lake Shore Hotel, which faces the lake; unfortunately, their room did not. They had, of course, many great homes in England, including Belvoir and the even more publicized Haddon Hall, but they saw no reason to dissipate their earnings in Chicago. Diana's role in *The Miracle* required her to remain motionless for nearly thirty minutes, which she did with exquisite beauty. [*The Miracle* was a German play by Karl Vollmöeller about a nun (Rosamund Pinchot) who flees a convent and is replaced by the Madonna (Diana Manners, as she was billed).] When asked how she remained immobile for such a long period of time, Diana always replied that she was thinking of how many new Haddon Hall bathrooms her immobility would be able to provide. Never have so many people lived on so little!

After two weeks in Chicago, *The Vortex* company pressed on to Cleveland, where the reception was a little more encouraging. But it was hardly tumultuous. Within three weeks, Noel and I were on our way across the Atlantic, and soon began my first personally conducted tour of London.

CHAPTER THREE

~

London

Noel's house in London came as a slight shock after the false elegance of the Hotel Des Artistes. Mrs. Coward, his mother, ran a rooming house on Ebury Street, and in spite of her son's newfound fortune, she stubbornly refused to give it up. Equally stubborn, Noel refused to give her up and retained a floor in these average lodgings, comprising living quarters and an office.

It was then that I met, with some trepidation, Lorn Loraine, who had been Noel's loyal secretary for many years and, for that matter, still is. Trepidation because it would have only been natural for her to resent the arrival of a moon-faced American who didn't, but might have, threatened her position in the ménage. To everyone's delight, and perhaps faint surprise, we took to each other at once. We became fast friends and remained so.

Noel must have seen Ebury Street with a fresh eye, because after his return from New York, he redoubled his efforts to get his mother to move. She resolutely refused, and he hit upon another plan, which may or may not have been wise, to take over two floors instead of one. He commissioned an old friend, a wealthy dilettante named Lord Latham, who was indulging in modern décor at the time, to redo the duplex. The results were somewhat ludicrous. In this staid, old-fashioned, routine boarding house, there suddenly appeared two floors of vermillion, orange, and pink, the most unexpected and unreliable colors of the period. The rest of the house remained the same, which only emphasized the unreality of Ned Latham's imagination in the suite modern. [Ned Latham was actually Edward William Bootle-Wilbraham (1895–1930), the Third Earl of Latham, a patron of the arts, a frustrated playwright, and one of Coward's first lovers and financial supporters. Latham squandered his entire estate on unprofitable theater ventures and died penniless at the age of thirty-five.]

Shortly after the renovation, Mrs. Coward elected to have a party. She never even told Noel until that same day, and when he offered her his elegant quarters, she emphatically refused and insisted that she host it in a sort-of lean-to at the back of the house. Without a trace of fear or embarrassment, she invited half the stars of London, including Fred and Adele Astaire and Jane Cowl, who by this time had arrived to play *Easy Virtue*. Whether out of kindness or perhaps a desire to impress, she had also invited her suburban relatives. The two groups definitely did not mix. I recall one of Noel's uncles saying to Adele Astaire in a thick, pompous voice, "Have you ever been to Canfield Cliffs?" Canfield Cliffs being one of the most unfashionable—in fact, squalid—resorts in England, Adele rose to the occasion and graciously smiled, "Alas, no." But the highlight of the party came when Noel's father, hospitable and ebullient, proffered a plate of sandwiches to Jane Cowl, who sat hung with jewels and covered with furs but resolutely silent the entire

Jane Cowl (1884–1950) was a popular actress beloved for her dark, limpid eyes and delicate fluttering gestures, which made her ideal for playing heroines in distress. But Cowl was also an accomplished classical actress, her Juliet considered the finest of her day. Born in Boston, she studied at Columbia and began her career under the aegis of impresario David Belasco, first appearing in his 1903 production of *Sweet Kitty Bellairs* and then in four of his other productions. Nevertheless. Cowl did not achieve fame until she played the wrongfully convicted Mary Turner in *Within the Law* (1912). She then scored another success as another wronged woman: Ellen Neal in *Common Clay* (1915).

Cowl starred in and cowrote *Lilac Time* (1917), *Information Please* (1918), and the hugely successful tearjerker *Smilin' Through* (1919). In addition to Juliet, her other classical roles included Shakespeare's Cleopatra and Viola. Her later successes included the mismarried heroine Larita in *Easy Virtue* (1925), the noble beauty Amytis in *The Road to Rome* (1927), a puppet come to life in *The Jealous Moon* (1928), glamorous actress Jenny in *Jenny* (1929), and dedicated writer Katherine Markham in *Old Acquaintance* (1940). Her last appearance was in a 1947 revival of *The First Mrs. Fraser*. Cowl made two silent films and five talkies, but the camera did not do her justice, so she concentrated on theater. To the end she remained a slim, dark-haired beauty who mesmerized her audiences.

afternoon, and said, "Have a tongue sandwich. That will make you talk!" In the pause that ensued, the party dissolved into giggles of laughter led by Noel himself.

Jane was a remarkable woman, the likes of which is seldom seen on the contemporary stage. She was a genuine star, as well as an accomplished performer. Unlike many present-day leading ladies, there were no jeans or sweatshirts for her. She wore jewels and furs, and was always beautifully dressed. She had loads of talent on stage, but like many actresses of that time, her main preoccupation was being a star. For example, when Jane arrived in London, she immediately took a large house in Grosvenor Square, and her entourage there included a butler, maid, masseur, secretary, and husband.

During rehearsals for *Easy Virtue*, Jane staged truly elaborate parties for the cast with an elegant embellishment of the peerage. And when we went to Manchester for tryouts, she continued her lavish entertaining at the Midland Hotel. Throughout her career, she lived in this lavish manner, and it was a sad and ironic twist that years later she was to end up penniless in Hollywood, where she eventually died.

The Manchester Watch Committee, the local censors, refused to pass the title, *Easy Virtue*, in spite of the fact that next door there was a film uninhibited by the committee called *Flames of Passion*. In consequence, it was simply titled "a new play by Noel Coward," since Noel stubbornly refused to give up the title, and the "Watchdog Committee," as we used to call them, was equally stubborn about allowing him to use it. The play, using the title *Easy Virtue*, was vociferously welcomed in London, however, and Jane immediately became the latest and most adored of the visiting stars, all of which

Easy Virtue is a 1925 melodrama by Noel Coward that was unusual in that it opened on Broadway and then played in London. John Whittaker (Robert Harris) brings his new bride Larita (Jane Cowl) to his English ancestral home, and it is clear that the stuffy family does not accept her. Details about Larita's past, involving a divorce case in which she was named, later come to light, and the family turns hostile. Larita defends herself in a pleasant, obliging manner, smashes a precious heirloom, and walks away from John and his family forever. Reviewers admired the British play's unsentimental quality and wit, and the Broadway production ran for four and a half months. In 1926, it enjoyed similar success in London. There was a silent film version in 1928, directed by Alfred Hitchcock and featuring Isabel Jeans as Larita. Eighty years later there was finally a talkie version of *Easy Virtue*, with Jessica Biel as Larita.

she earned, desired, and, I imagine, expected. [The West End production of *Easy Virtue*, produced and directed by Basil Dean, ran for 124 performances.]

There was a walk-on in the party scene, among many others, whose name at the time meant nothing to any of us: Adrianne Allen. I knew her later when she was married to Raymond Massey. Before that, Raymond had been married to the free spirit Margery Fremantle, and as he was always enormously influenced by his wife's tastes, marriage number one had been conducted along faintly bohemian lines. When they were divorced and Raymond married Adrianne, the picture altered. She had other plans, which included a house in Wilton Crescent, decorated by Oliver Messel and staffed with butlers and footmen. Elegant supper parties of several courses were frequently given, and Ray took to this setup as easily and casually as he had taken to the other. It was a happy household, and I had the pleasure of staying with them for several months in the greatest luxury. [Raymond Massey (1896–1983) was an imposing stage and screen actor who played a variety of roles but is most remembered for playing Abraham Lincoln on Broadway and in two films. Adrianne Allen (1907–1993) was a British character actress who appeared on both the London and New York stages and in movies and on television in both cities. Oliver Messel (1904–1978) was a British artist and outstanding stage designer; he painted an original oil portrait of Wilson that still belongs to the family.] Even this marriage subsequently ended in divorce, and one of the best switches of our day ensued. Ray married an intelligent and forceful lady from New Haven, Connecticut, Dorothy Whitney. Adrianne bided her time, and when a reasonable amount of shouting had died down, she quietly married Mr. Whitney. She kept the children from the previous marriages, including talented actress Anna Massey, and was a devoted mother and model wife, and she continued to develop her career as a fine actress. Noel used to call Adrianne "Planny," and the aforementioned history might tend to prove his point.

In 1934 and 1935, Adrianne and Ray worked together in one of my London performances. The play, a love triangle, was a serious one by Keith Winter called *The Shining Hour*. Keith had sent it to Ray, who induced Gladys Cooper to costar with him and then offered the package to me. Adrianne had an important part, which she played superbly. To the delight of us all, we had a hit. [The West End production of *The Shining Hour* ran for 213 performances, two and a half months longer than the Broadway mounting.]

Noel's next project following *Easy Virtue* in London was a play called *The Queen Was in the Parlour*. I mention this mainly as a matter of record, because although it was a fine production, headed by Madge Titherage and including Herbert Marshall, Francis Lister, and Lady Tree, it was not a conspicuous

The Shining Hour was a 1934 play by Keith Winter that starred popular actress Gladys Cooper. Mariella Linden (Gladys Cooper) marries into a Yorkshire family that has consisted of gentlemen farmers since Elizabethan times. She falls in love with her brother-in-law David (Raymond Massey), which drives David's wife Judy (Adrianne Allen) to suicide. Mariella and David run off together, disrupting centuries of family tradition. The British play was first produced by Max Gordon on Broadway, where it enjoyed a successful run of 121 performances, before opening in London with much the same cast. *The Shining Hour* was filmed by Hollywood in 1938, with Joan Crawford, Robert Young, and Margaret Sullavan comprising the love triangle.

success. [Actually, *The Queen Was in the Parlour*, produced and directed by Basil Dean, ran for a profitable 136 performances.]

In the meantime, Basil Dean—one of the most important, if somewhat irritating, producers in London—was planning to present *The Constant Nymph* and was anxious that Noel should play the part of Lewis Dodd. [Basil Dean (1888–1978) was an English writer, actor, and producer who was successful in London, on Broadway, and in the movies. He wrote a dozen plays and directed and/or produced twice as many films. Dean built the famous Ealing Studios in 1931 and ran the company until the war broke out.] Dean had already engaged a relatively unheard-of young man named John Gielgud for the part, and Noel was reluctant to take it away from him, as he thought it might cause some embarrassment. But Noel finally succumbed to Basil's persuasion and played it for a limited time with Edna Best, who gave an exquisite performance as the tragic Teresa. John behaved beautifully and agreed to follow in the role whenever Noel decided to leave. In preparation, Gielgud sat next to me in the stalls during each rehearsal. [What Wilson was probably not aware of was the fact that the young Gielgud was smitten with Coward and very jealous of Wilson's relationship with the playwright.]

Noel played it brilliantly. It was a great theatrical and personal success, although he always maintained that he was not essential to the production. And when Noel left after a few weeks, John took over, and it rolled triumphantly on. [Coward suffered a nervous collapse after playing in *The Constant Nymph* for three weeks. Gielgud played the leading role for nearly a year.] Of course, John became one of the theater's most remarkable actors. I knew him first when he was understudying Noel in *The Vortex*, and we became great

The Constant Nymph was a popular 1926 drama based on a best-selling 1924 novel by Margaret Kennedy. Basil Dean and Kennedy wrote the stage adaptation, which starred Noel Coward in one of his few hits not written by himself. The wealthy Englishman Sanger dies while summering in his Austrian chalet, and family members gather, including the late man's protégé Lewis Dodd (Coward). He falls in love with one of the cousins but soon realizes it was a mistake. He later falls in love with Sanger's daughter Teresa (Edna Best), and the two elope and go to Brussels but Teresa gets ill and dies. The 1926 London success was welcomed by the New York press later that same year, and audiences kept the drama on the boards for four months. Glenn Anders played Lewis on Broadway, and Beatrice Thomson was Teresa. *The Constant Nymph* was made into a silent film in 1928, starring Ivor Novello as Lewis, and then remade as a talkie in 1933, featuring Brian Aherne. Another remake came in 1943, with Charles Boyer.

friends sitting through those endless rehearsals of *Nymph*. Of course, the rest of his career is theatrical history.

In 1947, I had the honor of presenting John, in association with the Theatre Guild and H. M. Tennent, Ltd., in a season of two plays, Oscar Wilde's *The Importance of Being Earnest* and William Congreve's *Love for Love*. We primarily used the same cast for both productions. John directed. We had Pamela Brown, Adrianne Allen, and Cyril Ritchard in *Love*; Margaret Rutherford in *Earnest*; and Robert Flemyng in both. Mr. Wilde's comedy was an unmistakable hit, but Mr. Congreve's play was less well received. The audiences at the time may not have had an appetite for Restoration comedy. With Motley, Max Whistler, and Jeannette Cochrane dividing their designing talents, it was quite an aggregation. I am still amazed, however, that the management ended up with an undeniable, if somewhat minute, profit at the end of the season.

Three years later, under the same auspices, John appeared again in his production of Christopher Fry's *The Lady's Not for Burning*. The arrangements for this were made at Stratford-on-Avon while I was visiting John the previous summer. Again his costar was Pamela Brown, and among the supporting players was a brilliant young actor who has since proved his talents: Richard Burton. Oliver Messel designed a beautiful set, and the play, to my enlightening surprise—considering that it was in verse and scarcely on a popular theme—was a success. [*The Lady's Not for Burning* won the New York Drama Critics Circle Award and ran for a profitable 151 performances, with Burton making his New York debut.] There were some disasters, however. I recall

John Gielgud (1904–2000) was one of the most acclaimed British actors of the twentieth century and an accomplished director. While he was primarily known for his performances on stage and screen in Shakespeare roles, he also found success in a variety of other plays, from classical to theater of the absurd. A grand-nephew of Victorian-era actress Ellen Terry, the musical-voiced actor received his first recognition in 1926, when he replaced Noel Coward in *The Constant Nymph*. At the age of twenty-six, he played Hamlet for the first of many times. In fact, his portrayal of the Danish prince on Broadway in 1936 made him a star in New York. He returned to Broadway to reprise many of his London triumphs, in both classic and modern plays. Gielgud's most memorable stage performances include those in *The Importance of Being Earnest, Love for Love, The Three Sisters, Romeo and Juliet, Medea, Crime and Punishment, The Lady's Not for Burning, Much Ado about Nothing, The School for Scandal, Tiny Alice, Home, No Man's Land*, and his solo Shakespearean program *Ages of Man*. Gielgud directed some of these, as well as several other productions, perhaps most memorably Richard Burton's *Hamlet* in 1964.

Gielgud also appeared in more than 100 films and television dramas, often in later years in memorably eccentric character parts. Among his notable movie credits are *Secret Agent* (1936), *Julius Caesar* (1953 and 1970), *Richard III* (1955), *Becket* (1964), *The Loved One* (1965), *The Charge of the Light Brigade* (1968), *Murder on the Orient Express* (1974), *Arthur* (1981), *Prospero's Books* (1991), *Shine* (1996), and *Elizabeth* (1998). Gielgud received many honors during his long career, including a knighthood in 1953. He continued acting on the stage and screen until his death at the age of ninety-six. Gielgud's most distinguishing characteristic was perhaps his silver-toned voice, which was not bombastic, but mellow and musical.

one night at the end of the first act, while I was standing in the back of the theater, a husband and wife came stamping up the aisle as the man said, "This is the last time you'll ever do this to me!" Fortunately, that couple was in the minority, and the play ran for many months. The credit was mostly due to John and Pamela, who made a beautiful play come to life.

John is devoted to his work, and although he wisely demanded several thousand dollars a week from me for his Broadway appearances, he would gladly play Stratford-on-Avon for $60. His film salaries are monumental, but on the other hand, he did an entire season at the Lyric Hammersmith in London for what virtually amounted to cab fare, simply because there were certain plays he wanted to do. He has even persuaded actresses the likes of Pamela Brown, who have also cost me a pretty penny in my time, to do the same thing. [Pamela Brown (1917–1975) was a versatile British actress who played classical and modern roles on the stage and made many film and television appearances in her relatively short career.] John is courteous, charming, and, as the phrase goes, a gentleman and scholar. When you add his theatrical achievements to these qualities, it is easy to understand why he so richly deserved his knighthood.

It was during *The Constant Nymph* period that Noel introduced me to everyone of theatrical importance in London. He naturally knew them all and was anxious that I should know them too. There was Constance Collier, a warm and friendly hostess who gave endless supper parties peopled with the theater's elite. She was generous to her friends and even allowed famous dressmaker Charles James to design and fit his fabulous wardrobes in her bathroom. For some reason, he had not been allowed a permit to open a shop in England, but that was the sort of thing that never worried Constance.

Constance was a rare person and had been a famous beauty. Her theatrical career was the ne plus ultra of distinction, and she had been Forbes Robertson's leading lady at His Majesty's Theatre for years. I came to know her much later in numerous circumstances, in London, as well as

Constance Collier (1878–1955) was an accomplished leading lady in both classic and contemporary plays, but she is most remembered for her imposing grande dame roles, which she played in her later career on stage and in films. She was born Laura Constance Hardie in Windsor, England, and was on the stage at the age of three as a fairy in *A Midsummer Night's Dream*. She made her London debut in 1893 and had essayed many classical roles before coming to the United States for the first time in 1908, to appear as Anne-Marie in *Samson*, with William Gillette. Traversing the Atlantic, Collier managed a busy and successful career both on Broadway and the West End. Perhaps her most beloved role in both venues was that of Nancy in *Oliver Twist*, a part she returned to often. Two of Collier's other noteworthy roles were as matrons in comedies late in her stage career: the ditzy former actress Judith Bliss in *Hay Fever* (1931) and the outspoken Carlotta Vance in *Dinner at Eight* (1932). Although she had made her screen debut in 1916, in the massive epic *Intolerance*, Collier's scattered film career is mostly remembered for the stately ladies she played in such movies as *Anna Karenina* (1935), *Wee Willie Winkie* (1937), *Stage Door* (1937), *Susan and God* (1940), *An Ideal Husband* (1947), and *Rope* (1948).

Hollywood and New York. One Hollywood incident is worth reporting. She had been hired by MGM, technically as an actress, but ended up at a considerable salary as Louis B. Mayer's hostess. His wife was ill at the time, and Constance arranged his famous Sunday luncheons and innumerable dinner parties. I remember Mrs. Cole Porter, Linda, saying to me, "Darling, if you want to get anywhere socially in Hollywood, the queen of the town is Constance. So make sure she's your friend." Fortunately she was and had been for many years. Her appearances on the screen were somewhat ephemeral, but her influence in Hollywood high society carried more weight than even MGM's backlog of super-productions. In fact, the importance of her social value so impressed Jack Warner that he promptly engaged Elsa Maxwell to draft an acting contract with the inference that she would handle his parties as well. In the end, while film appearances by Constance were few, she handled the social affairs at that magnificent Warner house with her usual efficiency.

Ina Claire (1892–1985) was a svelte, blonde-haired, hazel-eyed beauty with a tipped-up nose and weak chin who was considered the finest high comedienne of her generation. She was born in poverty in Washington, D.C., and made her debut in vaudeville as a singing mimic in 1905. Her first New York appearance in 1909 won attention with her imitation of singer Harry Lauder. Claire toured in two-a-day vaudeville for several seasons before making her musical comedy debut in *Jumping Jupiter* (1911). After major roles in the musicals *The Quaker Girl* (1911), *The Honeymoon Express* (1913), and the 1915 and 1916 editions of the *Ziegfeld Follies*, she made her first appearance in a straight play, *Polly with a Past* (1917), and won such rave notices that she became one of the most sought-after comediennes in New York.

Claire consolidated her reputation as chorine Jerry Lamar in *The Gold Diggers* (1919), followed by sterling performances in *Bluebeard's Eighth Wife* (1921), *The Awful Truth* (1922), *The Last of Mrs. Cheyney* (1925), and *Our Betters* (1928). After touring in *Reunion in Vienna*, she played one of her best roles: the footloose painter Marion Froude in *Biography* (1932). Claire's last successes were in *End of Summer* (1936) and *The Confidential Clerk* (1954). Her film career was less prodigious, appearing in only eleven feature movies between 1915 and 1943. Claire reprised her Polly in the silent 1920 version of *Polly with a Past* and her Lucy in a 1929 talkie adaptation of *The Awful Truth*. Although she had a leading role in *The Royal Family of Broadway* (1930), she is best remembered by moviegoers as Grand Duchess Swana in *Ninotchka* (1939).

Many years later, when she was no longer involved with the film industry, Constance briefly fell upon rather difficult financial times. Ina Claire, with her persistent kindness—a characteristic not only of hers, but also of the theatrical profession in general—went to her friends to ask for contributions to alleviate Constance's temporary distress.

Ina had first suggested to Constance that she borrow from her devoted companion and housekeeper, Phyllis, adding the remark, "Servants always have more money than we have." But Constance replied in her famously resonant, drawling voice, "That's out of the question darling. I've milked her dry." And so Ina put her charitable giving plan into effect. Constance was never to know from what sources the contributions had come nor how much each had amounted to. She was simply to be given a lump sum "from her friends." I have no idea how much she realized, but I imagine it was considerable. I do know that the following spring, I lunched in London at Mrs. Somerset Maugham's, and Constance was one of the guests. We went down in the lift together, and I asked her if I could drop her anywhere in a taxi. "No," she replied, "but I can drop you, as I have my own car." And as we stepped out onto Park Lane, a rather large Rolls Royce drove up with a chauffeur behind the wheel. Ina's efforts were apparently very successful.

I was to know Constance again in her later years in New York. Her eyesight was failing, and she certainly wasn't as young as she had been. But with indomitable vitality, she took up dramatic coaching. Her favorite and most important pupil was Katharine Hepburn, who stood by her to the end. Constance used to brag to me, with a smile that enhanced her inevitable sense of humor, that she refused most applicants, limiting her teaching to those with "unmistakable talent." The list included Paulette Goddard, Mrs. Huntington Hartford, and Marilyn Monroe. It was obvious to both of us that irrespective of their histrionic abilities, each one of them had a nice, fat bank account. [Paulette Goddard appeared in several Broadway productions as a Ziegfeld girl and went on to achieve stardom in Hollywood. Her husbands included Charles Chaplin and Burgess Meredith. Huntington Hartford was heir to the A&P fortune and a famous philanthropist, producer, and art collector.] Constance died in 1955, beloved and bemourned. My personal sorrow at her passing can only be tempered by the fact that she had a rich, full life, which she enjoyed to the end.

Among the others whom I met through Noel's auspices was Gerald du Maurier. He was handsome, elegant, and one of the toasts of London. Of all his triumphs, his greatest achievement may have been that he uncovered Tallulah Bankhead. I had met her but hadn't seen her since the night she danced on a table in my Yale dormitory, an escapade that caused her student host to be dismissed from the university. [Gerald du Maurier (1873–1934) was a dashing British stage actor and producer. He was the son of writer George du Maurier and the father of novelist Daphne du Maurier.]

And then, of course, there was Ivor Novello. Ivor had been a childhood friend of Noel's but was presumably his theatrical rival. He wrote, composed, and starred in enormous musicals, but his public varied from Noel's in two ways: They were less sophisticated and larger. As a person, he was almost too good to be true. Always charming, he seemed to refuse to disagree with anyone on any topic. His friendship with Noel persisted throughout the years in spite of their unspoken yet undeniable difference of opinion on stagecraft.

Ivor's amiability was unbelievable. During the war he was arrested for illegally accepting gasoline for his car, but he emerged from prison without

Ivor Novello (1893–1951) was a popular matinee idol on stage and a romantic star on the silent screen who also had a successful career as a songwriter and playwright. He was born David Ivor Davies in Cardiff, Wales, the son of celebrated musician-teacher Clara Novello Davies, and educated at the Magdalen College Choir School. His first success as a songwriter came in 1914, with the beloved wartime hit "Keep the Home Fires Burning." This led to assignments writing books and scores for London musicals, among the most notable being *Theodore & Co.* (1916), *Arlette* (1917), *Who's Hooper?* (1919), *The Golden Moth* (1921), *Glamorous Night* (1935), *Careless Rapture* (1936), *The Dancing Years* (1939), *Perchance to Dream* (1945), and *King's Rhapsody* (1949), several of which he appeared in as well. Parallel to this was a distinguished career on the British stage as a writer, singer, and eventually a leading man in plays.

Novello made his screen debut in 1920 and found recognition the next year in *Carnival,* followed by memorable roles in such silents as *The White Rose* (1923), *Bonnie Prince Charlie* (1923), *The Rat* (1925), *The Lodger* (1927), *The Constant Nymph* (1928), and *The Vortex* (1928). Although he made a handful of talkies, by the 1930s he had returned to the theater and concentrated on plays and musicals until his death from a heart attack in 1951, at the age of fifty-eight. Novello wrote more than 250 songs, which have remained popular in England and can be heard in British films, among them "My Heart Is Singing," "Till the Boys Come Home," "We'll Gather Lilacs," and "Give Me Back My Heart," as well as the perennial favorite "Keep the Home Fires Burning." In Great Britain, the prestigious Ivor Novello Awards are given annually by the British music industry for composers, arrangers, and song publishers.

the slightest animosity toward his jailers or the judiciary that had been responsible for putting him there. He was a remarkable man, and everyone who knew him, plus the thousands who admired his work, was desperately shocked when he died in his fifties of a heart attack.

Noel had written a play during a holiday in Sicily called *This Was a Man*, and we went to New York to present it there first, this time without Gladys Calthrop or Noel's mother. Noel had thoughtfully dedicated the play to me, but it was a complete failure. It concerned a self-satisfied, overly confident, middle-aged Englishman, twisted around and made a fool of by two women. The plot was negligible, merely a satirical study of pomposity that is finally reduced to nothing. Francine Larrimore was the star, and the cast included Auriol Lee, Nigel Bruce, and A. E. Matthews. But on opening night, our overly fashionable audience began slithering one by one out of their seats. By the end of the evening there was no question that the play had been a big mistake.

Noel decided to whisk off to the Greenbrier in White Sulphur Springs to get away from it all. With his usual energy, within twenty-four hours he began writing a comedy for Marie Tempest, a charming period piece titled *The Marquise*. This play was subsequently dispatched to London, but without the author, who decided to avoid the directional routine for that moment. He was suffering from a nervous condition and wanted to get away, even farther than West Virginia this time. We entrained for San Francisco, where we spent two or three days before Noel sailed for China, with me waving good-bye from the pier in a highly emotional state.

I then joined Diana Cooper and her friend Rudolf Kommer for dinner that same evening. She was by now playing *The Miracle* in San Francisco. I remember her standing at a window in the Fairmont Hotel, looking out on

This Was a Man is a 1926 dark comedy by Noel Coward that struggled with the censors and had difficulty finding an audience. Portrait painter Edward Churt (A. E. Matthews) doesn't mind that his wife Carol (Francine Larrimore) has taken many lovers throughout the years, but when she has an affair with his best friend, Major Evelyn Bathurst (Nigel Bruce), it is too much. He asks Carol for a divorce and calmly goes off to lunch at his club, telling her, "There's always time to shoot yourself." The flippant attitude toward infidelity caused Lord Chamberlain to ban the comedy in England, so producer Basil Dean presented the play on Broadway, where it opened to indifferent reaction and only managed a one-month run.

The Marquise is a 1927 costume drama by Noel Coward that had a light touch and star appeal. French aristocrat Marquise Eloise de Kestournel (Marie Tempest), in eighteenth-century Paris, learns that her daughter (Eileen Sharp) has fallen in love with the son (Godfrey Winn) from her former marriage. To keep the half-siblings from marrying, Eloise finds new mates for them both, as well as one for herself. The charming play was well received in London and ran for 129 performances on the strength of the fine cast, particularly the star turn by Tempest. When *The Marquise* opened on Broadway later in 1927, it was poorly received, but there was high praise for Billie Burke's flighty, funny performance as the Marquise, so the piece ran ten weeks. Although the play was not made into a film, it showed up as a television drama several times: on Swedish television in 1964, on East German television in 1977, and on British stations in 1969 and 1980.

that fabulous harbor, and saying, "How unbelievably beautiful. So unlike our own dear Liverpool!" [Rudolf Kommer (1886–1943) was a Rumanian-born impresario who presented many of Max Reinhardt's theater productions.] Diana had to leave early for the theater, so I dined with Kommer and Raimund von Hofmannsthal—who had a small part in *The Miracle* and a large crush on Diana—and then took the night train back to New York. [Von Hofmannsthal was the son of Hugo von Hofmannsthal, author of *The Miracle*.]

A few months later, I joined up with Noel upon his return to New York. He had never reached China. Instead, upon his arrival in Honolulu, he suffered a nervous breakdown and had been taken in by the Walter Dillinghams, who at the time owned most of Hawaii. Noel stayed at their house for a few days, but the social whirl and the va and vien was so much for his frayed nerves that they lent him a full cottage on one of their numerous outlying plantations. Living alone in the Dillinghams's cottage, Noel was able to relax, and in time, he became completely well. [Walter Dillingham (1875–1963) was dubbed the Baron of Hawaii, having built and developed Pearl Harbor, the Ala Wai Canal, and urban Honolulu.] Soon after his return, we embarked together on the *Olympic*, en route to London. Noel naturally went at once to see his White Sulphur Springs play, *The Marquise*, which, by this time, had been running successfully for many months. Marie Tempest was assisted by her husband, Graham Browne, and Frank Cellier. The cast also included a juvenile, later to be widely known in British journalistic circles as Godfrey Winn. [Winn (1906–1971) was one of the most famous British correspondents during World War II.]

Noel had previously rented a country house called Goldenhurst, and when he found his mother happy and content there, he decided to buy it. We found that extensive renovations were needed, mostly instigated by me. Noel has always had a passion for houses, even though he ignores them as soon as they are acquired, and he can never be bothered by décor. He had, along with Goldenhurst, an elaborate studio in London and a flat in Paris, all of them eventually gone once he left England for tax reasons. He then established himself in Bermuda and bought two houses in Jamaica; at one point he had plans to build a third. Clearly he can't live in them all, but then there are a host of friends, well-wishers, and other satellites who keep them continuously and loudly occupied. Noel's great pride, among many, is that he need never travel with luggage exceeding a briefcase, as each of his homes is stocked with a complete wardrobe.

It was in the London studio apartment that I first coined a phrase that I have since regretted. It was morning, and the entourage was already ensconced, sipping coffee while waiting for Noel to descend from his quarters upstairs. When he finally arrived on the staircase, immaculate with a cigarette and red carnation, I unfortunately sardonically quipped, "Here comes the Master!" In spite of my sarcasm, the label was picked up by the group, and they have called him the "Master" ever since. He loves it, and ensuing entourages in later years also picked it up. Ironically enough, I became the only one close to him who refused to repeat the title. [In all that has been written about Coward, the origin of the nickname the "Master" has never been satisfactorily documented. Biographers only state that the expression was first used in the late 1920s. Coward only states that "it started as a joke and became true." This somewhat supports Wilson's claim that he created the moniker. Many years later, when a reporter asked Coward why he was known as the "Master," the playwright replied, "Oh, you know—Jack of all trades, master of none."]

While *The Marquise* was still running in London, it was translated into German for a presentation in Vienna. Noel was invited to the opening, and I went along with him. Naturally, it was unintelligible to us and particularly perplexing and somewhat shocking, as it had been written as an eighteenth-century fantasy, to see the heroine on a motorcycle, clad from head to foot in leather. The production was ultra-modern, practically atomic, but apparently highly successful. There were endless curtain calls, and Noel was summoned to the stage to take his bow. He made a speech in impeccable English, which must have confused the audience as much as the play had confused us.

Soon thereafter, we went to stay with Edward Molyneux, the famous fashion designer, who had the most beautiful house I have ever seen (with

the exception of a newer one he built some years later in Jamaica) at Cap
d'Ail on the Riviera. The house offered luxury, sun, and bathing, and even
featured a tennis court built out over the sea. It was also conveniently located
near Monte Carlo, where I made my first acquaintance with the Russian
Ballet. It was only a few miles from Edward's abode, just up the road, past
what later became Princess Grace's house on the right, to the Monte Carlo
Casino. The casino property included an exquisite theater, which Serge Diaghilev and his troupe used as a sort of New Haven tryout for their ultimate
seasons in Paris and London. The Ballets Russes was one of the most famous
ballet troupes ever created. They did *Le Chat* with isinglass scenery and costumes, *The Three-Cornered Hat*, and such old reliables as *Swan Lake*—all of
which at the time were entirely new to me. It was a charming way to go to
the ballet because during the time between acts, which one normally spends
at the Metropolitan in Sherry's Bar, one was allowed, even encouraged, to
wander to the gambling rooms to lose a few hundred francs before the bell
announced the next act. The ballet's star attraction, Vaslav Nijinsky, had
taken ill and retired to Switzerland, and Serge Lifar became the new star and
a special pet of impresario Diaghilev.

For me, learning to understand ballet opened up a new world of excitement. In addition, through Noel's influence, there were a series of lunches
with the great Diaghilev himself and whichever prominent members of his
company he favored at the moment. He was a rotund, bushy-eyed perfectionist, but a martinet with his dancers. Each and every one of them was terrified
of him. Socially, however, he was all amiability and wit. For a young man
from Trenton, New Jersey, it was an extraordinary treat. [Serge Diaghilev
(1872–1929) was probably the most colorful and famous impresario in the
history of ballet. He founded the Ballets Russes, created many stars, and premiered many major works. When Wilson met him, Diaghilev was at the end
of his career; he died two years later.]

The next stop was Venice, where Cole and Linda Porter had invited
Noel to stay, and he gently insisted that I should be included in the party.
They had a fabulous establishment on the Grand Canal called the Palazzo
Rezzonico, precisely where the poet Browning took Elizabeth Barrett after their well-known elopement. Poetry must have been very well paid in
those days, because it was one of the largest and most handsome houses in
Venice. In addition to being on the Grand Canal, it boasted a huge inner
courtyard, a ballroom, eight to ten drawing rooms, and I never knew how
many bedrooms. Noel and I occupied what was known as the "Pope's Suite,"
which included a sitting room facing the Grand Canal, two bedrooms, and a
relatively primitive bathroom. For some strange and never to be discovered

reason, the bath was almost permanently occupied by an elderly Italian lady, whose presence upset us considerably during the early period of our stay. A solution was finally reached, which was to pay no attention to her whatsoever and just go about one's business. She didn't seem to mind in the least. Monty Woolley, who was a close friend of Cole's, was another guest, and Hermann Oelrichs Jr. and his wife Dorothy (also known as "Dumpy" and later in life, the Princess Liechtenstein) took most of their meals there, although they had a large bridal suite at the Grand Hotel—quite rightly, as they were on their honeymoon. [Hermann Oelrichs Jr., was the son and heir of a vast shipping fortune.]

Each day we all went to the Lido to dabble in the famous, if somewhat tepid, Adriatic. That narrow strip of sand, littered with cabanas, somehow manages to attract the celebrities of the world. There was Diana Cooper, who by this time had finally relinquished *The Miracle* and apparently even Haddon Hall. Unlike her nearly naked contemporaries, she always appeared on the beach fully dressed and covered with heavy veils. Her skin was so exquisite and sensitive that no sun was ever allowed to touch it. I could never understand, under the circumstances, why she selected that particular spot for her holiday.

Walking up and down the narrow beach past the various cabanas, one could stop and chat with Elsa Maxwell, Princess San Faustino, Cecil Beaton, Princess Faucigny Lucinge, or the blue-haired Baron de Meyer—probably the most famous photographer of his day—and his equally blue-haired wife. Rudolf Kommer was there with Max Reinhardt, both of whom, in their shorts, looked like a couple of teddy bears. There was Lady Iya Abdy, Russian-born but English-married, and her ten-year-old son George, who many years later would achieve a magnificent physique and voice to be known on the American stage as George Gaynes. [The Finnish-born Gaynes (b. 1917) was a handsome leading man on the opera stage, Broadway, television, as well as in movies.]

A particular pleasure was running into Richard Rodgers and Lorenz Hart, who were on their first tour of Europe. They had already written *The Garrick Gaieties*, a charming show that gave enormous promise of their careers to follow. I had the pleasure of introducing them to Cole Porter, and there ensued many an evening of wonderful music, with Cole, Dick, and Noel taking turns at the piano and Larry Hart singing the lyrics he knew and, in some cases, even the ones he didn't. In any event, our time at the Palazzo Rezzonico with the Porters was a resounding and happy success, and many friendships began there that would continue for the rest of my career.

I was to work with Rodgers and Hart many, many years later, in 1943. They asked me to direct a revival of *A Connecticut Yankee*. They had long

Rodgers and Hart was arguably the first great musical theater team of the American musical theater. Composer Richard Rodgers (1902–1979) was born in New York and educated at Columbia, where he wrote music for college shows. Lyricist Lorenz Hart (1895–1943) was also born in Manhattan and educated at Columbia, where he wrote lyrics for campus theatricals. Hart left college to accept a job as translator for the Messrs. Shubert, providing English scripts and lyrics for foreign musicals. The two men teamed up in 1920 and their songs were initially heard on Broadway in *Poor Little Ritz Girl* (1920), but success did not begin to come until they wrote the song "Manhattan" for the first *Garrick Gaieties* (1925). What followed was a remarkable string of musical comedies, most of which were hits and produced song standards. Among the most notable of the Rodgers and Hart musicals are *Dearest Enemy* (1925), *Garrick Gaieties of 1926: The Girl Friend* (1926), *Peggy-Ann* (1926), *A Connecticut Yankee* (1927), *Present Arms* (1928), *America's Sweetheart* (1931), *Jumbo* (1935), *On Your Toes* (1936), *Babes in Arms* (1937), *I'd Rather Be Right* (1937), *I Married an Angel* (1938), *The Boys from Syracuse* (1938), *Too Many Girls* (1939), *Higher and Higher* (1940), *Pal Joey* (1940), and *By Jupiter* (1942). Most of their shows were turned into movies, although rarely with faithfulness to the original.

Rodgers and Hart wrote original scores for such films as *The Hot Heiress* (1931), *The Phantom President* (1932), *Love Me Tonight* (1932), *Hallelujah, I'm a Bum* (1933), and *Mississippi* (1935), as well as the London musical *Evergreen* (1930). Hart's last Broadway credit was writing some new songs for the 1943 revival of *A Connecticut Yankee*. After Hart died prematurely of alcoholism that same year, Rodgers worked exclusively with lyricist-librettist Oscar Hammerstein (1895–1960) for the next seventeen years, and they enjoyed the most successful collaboration in the history of American musicals. Hart was a master at polysyllabic and internal rhymes, as well as innovative lyric forms. His work was pervaded with his essentially misanthropic view of the world. Although personal problems, especially alcoholism, beset his later years, his gifts never waned. Rodgers's enticing use of melody and harmony, endless variety, and ability to capture a mood or an entire culture in a few notes are among the talents that made him one of the greatest musical artists in the United States.

since dissolved their partnership, and Dick had just teamed up with Oscar Hammerstein on their tremendous first hit, *Oklahoma!* But Larry and Dick had enjoyed so many years of success together that Dick must have felt that a return of their collaboration would be a friendly gesture, a kindness, and perhaps even another hit.

A **Connecticut Yankee** is a lighthearted 1927 musical comedy inspired by Mark Twain's satiric fantasy story *A Connecticut Yankee in King Arthur's Court*. At a party on the eve of his wedding, Martin (William Gaxton) flirts with Alice Carter (Constance Carpenter), which so infuriates his bride-to-be, Fay Morgan (Nana Bryant), that she knocks him unconscious with a blow from a champagne bottle. Martin dreams he is in King Arthur's court, where he falls in love with Alisande La Carteloise, who looks just like Alice, but where his wooing and attempts to modernize the medieval world are thwarted by Merlin (William Norris) and the villainous Morgan Le Fay, the fire-spitting image of Fay Morgan. When Martin awakes, he decides to marry Alice.

Herbert Fields wrote the clever book, and the score by Rodgers (music) and Hart (lyrics) included the song standards "My Heart Stood Still" and "Thou Swell." Lew Fields produced the original 1927 Broadway production, which ran for a very profitable 418 performances. *A Connecticut Yankee* was successfully revived in 1943, with a few new songs by Rodgers and Hart. Wilson directed the production, which featured Dick Foran, Vivienne Segal, and Julie Warren, running seventeen weeks. Hart died of alcoholism and exposure five days after the production opened.

Larry was a wonderful guy: short, dark, a little homely, and inevitably puffing on a huge cigar. He was warm and friendly and would give you the shirt off his back, or the pants off his backside. He went to work on the revival with his usual vim and vigor, adding two new numbers to the original score. One was "Why Can't You Do a Friend a Favor?" and the other "To Keep My Love Alive." This second song was immaculately performed by Vivienne Segal and, I believe, one of Larry's greatest lyrical achievements. It was the last song he ever wrote.

We went through the usual preliminaries in Philadelphia, but it was there that we began having trouble with Larry's health. Not personal trouble ever, but his addiction to the local bars caused a certain amount of concern. Dick finally moved him into a room at the Ritz with Herbert Fields, author of the book on which the play was based, and Fields was elected Larry's guardian and nurse. This arrangement functioned satisfactorily until one night when Herbert was away and Larry ended up outside in the pouring rain. He was in his bare feet with no jacket and quite naturally caught pneumonia. The next day we rushed him to a hospital in New York. A week later, at our Broadway opening at the Martin Beck Theatre, Larry suddenly and unexpectedly appeared. He had broken out of the hospital to attend but was unable to make it through to the end. He returned to the hospital and tragically passed away five days later. [Accounts of Hart's activity during those last five days vary. Some friends recount that he was missing for a few days and they looked everywhere. Hart's sister-in-law, Dolores Hart, claimed he was with her. What is pretty much known is that Hart was so drunk and disorderly at the opening of *A Connecticut Yankee* that some ushers, not knowing who he was, ejected him from the theater.]

A Connecticut Yankee was a success, and after a season in New York, it continued on the road for many months. It was sad that Larry wasn't around to know that "To Keep My Love Alive," the song he wrote for Vivienne, was the hit of the show. [Although the revival of *A Connecticut Yankee* was Wilson's only professional association with Richard Rodgers, the two men were friends for many years, the Rodgers often being guests in the Wilson country house Pebbles in Connecticut. Wilson hosted a star-studded party there for Rodgers's fiftieth birthday on June 28, 1952. Moreover, Wilson hired Rodgers's daughter Mary as an intern at the Westport Country Playhouse. A young Stephen Sondheim was also a Westport apprentice that summer.]

Noel, of course, never stopped writing, and it was at some point during the period with the Porters in Venice that he conceived a play called *Home Chat*. When it was submitted for Lord Chamberlain's approval, he refused to pass a line that had been allotted to Madge Titheradge. She was to describe a train wreck, saying roughly, "I found myself sitting by the side of the tracks, relatively uninjured, but with a lavatory seat around my neck." It was immediately ruled out, which always upset me, as I thought it totally harmless and amusing. [*Home Chat*, produced and directed by Basil Dean, opened in the West End in 1927, and ran for only thirty-eight performances.] Unfortunately, the show was not a great success, and as usual, Noel took the brunt of it. As he cannot be restrained from making a curtain speech, regardless of the reception, he strode onto the stage in spite of the halfhearted "boos" and suavely faced the audience. Someone from the gallery shouted, "We expected better," and Noel, doing one of his courtly bows, replied, "So did I!" The notices, as anticipated, were not good, and the play limped along for a limited period before subsiding into oblivion.

CHAPTER FOUR

~

New York

Basil Dean, Noel's employer during *The Constant Nymph*, wanted to present a play called *Sirocco*, which Noel had written in 1921 and reluctantly discarded. But Ivor Novello, no doubt egged on by Basil, became interested in playing it, and Noel finally allowed it to be done. It dealt with a resident of the Italian Riviera and his relations with a visiting English girl. Ivor, of course, played the Italian lead, and a comparative newcomer, Frances Doble, was the lovely tourist on holiday. It was an excellent production but proved to be one of the few major catastrophes of Noel's career. By the end of the performance, the bedlam of booing was so violent that even Mrs. Coward, who was sitting next to me and was deaf, sensed the difference between applause and the unrestrained abuse pouring from the gallery and upper circle.

Noel again took it on the chin, going onto the stage to experience an indescribable attack, heightened by the stalls screaming to the gallery to "shut up" and the gallery screaming back to "shut up" themselves. The reaction was so out of proportion that many of us believed that it had been planted and planned. Ivor behaved quite calmly, and the joke that saved our sanity was unwittingly made by Frances Doble. As she was young and inexperienced, the audience was quietly polite when she stepped forward. There was even a smattering of applause. She fixed that by innocently saying, "Ladies and gentlemen, this is the happiest moment of my life!" at which point the general tumult began all over again. When Noel started out the stage door, he was literally attacked and spat upon until he was forced to retreat back into the theater. He then made a private exit from another door. The notices played

Sirocco was a notorious flop by Noel Coward more remembered for its infamous opening night than itself. The drama, about a wealthy Italian (Ivor Novello) and his affair with a young English girl (Frances Doble), opened in London in 1927, in a production directed by Basil Dean. At the curtain call, the booing and catcalls were so furious that some, including Dean and some of the cast, mistakenly thought they were cheers. Legend has it that Coward was physically attacked and spat upon as he left the theater that night. Novello and the rest of the cast hung on for twenty-eight performances. This production was the only time Novello and Coward's professional paths crossed.

along with the general reaction and with an almost unreasonable pleasure. But everyone concerned in the production behaved with admirable fortitude until the play closed two or three weeks later.

To escape from it all, Noel and I spent a week in another of Edward Molyneux's magnificent houses, this time in Neuilly. Then we went on to St. Moritz to spend the Christmas of 1927 and New Year's of 1928 in that charming, snow-swept crow's nest, so remote from the London theater.

Smarting from his recent humiliation, Noel behaved with impeccable honesty. He had a contract with two London managers, McCleod and Mayer, to appear in *The Second Man* by S. N. Behrman. One year earlier, in New York, the play had been done by Alfred Lunt and Lynn Fontanne, and they had recommended it to Noel as a highly suitable vehicle for him in London. Noel had a separate contract with Charles Cochran to create lyrics, a score, and a book for a new revue. Noel contacted both parties with the suggestion that, in light of the recent *Sirocco* unpleasantness, both produc-

The Second Man is a clever and knowing 1927 comedy that launched the careers of playwright S. N. Behrman and leading man Alfred Lunt. Clark Story (Lunt), a novelist and carefree hedonist, proposes to marry the rich, understanding widow Mrs. Kendall Frayne (Lynn Fontanne), but his plans are sidetracked when he hears (wrongly) that his lover, Monica Grey, (Margalo Gillmore) is pregnant. Seemingly accepting of his fate, he ruefully tells Monica's disappointed suitor, scientist Alistin Lowe (Earle Larimore), how dreary the prospect of marriage to Monica appears to him—"Her talk is not small. It is infinitesimal." Monica and Clark inevitably recognize that they are wrong for one another. She leaves Clark and is reconciled with Alistin, while Mrs. Frayne also drops Clark. The play ends with Clark laying plans to get back in Mrs. Frayne's good graces.

Although many critics complained about the slight plot of the Theatre Guild's offering, most agreed that the characterizations and dialogue were first rate. Lunt's portrayal of a charming yet unscrupulous cad was the talk of Broadway, and he became a stage star in the role. The play ran for 178 performances in New York and was then presented in London in 1928, with Noel Coward as Clark Story, where it was also well received. Because of the piece's Coward-like brittle dialogue, many assumed that the British playwright-actor had written Behrman's script. A film version released by RKO in 1930, titled *He Knew Women*, featured Lowell Sherman as Clark and Alice Joyce and Frances Dade as his love interests.

tions be postponed. They refused to accept any such idea, and so, with the snow clinging to our boots and icicles to our eyelashes, we started back to London for Noel to go to work again. We approached *The Second Man* with a certain amount of trepidation, not because of the play itself, which was witty and well written, nor because of the cast, which included Zena Dare, Ursula Jeans, and Raymond Massey, but because of the eventual reception, which, considering recent circumstances, could not be predicted.

On the first night, we trooped into the theater with butterflies in our stomachs and a sick feeling of dread. As it turned out, we needn't have bothered, because the play was enthusiastically received and there wasn't a trace of the antagonism that had greeted the previous venture. We went home happy that it had gone so well. In addition, we were deeply relieved that the cabal had apparently abated. Noel had been restored to his proper position as an idol of the British public.

Sam Behrman—a short, nervous, and superficially shy man—attended the opening of *The Second Man* and expressed great delight with the production

Charles B. Cochran (1872–1951) was a British theatrical producer most known for his musicals in the 1920s and 1930s, and for discovering such stars as Gertrude Lawrence, Jessie Matthews, Evelyn Laye, and Noel Coward. The Oxford-educated Cochran worked as an actor and then a press agent in the United States before returning to Britain in 1917, finding success with his first London production, *The Better 'Ole*. Although he produced many plays, he was most successful with musicals on both the London and New York stages. Long associated with Coward, Cochran presented several of his musicals, comedies, and dramas, most memorably *This Year of Grace* (1928), *Bitter Sweet* (1929), *Private Lives* (1930), *Cavalcade* (1931), and *Conversation Piece* (1934).

and the performances. He made it a habit to pop in on many subsequent nights. There was one particular evening in Noel's dressing room when the Duke of Connaught appeared. He was charming, of course, but a little pomp-ous, and made a great many references to his grandmother, Queen Victoria, and his innumerable royal relatives. After he left, Sam said, in his wonder-fully dry delivery, "Who is that guy? I must say he seems well connected."

Even during the run of *The Second Man*, Noel started on the monumental chore of creating the revue for Cochran. This was eventually to be named *This Year of Grace*. The title had been conceived by Noel's secretary, Lorn. Many people considered it extremely inadequate, but it actually survived to become one of the greatest revue titles of all time. We went through the usual days of auditions and tryouts until the casting eventually took shape.

S. N. Behrman (1893–1973) was a highly respected American playwright who had many hits in his day but is infrequently produced today. He was born Samuel Nathaniel Behrman in Worcester, Massachusetts, and studied at Clark University, before enrolling in Professor George P. Baker's 47 Workshop at Harvard. Behrman worked as a book reviewer, play reader, and press agent before turning to playwriting. His first two efforts, written with others, never reached New York, but he found success with his first solo effort, *The Second Man* (1927). Behrman did not repeat that success with *Love Is Like That* (1927), *Serena Blandish* (1929), *Meteor* (1929), and *Brief Moment* (1931), but he triumphed with what is considered his finest work: *Biography* (1932). Somewhat less applauded were *Rain from Heaven* (1934) and *End of Summer* (1936), although the latter has enjoyed many revivals throughout the years. In 1937, Behrman adapted Jean Giraudoux's *Amphitryon 38* for the Lunts, for whom he also wrote *The Pirate* (1942) and *I Know My Love* (1949). Among his other notable stage works are *No Time for Comedy* (1939), *Jacobowsky and the Colonel* (1944), *Dunnigan's Daughter* (1945), *Jane* (1947), and the book for the musical *Fanny* (1954) with Joshua Logan. His last play, which he called a "serious comedy," was *But for Whom Charlie* (1964).

Behrman was also active in Hollywood, where several of his plays were turned into movies. He contributed to many original screenplays, including *The Sea Wolf* (1930), *Daddy Long Legs* (1931), *Rebecca of Sunnybrook Farm* (1932), *Hallelujah, I'm a Bum* (1933), *Queen Christina* (1933), *The Scarlet Pimpernel* (1934), *A Tale of Two Cities* (1935), *Love Affair* (1939), *Two-Faced Woman* (1941), *Quo Vadis* (1951), and *Ben-Hur* (1959). Behrman, who often added a political slant to his stories, is considered one of the best American playwrights of high comedy.

Tilly Losch (1903–1975) was an accomplished dancer and choreographer who was as famous for her infamous marriages as her stage and film performances. She was born in Vienna and studied ballet as a child at the Vienna Opera. By the time she was eighteen, Losch was prima ballerina for celebrated dance companies in Vienna and Berlin. She made her New York debut in 1927, as a featured dancer in *A Midsummer Night's Dream*, and the next year Losch made her first London appearance in the Noel Coward musical revue *This Year of Grace*, which she also choreographed. On Broadway she danced in and choreographed the revue *Wake Up and Dream* (1929) and danced opposite Fred Astaire in *The Band Wagon* (1931). Losch also appeared in four movies, making an impression as sultry dancer Irena in *The Garden of Allah* (1936), the bratty Lotus in *The Good Earth* (1937), and the heroine's mother Mrs. Chavez in *Duel in the Sun* (1946). Her unsuccessful marriages to two British lords made for colorful copy in the newspapers. To escape her depression from her failed marriages, Losch turned to painting, and her portraits were highly praised and can be found in notable art museums.

Cochran had imported Tilly Losch, whom he had discovered somewhere in Central Europe. She ended up being a resounding success but was indifferent to the concept of rehearsals. It was during this period that Noel made the remark, of course untrue, that Tilly had promised her grandmother on her death bed "never, never to dance."

Tilly was an interesting woman and a magnificent dancer with a style very much her own. She relied on a series of rhythmic, somewhat plastic poses of great beauty and subtlety rather than the frenetic activity that choreographers would sometimes demand. Her private life, however, turned out to be less restrained than her dancing. She married Edward James, who was young, rich, and eccentric, and also an important collector of modern painting, notably works by Salvador Dalí and Pavel Tchelitchew. James specially designed a magnificent bedroom for Tilly at his elegant house, but it was apparently a room he rarely entered, as shortly thereafter they ended up in an unpleasant divorce suit. He accused her of many things, and she accused him of many quite different things. It must have been a matter of money or the case never would have reached the courts. Important witnesses were called, including Adele Astaire and Prince Serge Obolensky. What they testified I cannot say, but Tilly lost her case and Edward emerged with the benediction of the magistrate and a clean bill of health. [He accused Losch of infidelity with the Prince, and she accused

James of homosexuality.] Some years later, Tilly married Henry Herbert, Earl of Carnarvon, whose father sponsored the expedition that discovered King Tutankhamun's tomb. He was probably as rich as Edward but far less eccentric. Herbert owned several large and pompous houses, where Tilly tried her level best to play "lady of the manor." Perhaps due to the Earl's lack of eccentricity, they too would eventually separate, and Tilly settled in New York, where she took up painting, which she did extremely well, and lived simply and quietly—and alone.

During the rehearsals for *This Year of Grace*, it amazed me that Noel had the energy to put in six or seven hours a day in that dust-shrouded theater and still go on at night to perform in the brittle, high-spirited Behrman comedy. *This Year of Grace* opened in Manchester—although without the benefit of the author-director, except on hasty weekends—and eventually came to the London Pavilion in March. It was a beautiful show and an immediate success. In addition to Tilly's triumph, there were Maisie Gay, who was actually the star, and Sonnie Hale and Jessie Matthews. The notices were ecstatic, and Noel was well back where he belonged.

The success of *This Year of Grace* inspired Cochran and his American associate Archie Selwyn to attempt to duplicate the hit in New York. It was obviously impossible to disturb the London company, so they eventually arranged for Beatrice Lillie to take over Maisie Gay's roles, and Noel agreed to assay the material he had created for Sonnie Hale. There were a few new scenes, but in general the show followed the pattern of the London production and sailed off to the United States to open at the Selwyn Theatre.

This Year of Grace was a delightful 1928 musical revue by Noel Coward popular in both London and New York. Coward did not appear in the show in the London version, but he wrote the sketches, as well as the songs, which included three that have become standards: "A Room with a View," "Dance, Little Lady," and "World Weary." The cast featured Sonnie Hale, Maisie Gay, Jessie Matthews, Sheilah Graham, and Tilly Losch. Coward directed and Charles B. Cochran produced the show, which was billed as *Cochran's 1928 Revue* until it opened in the West End as *This Year of Grace*. The reviews were enthusiastic and business was brisk, so when Broadway producer Arch Selwyn wanted to produce the revue in New York, a new cast headed by Coward and Beatrice Lillie was formed. The American production opened later that same year and was warmly welcomed by the press and the public. The London show ran for ten months and the Broadway version five months.

Beatrice Lillie (1894–1989) was a uniquely inspired comedienne who retained her regal and ladylike demeanor while doing outrageous things like roller-skating dressed in an evening gown or marching out of formation with a chorus of soldiers. A tiny, slender woman who wore her hair in a mannishly short bob, she was generally recognized as the greatest comedienne of her era. Lillie was born in Toronto, where she was a child performer. When she was a teenager, her family moved to London, where she began performing in music halls. By 1914, she was being featured in London revues and became a star for her comic antics and singing in *Charlot's Revue of 1924*. When the show went to Broadway, she endeared herself to American audiences and remained a favorite for four decades. Most of Lillie's stage appearances were in revues, but she also triumphed in a handful of comedies and book musicals. Among the highlights of her London and Broadway theater career were *Charlot's Revue of 1926: Oh, Please!* (1926), *She's My Baby* (1928), *This Year of Grace* (1928), *Walk a Little Faster* (1932), *At Home Abroad* (1935), *The Show Is On* (1936), *Set to Music* (1939), *Seven Lively Arts* (1944), and *Inside U.S.A.* (1948), culminating in *An Evening with Beatrice Lillie* (1952).

After the failure of the *Ziegfeld Follies of 1957*, Lillie succeeded Rosalind Russell in *Auntie Mame* and then played the wacky medium Madame Arcati in the musical version of *Blithe Spirit* entitled *High Spirits* (1964). She appeared in half a dozen movies but was never comfortable performing without an audience. Her film credits include *Exit Smiling* (1926), *On Approval* (1944), *Around the World in Eighty Days* (1956), and *Thoroughly Modern Millie* (1967). She was more effective on television, where she was a guest on variety shows with a live audience.

Bea Lillie is, of course, one of the funniest women in the world, which is fascinating when one realizes she has had a rather tragic personal life. She lost her husband, Sir Robert Peel, and many years after his death, her son, whom she absolutely worshipped, was killed in World War II. In spite of what she must have felt, Bea remained brittle and witty, and always put on a magnificent façade to conceal her grief. To work with her was stimulating. Her boyish face and figure were always animated and gay, and devoid of any of the airy pretentiousness often affected by stars of her stature.

The dress rehearsal on the afternoon of the opening of *This Year of Grace* was practically disastrous. The scenery fell down, the lights would not operate properly, and we were all convinced that nothing but catastrophe lay ahead. The cast was in a state of desperation and nervousness. I went home and drank some gin, took a bath, put on a dinner jacket, and went back to the Selwyn Theatre prepared for the worst. As can happen in the theater, contrary to our fears of that afternoon, the show was a terrific success. Bea's rendition of "World Weary" and Noel's "ballet announcements" were the high points of the evening. Owing to its persistent popularity, the New York run of *This Year of Grace* was extended. Noel had originally agreed to play it for only three months, but he succumbed to management's blandishments to extend. It was probably the personal pleasure he took from appearing in a musical he had always adored. It couldn't have been the additional revenue, as his indifference to money when he is not enthusiastic about what he is doing is legendary.

Noel's real love on stage has always been singing, although—let's face it—he's not very good! In the early musicals that he wrote and directed, he always managed to nip off on odd afternoons to record the songs before the cast had a chance to get anywhere near the microphone. This addiction to vocalization culminated in the mid-1950s with his decision to appear at the Café de Paris in London. This being his first nightclub appearance, I was horrified and tried to dissuade him. My wife Natasha and I flew over for his opening, only to find that I was gravely mistaken. His voice was still not of Metropolitan quality, but his wit, timing, and delivery were such that, taken all in all, it was the greatest nightclub performance I had ever seen. He was appearing at the same time in George Bernard Shaw's *The Apple Cart* at the Haymarket Theatre, but when my wife and I would visit him in his dressing room, it was apparent that his heart wasn't really with Shaw, but on the small stage of the Café de Paris. On the heels of that success, Noel was approached with a new proposition involving enormous amounts of money to take on a nightclub act in Las Vegas. He loved it and quickly decided to cancel the intended New York production of *Nude with Violin* and accepted their offer to compete with the slot machines—which he defeated with casual ease.

The next project—and an ambitious and successful one it was—following *This Year of Grace* was *Bitter Sweet*. It was a romantic light opera for which Noel wrote the book, lyrics, and music, and Charles Cochran produced. The preparations for its London production were complicated, so much so that it did not reach the stage until spring of the following year, 1929, during which time Noel madly wrote and composed, and carried out endless auditions. Noel's methods when writing a musical were distinctly his own. Naturally, the basic idea was carefully conceived, but during the actual writing he would dash from lyrics to music to book, not completing each phase one at a time, but moving about as his whims and instincts prompted. The only thing that he could not do was actually orchestrate the score. He would play the numbers on a piano and an arranger would weld them into the final

Bitter Sweet is a decidedly old-fashioned 1929 operetta by Noel Coward that found success in London and New York, and is still produced today. In her posh Grovesnor Square residence, the Marchioness of Shayne (Peggy Wood) helps her young niece, who cannot decide whether to marry for love or social position, by telling her own story in flashback. In 1875, when she was Sarah Millick, she was engaged to the Marquis of Shayne (Alan Napier) but in love with her music teacher, Carl Linden (Georges Metaxa). The two elope to Vienna and are happy until Carl is killed in a duel five years later. Sarah goes on the stage to support herself, becomes a famous prima donna, and weds the patient Marquis.

An obvious throwback to the operetta formula of decades earlier, *Bitter Sweet* was an audience favorite, and the old-style songs became hits, in particular "If Love Were All," "I'll See You Again," and "Ziguener." Coward directed Charles B. Cochran's London production, which ran for a surprising 697 performances. Broadway impresario Florenz Ziegfeld opened his production four months after the London premiere with Evelyn Laye as Sarah, and the reviews were highly favorable. But the New York presentation of *Bitter Sweet* had the misfortune of opening less than a month after the stock market crash, so the production only managed a five-month run. Two film versions were made: a British movie in 1933, starring Anna Neagle and Fernand Gravet, and an MGM version in 1940, with Jeanette MacDonald and Nelson Eddy.

orchestration. Incidentally, this approach was also true of Cole Porter and Richard Rodgers. [Few theater composers have written their own orchestrations. George Gershwin, Kurt Weill, and Leonard Bernstein are the notable exceptions.]

All available English stars, including Gertrude Lawrence and Evelyn Laye, were sought after for *Bitter Sweet*, but they were all unavailable for various reasons, so Noel turned his eye to the United States and decided on Peggy Wood. As it turned out, this was an extremely wise decision. Peggy, in the role of Sarah, looked exactly right, sang like a dream, and, more importantly, acted like an actress. The part called for her to start as a young girl who eloped with her music teacher, sung by Georges Metaxa. What followed was a sequence of financial difficulties, forcing Sarah to assist her husband by singing in a Vienna café. The second act culminated in a duel over her "favors," in which her husband was killed. By the third act, having quelled her grief, she married well and became Lady Shane. Her final exit, walking with a cane with her head held erect, was deeply moving.

Peggy Wood (1892–1978) was a striking soprano beauty who appeared in plays and musicals in New York and London in the 1910s and 1920s, graduated to nonmusical roles in the 1940s, and became famous for her television appearances in the 1950s. She was born in Brooklyn, the daughter of a newspaperman, and made her Broadway debut in the chorus of *Naughty Marietta* in 1910. Wood was a stage star by the time she played the aristocratic Ottilie in the classic operetta *Maytime* (1917). After appearing in other musicals, plays, and Shakespeare revivals, Wood created the role of the heiress Sarah in Noel Coward's *Bitter Sweet* in London (1929). Most of her stage work was in New York, where she continued to act until 1970. Among her other memorable roles were Portia in *The Merchant of Venice* (1928), the Vienna aristocrat Rosalinde in *Champagne Sec* (1933), Mrs. Foresight in *Love for Love* (1940), authoress Mildred in *Old Acquaintance* (1940), the frustrated second wife Ruth in *Blithe Spirit* (1941), the classy Donna Lucia in *Charley's Aunt* (1953), Clytemnestra in *Electra* (1961), and the daffy Mme. Constance in *The Madwoman of Chaillot* (1970). She found most recognition for eight years as the struggling Swedish Mama in the television series *I Remember Mama*. Wood acted in a dozen movies but is most remembered for her final screen portrayal, Mother Abbess in *The Sound of Music* (1965).

There were the usual minor rehearsal problems, which came to a climax during the final run-through at two o'clock in the morning. Cochran came to Noel to ask him if he could speed things up, as the company was on double-time and the orchestra on triple-time, and the rehearsal was running into pretty big money. Noel smilingly agreed, left his seat in the front of the dress circle from which he always directed, and went onto the stage to talk to Peggy for practically half an hour. Upon his return to our balcony perch, I asked him what they had been discussing for all that time. "Nothing really, nothing at all," Noel replied. "I simply wanted to show Cocky that I will run rehearsals the way I want to!"

These minor incidents were happily obliterated the next night when the show was a smash hit. It ran for more than two years at what was then called His Majesty's Theatre. Meanwhile, Cochran decided on an immediate American production. By this time Evelyn Laye was available to play Sarah, and Cochran arranged with Flo Ziegfeld not only to coproduce the play, but also house it in his theater. The leading man was a little more difficult to cast; however, Princess Jane San Faustino suggested—nay, insisted on—a handsome young Roman with a beautiful singing voice whose name I can't recall. Unfortunately, he couldn't speak English, although he swore that he could learn it in "no time." [Born Jane Allen Campbell (1865–1938) in Montclair, New York, the beautiful international socialite became the Princess of San Faustino when she married an Italian count in 1897.]

We rehearsed the play in London, as it was during the days, long since past, when American Equity allowed a play to be cast and rehearsed in a foreign country and brought intact to the United States. The company was dispatched on a slower boat, while the big brass were ensconced on the *Mauritania*. The voyage, otherwise uneventful, was enlivened by the presence of Ina Claire, who was on her honeymoon with John Gilbert. A gay and tumultuous honeymoon it was, and we forgot about *Bitter Sweet* and concentrated on the happy couple. Between their champagne-inspired love scenes, there were violent intermissions during which they hurled invectives and frequently odd pieces of crockery at one another, inevitably followed by a little more champagne and an amorous reconciliation.

During that cruise, John's first talking picture had been released and was apparently *not* a success. I remember so well the cruelty of the studio, which even took the trouble to send a man down to the boat to greet him with his bad notices. This caused a virtual collapse, and the party we had planned to

John Gilbert (1897–1936) was a dashing and handsome silent screen star whose career collapsed when talkies came in. With his trim mustache and imposing good looks, Gilbert was the very image of a romantic leading man in the silent movie era. He was born John Cecil Pringle in Logan, Utah, into a family of actors and as a child traveled throughout the country with his parents. He was still in his teens when he started appearing in minor roles in the movies. By 1925, he was a screen star thanks to such films as *He Who Gets Slapped* (1924), *The Merry Widow* (1925), and *The Big Parade* (1925). Gilbert became a romantic idol both on and off the screen when he was paired with Greta Garbo in *Flesh and the Devil* (1926), and they re-created their screen electricity in *Love* (1927), *A Woman of Affairs* (1928), and *Queen Christina* (1933). But the volatile actor, who suffered from alcoholism and depression, often quarreled with the studio heads and was purposely given weak films to fulfill his contract. Hollywood legend has it that Gilbert's voice was thin and nasal, and that talking pictures destroyed him. In fact, he had a deep and expressive voice, as witnessed in his performance in the sound film *Queen Christina*. Gilbert's heavy drinking and careless lifestyle led to a heart attack in 1935, and no studio would hire him. He died the next year at the age of thirty-eight.

celebrate our arrival was canceled and John put to bed, with Ina looking after him. Shortly thereafter, the studio began urging him to break his contract, but he stubbornly refused and insisted on returning to Hollywood to resume work. They proceeded to subject him to a series of humiliations that were varied, constant, and viciously ingenuous. They would phone him in the middle of the night to film a swimming-pool sequence that never did, and was never intended to, reach the screen. On one occasion, he had a highly publicized fistfight with a writer in front of the Mocambo nightclub. The studio had seized on the notion of starring the writer, who had never acted in his life, in their next picture, and forcing John to appear with him in a supporting role. John resolutely accepted this and the studio's other indignities, but their process of erosion eventually proved effective. He was not yet forty when he died of a heart attack in 1936.

Upon the arrival of the *Bitter Sweet* company in New York, we reestablished rehearsals at the Ziegfeld Theatre, which was to become our eventual home. They were generally routine, except for the moment when Ziegfeld—suave, elegant, and possessing an acute sense of his own importance—sent word to Noel that he would not be allowed to smoke while rehearsing. Noel gracefully accepted the ultimatum and simply got up and walked out of the theater, only to be pursued down Seventh Avenue by Ziegfeld himself, imploring Noel to return to work. From then onward, Ziegfeld remained ensconced in his handsome suite (later to be occupied with considerable publicity by Billy Rose) at the top of the theater, and a large, sand-filled urn, obviously borrowed from the lobby, was placed next to Noel's seat for use as an ashtray. Rehearsals proceeded in comparative calm.

It wasn't until Boston that we realized that Jane San Faustino's brilliant Roman could only do harm to the play. In spite of his excellent voice and earlier assurances, he had not been able to master intelligible English. Thus, on the night before the premiere, it was universally decided that he could not open. Amazingly, he elected to fight the decision and hired a lawyer, who obtained an injunction to block opening night in Boston. Ziegfeld replaced the actor and simply ignored the injunction. The theater, through management's influence, was surrounded by police, and the play opened to enormous success under the protective arm of the law.

Despite the Boston sellout, some minor disagreements set in between Noel and Ziegfeld. The latter felt, based on his many years of experience in this type of entertainment, that the production could be spruced up with a series of beautiful girls wandering on stage at various times—in other words, a proper Ziegfeld production. Noel's view differed, and so, with characteristic stubbornness, he flatly refused. This caused Ziegfeld to return to New York with an apa-

Florenz Ziegfeld Jr. (1867–1932) was the most famous of all American showmen, his name still synonymous with glamour and opulence. He was born in Chicago, where his German immigrant father ran a music conservatory. As director of musical events for the 1893 Columbian Exposition, the elder Ziegfeld sent his son to Europe to secure talent. Instead of hiring distinguished musical figures, the young Ziegfeld signed music hall performers and circus acts. In 1893, he also became manager of strongman Eugene Sandow, and his promotion of the muscle man established his own name, too. Ziegfeld's first Broadway production was an 1896 revival of *A Parlor Match*, which featured his first wife, Anna Held. Among his subsequent productions, mostly vehicles for Held, were *Papa's Wife* (1899), *The Little Duchess* (1901), *Mam'selle Napoleon* (1903), *Higgledy Piggledy* (1904), and *A Parisian Model* (1906). Even in these early productions he began to earn a reputation for offering a chorus line of beautiful girls in sumptuous costumes.

Ziegfeld's next production was the *Follies of 1907*, which initiated the famous *Ziegfeld Follies* series. His other musical productions included *Miss Innocence* (1908), *A Winsome Widow* (1912), *The Century Girl* (1916), *Sally* (1920), *Kid Boots* (1923), *Annie Dear* (1924), *Betsy* (1926), *Rio Rita* (1927), *Show Boat* (1927 and 1932), *Rosalie* (1928), *The Three Musketeers* (1928), *Whoopee* (1928), *Show Girl* (1929), *Bitter Sweet* (1929), *Simple Simon* (1930), *Smiles* (1930), and *Hot-Cha!* (1932). He also produced a number of nonmusical plays, including *Rose Briar* (1922), for his second wife, Billie Burke.

Ziegfeld's personal extravagances were as well publicized as his shows—among them his penchant for sending long telegrams to people within reach of his phone. His productions were the costliest of their day and praised not only for their richness, but also for their tasteful visual beauty, especially those designed by Joseph Urban. He got involved with Hollywood for a time, most memorably as producer of *Rio Rita* (1929) and *Whoopee* (1930). Ziegfeld was a shrewd businessman in many ways, but his excesses eventually led to bankruptcy and he died at the age of sixty-five, deep in debt.

thy that virtually amounted to washing his hands of the entire production. He must have been secretly gratified, however, when news came through of our success in Boston, and his chagrin didn't last. Police cordons, this time for traffic only, greeted our New York opening, and tickets were going for $200 a pair.

In addition to his suite on the top floor, Ziegfeld had a private box from which Noel, Gladys Calthrop, and I witnessed the performance, surrounded by caviar and champagne (compliments of the management). In the end,

Bitter Sweet was less well received than it had been in London, although what Peggy Wood accomplished in the original was repeated by Evelyn Laye in New York. Within a week, having launched the show and completed his job, Noel boarded a train for San Francisco and from there embarked on one of his periodic trips throughout the world.

CHAPTER FIVE

~

Larry, Tallulah, and Friends

Naturally, even though on holiday and in transit, Noel was as restlessly active as ever. In Singapore, he played *Journey's End* with a local touring company called "The Quaints." [*Journey's End* is a World War I drama by R. C. Sheriff that was first presented in London in 1928.] Among the cast was a young man, much to be heard of later, named John Mills. More importantly, it was on this trip that Noel wrote a little play called *Private Lives*, for which he had in mind himself and Gertrude Lawrence—a good combination indeed. He sent her the play and received a cable, which was something of a classic: it simply read, "Nothing wrong that can't be fixed." Upon his return to England, she promptly signed, and we immediately went into rehearsals. After a short provincial tour, opening in Edinburgh—that most charming and dour of cities—it was blatantly clear that indeed nothing had to be fixed. The play was an unqualified success.

The cast was small but elegant. Adrianne Allen, who was, at that point, still Mrs. Raymond Massey, played Sibyl, and the stuffy, dreary role of Victor was beautifully embellished by Laurence Olivier, who rose above his miscasting with an aura of his eventual eminence. At the time, Larry was married to actress Jill Esmond, and it was to be many years before his path crossed that of Vivien Leigh.

Oddly enough, I was seeing Vivien all the time. She too was married, to a young lawyer in London, but had an eye on the theater with, as yet, no particular success. She was a frail, exquisite creation, with a passion for dancing. And that's where I came in. I'm not sure, but I think we first met

Private Lives is one of Noel Coward's most popular plays, still appealing to stars and audiences in English-speaking countries. Englishman Elyot Chase (Noel Coward) is honeymooning with newlywed Sybil (Adrianne Allen) at the same French hotel where his ex-wife Amanda (Gertrude Lawrence) and her new husband Victor Prynne (Laurence Olivier) are staying for their honeymoon. It doesn't take long for the old flame of romance between Elyot and Amanda to billow, and they run off to Paris together, followed by their puzzled spouses. Elyot and Amanda soon begin fighting with one another again, as well as with Sybil and Victor, but they eventually realize they still belong together.

Coward directed the 1930 London comedy, produced by Charles B. Cochran. The press adulated the witty dialogue and vivacious performances, even if the plot was far from unique. The three-month run quickly sold out, and most of the cast went to New York, where the play opened on Broadway in 1931. The reviews for the play and the players were again enthusiastic, and the comedy ran for nearly nine months. The Broadway production might have run even longer, but Coward and Lawrence returned to London, and their replacements were not nearly as effective. The 1931 Hollywood film version stars Norma Shearer and Robert Montgomery in the Coward and Lawrence roles, with Una Merkel and Reginald Denny as their new spouses. The movie, which lacks the British sense of humor, was not successful. There have been countless stage revivals and television and radio versions throughout the years. *Private Lives* is, in many ways, the quintessential Coward comedy.

in Ivor Novello's dressing room when she was appearing with him in *The Happy Hypocrite*. We became fast friends, and our dancing sessions began. We would start off our evenings at London's more routine places—The Ritz, Claridges, or The Savoy—until they closed at one a.m. which was the law. But London had a nest of places called "bottle clubs," which managed to appease the law by limiting their clientele to "members only," and it was there that we would continue whirling about until four or five in the morning. I would then take her home in a taxi, chastely kiss her on the forehead on her doorstep, and send her in to her husband, who was presumably sound asleep. I never saw him, and what's more, I never met anyone who had.

It was some time after that when Vivien and Larry finally met at a film studio outside London. The reaction was, to say the least, definite. She divorced her husband, he divorced Jill Esmond, and shortly thereafter they came to stay with my wife and me at our home in Connecticut. As far as I could see, the idea was a great success, as they were blissfully happy, and after

Laurence Olivier (1907–1989) is considered by many to be the finest British actor of the twentieth century for his classical and modern roles on stage, in films, and on television. He was born in Dorking, England, the son of a minister, and began acting as a boy in school productions. His professional career began in Birmingham in 1926, and he was soon a West End romantic leading man, his dark and handsome looks making him something of a matinee idol. Olivier found a different and wider audience for his superb acting in Shakespeare and other classic roles. His popularity became international with such films as *Wuthering Heights* (1939) and *Rebecca* (1940), but despite his sixty movies, Olivier's first love was the stage, and he returned to it frequently, always pushing himself to try new characters, playwrights, and challenges. In his later years, when he suffered from ill health, he concentrated on films and television dramas. Olivier was also a highly respected director and theater manager, running the National Theatre for several years. Among his many distinguishing acting characteristics were his commanding presence, versatile vocal range, and dynamic sense of danger and excitement.

the period of time required by the British government before a divorce decree is final they were eventually married.

We opened *Private Lives* in a new theater in London called the Phoenix, a beautiful, somewhat unfinished edifice at the time that is now one of the more desirable playhouses in the West End. The success of *Private Lives* is history. Initially, however, Noel had agreed to play it for only three months,

Vivien Leigh (1913–1967) was one of the cinema's most beautiful and talented stars, who also had an extensive stage career. Born in Darjeeling, India, to British parents, she was educated in various schools throughout Europe before studying acting in London and Paris. Leigh made her screen debut in 1935, and within a few years she was getting featured roles in British films. Her portrayal of Scarlett O'Hara in *Gone with the Wind* (1939), her first Hollywood film, propelled her to the top ranks of the movie industry, and she was given many memorable roles, for instance, *Anna Karenina* (1948), Blanche DuBois in *A Streetcar Named Desire* (1951), and Mary Treadwell in *Ship of Fools* (1965). Yet, Leigh wanted a theater career, especially after she married Laurence Olivier in 1940, and she played many classic and modern roles on the London and New York stages. Her life and career were damaged by physical and mental illness, and she died at the untimely age of fifty-three.

and so we sold out and closed as we had opened—to capacity. The New York run was yet to come. Noel again limited his appearance to three months, but with his tireless energy he had already started on the idea of *Cavalcade*. He always excused himself for limiting his acting seasons on the grounds that he was first a writer and second an actor; however, with the New York production of *Private Lives*, there evolved a new position for me.

Noel had felt for a long while that being his personal representative was not sufficient and had in mind that my career goal should be to become a producer. We both agreed that I should learn the business as I had on Wall Street—from the ground up. Although Archie Selwyn was the actual producer, at Noel's suggestion I became the "company manager" and worked in the box office. This meant being present at the theater nightly, managing the box office personnel—who were skating on thin ice—and being in charge of the general business of the production. It was indeed my first step toward becoming a producer and a very useful one.

The play opened in New York in January 1931, at the Times Square Theatre on 42nd Street. Like most of its neighbors in that district, it has since become a rather dubious, second-run movie house. At that time, however, 42nd Street represented what 45th Street does today. There were the Times Square, the Selwyn, the Lyric, the Eltinge, the Apollo, and the Liberty, all housing the most important plays in town. Then, of course, there was the New Amsterdam, which also became the movie house where Ziegfeld produced his famous *Follies*, in addition to such shows as *Sally*, *Sunny*, and many others. It was also at the New Amsterdam that Max Gordon presented the best revue I ever saw, *The Band Wagon*, with the Astaires, Frank Morgan, and—surprise, surprise—Tilly Losch. Mr. Ziegfeld went even further. He built a restaurant-theater on top of the building. After seeing such stars as Will Rogers, Eddie Cantor, and the like, audience members could ride up in a plush elevator and see them again, assuming they could afford it. As a bonus, there would also be the customary array of Ziegfeld beauties, headed by the famous "Dolores," arranged in seductive tableaux by Ben Ali Haggin. Forty-Second Street was indeed a street of glamour. It was sad for me in later years to walk it and observe nothing but decay and decrepitude. [Today the Times Square Theatre remains closed on 42nd Street, still awaiting renovation. Remnants of the old Lyric and Apollo theaters were used in creating a new playhouse called the Ford Center in 1996; in 2014, the space was renamed the Lyric Theatre. The Selwyn Theatre was restored in 1997 and is currently called the American Airlines Theatre. The New Amsterdam Theatre was restored by the Disney company in 1997 and is home to most of their stage musicals. The Liberty

Theatre is now a restaurant and retail space, and the Eltinge Theatre was turned into a movie cineplex in 1998.]

Private Lives was sold out for its three-month engagement even before we opened, and we optimistically assumed that Noel would prolong its run, but we assumed wrong. At the end of the agreed limitation, he quietly refused to continue. It was a distressing loss of revenue, of course, as he had his actor's salary plus his royalties, but instead of running three years, as it easily could have, three months had been agreed upon and three months it was. Gertie beetled off to London and Noel and I to Nassau, where he bounced about in the sea, apparently unconcerned about the gold mine left behind. The play was to remain in our lives for a long, long time. It was seized upon by summer theaters, and so solid was its construction that apparently no actor or actress could destroy it. It brought in a steady income from the most remote and unlikely places.

Several years later, even Tallulah Bankhead asked if she could take *Private Lives* on the summer circuit. It was a bold request and presented a slight problem, as Noel and Tallulah had not been on good terms for years, dating back to the 1920s and a London play called *Fallen Angels*. At that time, Noel was only twenty-five and far from famous, but he was commissioned by the owner of the Globe Theatre in London to write a play for Margaret Bannerman, who was the proprietor's favorite actress. He wrote it, and rehearsals proceeded under his direction. The play is a farce constructed for two women, and Edna Best was engaged as Bunny Bannerman's vis-à-vis. Things seemingly went smoothly until the last week of rehearsals, when Bunny decided that her part should be larger than Edna's. [Margaret "Bunny" Bannerman (1896–1976) was a Canadian-born actress on stage and screen. Edna Best (1900–1974) was a British-born actress who began her career on the London stage but spent most of it in the United States in movies and on Broadway.] Noel must have been as stubborn then, even in his unproved youth, as later, because he resolutely refused to make any alterations. When Miss Bannerman threatened to leave the show, he told her to go and do so. As the play was only three days away from opening, finding a replacement presented a serious problem. They finally settled on Tallulah, a relatively unknown actress at the time. She miraculously learned a lengthy part in forty-eight hours and went on opening night word perfect and with enormous success.

Fallen Angels, concerning two married women and their mutual French lover, caused a scandal and was attacked by press and pulpit. This naturally increased ticket sales from average to capacity. By modern standards, *Fallen Angels* is as harmless as "Uncle Wiggly," but at the time it was considered immoral, degenerate, and a menace to the welfare of a nation. Noel bore this attack with

Tallulah Bankhead (1903–1968) was a distinctive, throaty-voiced, highly mannered American actress who starred on the Broadway and London stages and gave some memorable screen performances as well. Born in Huntsville, Alabama, the niece of a U.S. senator, she used her family's influence to land a walk-on part in her first Broadway show, *Squab Farm* (1918). After a brief fling in silent films, Bankhead replaced others and originated parts in *Nice People* (1921) and *The Exciters* (1922), but her career seemed stalled, so she left for England, where, for the next eleven years, she played increasingly important roles, as in Noel Coward's *Fallen Angels* (1925).

When Bankhead returned to the United States in 1931, she found modest success in *Forsaking All Others* (1933), *Dark Victory* (1934), a revival of *Rain* (1935), and *Something Gay* (1935). She had better luck in *Reflected Glory* (1936) but was roundly panned as the Queen of the Nile in a revival of *Antony and Cleopatra* (1937); however, her greatest performances soon followed, including Regina Giddens in *The Little Foxes* (1939), the sibyl-like servant Sabina in *The Skin of Our Teeth* (1942), and Amanda Prynne in a free-slugging revival of *Private Lives* (1946), a character she played in various venues for four years.

Bankhead's later stage roles were in *Foolish Notion* (1945), *The Eagle Has Two Heads* (1947), *Dear Charles* (1954), and *Midgie Purvis* (1961). Her last Broadway appearance was as a typically deluded Tennessee Williams lady in his *The Milk Train Doesn't Stop Here Anymore* (1964). Bankhead did not like Hollywood but made sixteen movies because the money was so tempting. Her noteworthy screen performances were in *Tarnished Lady* (1931), *The Cheat* (1931), *Devil and the Deep* (1932), *Lifeboat* (1944), and *Royal Scandal* (1945). In her last years, when major Broadway success eluded her, she regularly appeared on radio, calling everyone "dahling" in her deep baritone voice and seemingly behaving like a parody of herself.

fortitude, but when he went to the theater several weeks later, he discovered, to his horror, that Tallulah had "kicked it up" to an alarming degree. After, I presume, proper deliberation, he took out a paid ad in the London papers confirming the opinion of the church and the media, and publicly blaming Tallulah for her overly enthusiastic improvisation of the role. This started the feud that would last nearly twenty years. And Noel's secretary, Lorn Loraine, and I were included in the vendetta, even though we had known Tallulah personally for a long time. This imposed banishment resulted in my not seeing her for many years, but when she returned to New York, we resumed our early friendship. When, years later, she asked to do *Private Lives*, Noel's wound had sufficiently healed, and he gave his somewhat reluctant consent.

Fallen Angels is an acerbic 1925 comedy by Noel Coward that caused some censorship problems because of its flippant attitude toward drinking. Julia Sterroll (Tallulah Bankhead) and Jane Banbury (Edna Best) were once in love with dashing Frenchman Maurice Duclos but have since been happily married to other men. When the two women hear that Duclos is back in Britain, they meet at Julia's flat while their husbands are golfing and wait for their old flame to arrive. They drink while they wait and are soon plastered, becoming nostalgic, then belligerent, by the time the Frenchman shows up. While some audience members found the play in poor taste, enough enjoyed the slight comedy to let it run for 158 performances. A New York production in 1927 featured Fay Bainter and Estelle Winwood as the tipsy heroines. Critics approved of the two actresses but thought the nearly plotless play tiresome and inconsequential, so it ran for only a month. It would be decades before the comedy enjoyed successful revivals in London, on Broadway, and regionally. *Fallen Angels* was adapted for television in 1963 and 1974.

That particular revival of *Private Lives* was phenomenally successful. Tallulah was paid an enormous salary and toured the summer theaters at capacity business. I then decided to take it to Chicago for a few weeks as a speculative production. To our delight and amusement, it ran there for a year. Donald Cook was her costar, Buff Cobb played the Adrianne Allen role, and Phil Arthur took over the part originally done by Laurence Olivier. It was an interesting period for me, as it necessitated regular trips to Chicago every three weeks or so. There were two identical theaters there—the Selwyn and the Harris—both adjoining, with a single alleyway leading to the two stage doors, as close together as a French farce. I had the Lunts playing O *Mistress Mine* in one theater and Tallulah across the alley in the other. This caused considerable difficulties on my periodic road trips, as I only had to visit Lynn Fontanne's dressing room to be promptly summoned to Tallulah's and vice-versa. It made for many busy evenings. At one point, Noel arrived en route to Hollywood, and the reconciliation with Tallulah was completed in person. She gave him an Augustus John portrait of an unknown young man; they spent a day together at the local amusement park, and one could tell that the wounds were unmistakably healed. She did fall back onto shaky ground when she decided to inform Noel that his "lousy play wouldn't run one night if she weren't in it," but even this he accepted with patience and impeccable manners.

After the Chicago engagement, undimmed by her outspoken view of the play, we took it on an elaborate tour of all important points West, ending up in Los Angeles and San Francisco. One member of the cast was an understudy named William Langford. Until the California run, I don't think Tallulah had even given Langford a second glance. In San Francisco, however, she suddenly discovered him, and from then onward Phil Arthur, whom Langford was understudying, was on the skids. Tallulah phoned me to say that Arthur had become unsatisfactory and totally incompetent, and that she had found a brilliant young man to replace him. According to her, Langford's credits were apparently endless. He had even played Hamlet in high school. She requested—nay, insisted—that he take over for Phil Arthur immediately. As the San Francisco run was nearing its close, I gave in but demurred when she suggested that Langford also be signed then and there for the New York engagement that we had decided to take a shot at. Three days later, she phoned again to report that she had developed severe laryngitis and would not be able to perform for several days. The remedy for this illness was somewhat curious. If I would agree that Mr. Langford could play the part in New York, her voice would miraculously and immediately return. There was nothing to do but acquiesce, and we opened in New York with Mr. Langford, who was competent and highly uninteresting, and *Private Lives* went on to enjoy a third year at Plymouth Theatre.

Tallulah's performances varied each night, which was a key ingredient in her popularity with the audience. Sometimes she was raucous, sometimes charming, and sometimes downright vulgar. Contrary to Martin Manulis's direction (no one *ever* truly directs Tallulah), she frequently whooped it up beyond the bounds of the script, a script which, heaven knows, had already given her ample opportunities. But the Bankhead fans loved the unpredictability and flocked to see her night after night. Considering that we had started out taking a chance on summer stock, *Private Lives* starring Tallulah Bankhead proved resilient and must have finally redefined her idea of a "lousy play."

It is difficult to write about Tallulah. Everything writeable about her has already been written by her or her publicist, Dick Maney, but there are a few observations that may have been omitted from the *Encyclopedia Bankhead*. She is a warm, overly generous person, but gregarious to a point of exhausting herself and everyone around her. It is essential that she is constantly surrounded by a half-dozen people, to whom she gives food and drink lavishly, and the cover charge is merely the necessity of listening to her conversation, as unflagging as Ina Claire's. Unlike most actresses, her monologues are, oddly enough, not about herself. What one had to listen to, however, was always about "Daddy," who was speaker of the House of Representatives, or Uncle X, who was in the Senate, or Auntie Y or Auntie Z of Huntsville,

Alabama—stories she repeated so constantly that I'm sure I could tell them myself and not miss a word.

At her country house in Bedford Village, New York, there was a steady group of satellites (Estelle Winwood, Glenn Anders, Mildred Dunnock, Edie Van Cleve, and others), which enjoyed her hospitality and listened with patience and even enthusiasm to stories they must have heard a thousand times before. Such was Tallulah's aversion to losing even one member of the audience, however insignificant, that she would quietly nip the keys out of one's car when no one was looking rather than lose another ear. Life at the Bankhead ménage was somewhat irregular since Tallulah had another aversion: bed before dawn. Consequently, lunch was served around three p.m., and dinner (which I never stayed for, as I lived nearby) must have happened around nine or ten at night.

Estelle Winwood made a particularly typical comment one afternoon. The members of the entourage had experienced a rather stormy night and were definitely not feeling their best the following day. Thus, Estelle slipped off to Bedford Village and returned with, of all things, a bag of mushrooms. "I brought these as I thought they would cheer us all up," she said in her vague, evanescent way. How a bag of mushrooms could possibly cure a hangover was, and still is, a mystery to me, but it apparently sufficed.

The trying times with Tallulah were not at Bedford, or even in New York, but rather on the preliminary tours of the many shows we did together. On these occasions, she would insist on the entire touring company's presence at her late-hour sessions. People were commandeered to her hotel suite, and after receiving food and drinks, her monologue would resume. There was one particular incident during the tour of *Private Lives* that kept us up a little later than usual. She was staying at the Ambassador East in Chicago, where she had formed a warm friendship with Dave Garroway, at that time a disc jockey for Chicago radio. [Dave Garroway (1913–1982) was later founding host of the *Today* show on NBC-TV and a nationally known, beloved commentator.] Unfortunately, his nightly show began at midnight and continued until two a.m. He had developed a gratifying habit of dedicating records he played to Miss Bankhead (whom he called "Tiger"), and the assembled gathering was naturally required to listen to the entire broadcast, not so much for the records as for the dedications. After two o'clock, there would be the typical lapse of time to give Mr. Garroway a chance to get to the hotel suite, followed by, out of politeness, additional time to sit and chat for a reasonably social period. By now it was after three o'clock, of course, and the various guests would stagger out, giving appropriate thanks for the evening. But it *was* after three!

One of the dominant figures in Tallulah's life was a Mrs. Dola Cavendish, a rich Canadian whose sole interest seemed to be to serve Tallulah. It was even bruited about that she paid for the privilege under the somewhat ambiguous heading of "Expense Money." [Dola Cavendish (1903–1966) was the daughter of the lieutenant governor of British Columbia and a celebrated beauty and socialite in Canada. During World War II, her assets were frozen in Canada, so she lived with Bankhead in the United States. The two were close and volatile friends but not lovers, as many assumed.] Dola was fantastically devoted to our star, serving as a companion and, frequently, a maid. She was also recurrently fired but always—in sometimes mysterious ways—returned. The opening of *Private Lives* in Toronto, for instance, coincided with one of Dola's periodic dismissals. Out of the blue on the night of the opening, Dola appeared uninvited and declared how she couldn't allow Tallulah to open in Canada without being present. As she lived thousands of miles away in Saskatchewan, her appearance was *somewhat* of a gesture.

Our next date was Detroit, but Dola insisted on our staying just across the river in Windsor, so she could continue using Canadian currency to help cover expenses—not only for Tallulah, but also for a large part of the company. Trips across the bridge were made after each performance. When Canadian Customs officials stopped us to ask if we had anything to declare, Tallulah would invariably reply, "Nothing but scotch, bourbon, gin, cocaine, and heroin." This was, of course, not true, but it amused the customs inspector to such an extent that we always sailed through without any trouble.

Dola's devotion was perhaps best exemplified by one particular incident. She had bought an expensive fur coat, and upon her arrival home, Tallulah immediately asked for it and, of course, instantaneously got it. Dola timidly asked permission to buy another and this was granted, but only under the condition that it be an imitation. From then onward, Tallulah went about exhibiting her coat, vociferously explaining that Dola's was a bogus copy and hers was real. But considering that they both belonged to Dola, I think the situation had a certain ironic flavor.

The "Cronin Episode" was, of course, front-page news for weeks. Evelyn Cronin was officially Tallulah's maid and secretary. She was an ex-vaudeville actress who, for some reason, had enormous influence on her. I remember one Christmas day when Tallulah called all the way from New Orleans just so that Evelyn could sing to me over the phone. Tallulah's devoted dependence was so great that when her favorite stage manager—whom she always insisted should be in charge of any production in which she appeared—informed her that Evelyn was doing some quiet pilfering around the theater, he was promptly fired and never allowed to enter her orbit again.

Dola subsequently overcame her shyness enough to murmur in Tallulah's ear that Evelyn was also stealing from her, and so *she too* was sent packing for her pains. The company manager later came to me with the same story, but when I asked him why he didn't tell Miss Bankhead, his laconic answer was, "And what, lose my job?"

The unpleasantness and true facts eventually came out. Tallulah pressed charges, and the trial broke. It was much more serious than any of us had imagined. Evelyn Cronin had been doctoring checks at an alarming degree, adding extra zeros and converting, say, $60 into $600, or in other cases, making even more astronomical returns. Tallulah was magnificent in this dilemma and went daily to court. She was often forced to listen to accusations from her former favorite as to drinking, drug-taking, and irregular sexual activities. She took it in with indomitable fortitude that was nothing short of remarkable. One day during the trial, she said to me, "Darling, I have always been a great actress, but now I'm Joan of Arc!" Her courage paid off. She won her case but was still out of pocket for about $60,000, which had already been spent and could scarcely be reclaimed. It was at this point that Dola stepped into the picture again, sending Tallulah a check for the full amount of her losses. She even threw in a Cadillac for good measure, ensuring that she once more returned to the fold.

There were other plays and experiences with Tallulah, before and after *Private Lives*. One was *Foolish Notion*, produced by the Theatre Guild in 1945, which I was hired to direct. Our star was highly cooperative, and the author, Philip Barry, was certainly one of the most considerate people with whom I have ever worked. He would sit silently all day with never an interruption, quietly making notes that we would discuss at the end of rehearsals. He was an unassuming and brilliant man, but he too had his troubles with Tallulah.

Foolish Notion is a 1945 comedy by Philip Barry that was lacking in the author's usual wit and human insight. When it is clear that his actress-wife Sophia Wing (Tallulah Bankhead) has fallen in love with her longtime leading man Gordon Roark (Donald Cook), Sophia's husband Jim (Henry Hull) goes off to war. After being missing in action for five years, he is presumed dead. Just as Sophia and Gordon are about to wed, word comes that Jim is alive and returning. After much fretting and imagining of what he will be like, Jim arrives with a new love of his own, leaving everyone happy. With the Theatre Guild's subscribers and the popularity of Bankhead, the advance sale was hefty, but disappointed reviews and word of mouth limited the run to less than four months.

She had accepted the play on the strength of the first two acts, with the understanding that a new, third act, more to her liking, was eventually to come to life. But during rehearsals, the new act did not appear, and it also failed to materialize during a lengthy preliminary tour. The tension increased steadily, and the bust-up came in Baltimore, when, after opening night there, she attacked and abused not only Philip's play, but also his lineage, background, and consequent inability to "write a play for a lady." He behaved beautifully, visibly restraining himself, and when the attacks were over, he safely returned to his hotel room. Mrs. Barry, Philip's wife, called me in great distress to say that Philip was extremely ill. He had a fiendish Irish temper, and bottling it in during Tallulah's tirade, he had actually burst a blood vessel in his nose and had to be taken to Johns Hopkins Hospital for treatment. Tallulah sent flowers to the hospital but still refused to speak to him. The fight wasn't finished.

Philip Barry (1896–1949) is generally considered the American theater's finest playwright of high comedy. Born in Rochester, New York, he was the son of old Irish-Catholic stock. Young Barry was a frail child with defective eyesight. Yet, despite his myopia, he became an avid reader and a precocious wit, entering Yale in 1914 and eagerly plunging into campus literary activities. During World War I, he was rejected for military services but served in the Communications Office of the State Department in London, where he became a lifelong Anglophile. Returning to Yale after the war (as Wilson was beginning his studies there), one of his plays won a prize offered by the school dramatic society, and even with strident family objections, he enrolled in George Pierce Baker's famed 47 Workshop at Harvard. Barry was still a student when his play *You and I* (1923) was a hit on Broadway. This was followed by such notable works as *Paris Bound* (1927), *Holiday* (1928), *Hotel Universe* (1930), *Tomorrow and Tomorrow* (1931), and *The Animal Kingdom* (1932).

Deeply saddened by the death of his baby daughter, Barry took darker turns in his next plays: *The Joyous Season* (1934), *Bright Star* (1935), and *Here Come the Clowns* (1938). Returning to the sort of high comedy the theater expected of him, Barry enjoyed his greatest success with *The Philadelphia Story* (1939), but the rest of his career was anticlimactic, filled with lesser works, for instance, *Liberty Jones* (1941), *Without Love* (1942), *Foolish Notion* (1945), the adaptation of Jean-Pierre Aumont's *My Name Is Aquilon* (1949), and the unfinished *Second Threshold* (1951), which Robert Sherwood completed with little success. Barry's strange interplay of wit and despair gives his best works a dramatic tension and meaningfulness unique in American theater.

It was in Washington one week later, after Philip was released from the hospital, that the real fireworks began. The procedure was a little bizarre, to say the least. Lawrence Langner and Terry Helburn, the heads of the Theatre Guild, and Phil, would come for conferences in my suite, while Tallulah resolutely remained in hers. The Willard Hotel is a block square, and our rooms couldn't have been farther apart. Phil would write down proposed suggestions, and as messenger boy, I would take them to Tallulah and return with her word as to what she would accept. This went on for an indefinite period until I ultimately asked hotel management for a scooter, as the recurrent trips on foot were wearing me out. We finally arrived at a compromise, and the play opened in New York with some success.

Foolish Notion had an interesting cast: Henry Hull and Donald Cook, who were well known, and two comparative newcomers, Maria Riva and Mildred Dunnock. Time has proven that we chose them well. *Foolish Notion* turned out to be one of Philip Barry's last plays, and it was a sad day for all of us when, four years later, he passed away.

Another project with Tallulah was *The Eagle Has Two Heads*, an adaptation of Jean Cocteau's romantic melodrama. It had been an enormous success in England, and Tallulah wanted to play it there. Whether she was most intrigued by the idea of playing a queen or the fact that she had a twenty-minute monologue in the first act is a moot point. The production was

---

The Eagle Has Two Heads is the most common English title for Jean Cocteau's philosophical play *L'Aigle a Deux Têtes* (1946). For fifteen years, the queen (Tallulah Bankhead) of a mythical country has been in mourning for her husband, who was assassinated on their honeymoon. A radical poet named Stanislas (Helmut Dantine) sneaks into her bedchamber to assassinate her as well, but the two fall in love. Realizing the futility of his actions, Stanislas takes poison and follows the queen's order and shoots her. The drama was first performed in Brussels in 1946, and later that year it was produced in London, with a translation by Ronald Duncan. Eileen Herlie and James Donald played the queen and the assassin, and although Cocteau did not like it, British audiences were intrigued enough to let it run. Tallulah Bankhead starred in the 1947 New York production, which was produced and directed by Wilson. Only Bankhead's frenzied performance was applauded, and her popularity allowed the existential drama to hang on for a month. A French film version of *L'Aigle a Deux Têtes* was made in 1948, featuring Edwige Feuillere and Jean Marais, who had starred in the first Paris production.

Marlon Brando (1924–2004) is considered the preeminent Method actor of the American theater and American film. He was born in Omaha, Nebraska, and, after being dismissed from military school, attended the Dramatic Workshop at the New School for Social Research in Manhattan and studied acting with Stella Adler and Elia Kazan. Brando appeared in summer stock, made his New York debut in 1944, and was first noticed two years later as the poetic Eugene Marchbanks opposite Katharine Cornell in *Candida*. He dazzled theatergoers with his dangerous, electric brute Stanley Kowalski in *A Streetcar Named Desire* and jump-started his movie career when he re-created his performance on film, never returning to the theater. Among his many notable movie credits are *Julius Caesar* (1953), *The Wild One* (1953), *On the Waterfront* (1954), *Guys and Dolls* (1955), *Sayonara* (1957), *The Godfather* (1972), *Last Tango in Paris* (1972), and *Don Juan DeMarco* (1994). Brando was the finest embodiment of the Method, bringing an intensity of feeling to his characterizations, which many lesser actors would copy with embarrassing results.

magnificently designed by Donald Oenslager and boasted Clarence Derwent in an important supporting role, and Tallulah looked superb in her Aline Bernstein costumes. She gave a brilliant performance, culminating at the end of the last act, when, having been shot, she fell down a flight of sixteen stairs. The show had, however, two major distinctions, in my recollection: First, we actually released Marlon Brando, who was not getting along with our star, and replaced him with Helmut Dantine, who was, and second, it was a colossal flop.

I have long had enormous respect for Marlon Brando's talents. Prior to *Eagle*, I offered him a part in a play, which he simply sent back in the mail with a polite refusal. Shortly afterward, I made a second try to engage him for an important role in Noel Coward's *Present Laughter*. He came to my office in Rockefeller Plaza, took away the script, and returned forty-eight hours later, literally throwing it in my face with the remark, "Doesn't Mr. Coward know there's a war on?" But that same year, he finally succumbed to playing the poet in *Eagle*. He played it beautifully, of course, but there were moments when his personal behavior was, to say the least, somewhat disconcerting. One day, I arrived in the waiting room of Penn Station, en route with the company to Wilmington, to find Marlon sitting on his luggage pounding on a pair of bongo drums, which I was to learn invariably traveled with him.

And then during our tryout engagement in Wilmington, another incident occurred that to this day leaves me puzzled. Marlon failed to appear at the theater for a dress rehearsal, and after a considerable amount of waiting—with the cast milling about impatiently and Tallulah absolutely fuming—I went to his hotel to find out what had happened. I knocked on his door once, twice, and even three times, with no response. I went in and there was Marlon sound asleep on the bed, rigged out from head to foot in a football uniform: helmet, shoulder pads, and even spikes. In spite of his eccentricities, we got along well, but, as I said, Tallulah and Marlon did not. Before we reached New York for opening night, Marlon had departed—bongo drums, football uniform, and all—however, it is no surprise to me that he has done very well for himself since, perhaps even surpassing Miss Bankhead.

My final mutual venture with Tallulah, in 1957, was also dogged by disaster. It was *Eugenia*, an adaptation by Randolph Carter of a Henry James novel, *The Europeans*. Pictorially, it was a lovely show, with sets by Oliver Smith and costumes by Miles White, but the excellence of the production failed to allay our other difficulties. Tallulah fell in her bathtub the day before rehearsals began, broke two ribs, and was sent to Lenox Hill Hospital. The company proceeded as best they could without her. Then in Philadelphia, she broke her hand so seriously that it was necessary to cancel the entire second week of our engagement there. Again, we continued to rehearse, although the schedule was hardly conducted along the usual lines. The company—under Herbert Machiz's direction—would be summoned at midday to the theater, but with Tallulah unable to appear. Consequently, by the end of the afternoon, the cast would religiously file into the Warwick Hotel for a second session with our convalescent star. Chairs were brought in, and they all sat solemnly around her bed, reciting their lines in a pitch-black room; she had imported special dark curtains to shut out every ray of light. As if darkness were not enough, she also insisted on keeping the television going full blast.

Eugenia is a 1957 play by Randolph Carter that dramatized Henry James's 1878 novel *The Europeans*. Eugenia, Baroness of Munster (Tallulah Bankhead), arrives in Boston with her brother, Felix Da Costa (Scott Merrill), to seek security and freedom in a country known for open-mindedness. Felix marries an American and stays, but the baroness finds she cannot deal with New England hypocrisy and returns to Europe. The talky play struck critics as false and melodramatic, and even Bankhead's fans were not interested, so the Wilson production closed after twelve performances.

The following week in Baltimore presented no serious considerations, except that business wasn't very good. But after we opened in New York, Tallulah fell in her bathtub again, suffering severe lacerations of the head, and so the first Saturday matinee had to be canceled. As the critics' reaction was not too enthusiastic and advance ticket sales virtually nonexistent, it was clear that it would be wiser not to continue, and so I was forced to post the closing notice.

Despite our various problems throughout the years, it has always been stimulating, to say the least, to work with Tallulah. I only regret that our last few ventures came to such unfortunate ends. [Despite her difficulties, Bankhead clearly had a special fondness for Wilson or she would not have returned to work with him on so many occasions. Writing in her autobiography in 1952, Bankhead declares, "Jack's my favorite producer—charming, tactful, alert."]

CHAPTER SIX

~

Cavalcade

During those tenuous formative years, Noel and I returned in May 1931, to London, where he finally embarked on the serious construction of *Cavalcade*. It was a monumental concept, and Charles Cochran had decided on the Drury Lane as its home. This was not only one of the largest theaters in London, but also one of the most efficiently constructed. Its enormous stage was equipped with six hydraulic elevators, and the possibilities they offered were a definite challenge not only to Noel, but also to Gladys Calthrop, who did a superb job of designing. There were an endless number of extremely elaborate sets and nearly four thousand costumes, as the play covered a span of thirty years of English history. In addition to the principal cast, the company boasted more than three hundred extras. Auditions were interminable and rather pathetic, since more than 1,000 actors applied, some of them stars from another era. Amazingly, they were willing—or perhaps forced—to accept thirty shillings a week merely to walk on in this production. By September, we were finally ready for rehearsals to begin.

Noel may have been nervous, but he never showed it. He came up with a unique system of direction that worked without a hitch. As he could not possibly know the names of everyone in that huge cast, he had numbered placards hung around the extras' necks so that he could speak to them by number, using a microphone from his usual dress-circle perch. For the crowd scenes, he hit upon a trick where he would outline the idea of the action and ask them to behave as they would if placed in a similar situation. Nine times out of ten this worked with enormous success. His delegation of responsibility somehow

Cavalcade is a pageantlike epic play by Noel Coward that was a major hit in 1931, but because of its production demands, it has rarely been produced since then. The episodic plot follows the Marryott family and their servants from 1900 to 1929, as characters grow, change, and are affected by historical events. With its many characters and locations, and progression through three decades of British history, *Cavalcade* can be best described in today's terms as a period television miniseries on stage.

The original cast and crew numbered more than four hundred, and the Drury Lane Theatre's large stage was filled with many set and costume changes. Coward directed the massive production and wrote two songs, which were heard along with familiar songs from the different periods. The London production was roundly applauded and ran for 405 performances. Because of its strong British sentiment, *Cavalcade* was not deemed practical for a Broadway production, and the play has never been presented in New York. An impressive production by the Shaw Festival in Ontario, Canada, was a hit in 1985–1986. The 1933 British film version was a success and won the Oscar for Best Picture, so perhaps *Cavalcade* was not too British for American audiences after all.

heightened their enthusiasm and imagination. The scenes, which would have been endless and practically unmanageable had each actor been personally directed, excitingly came to life.

During those weeks, it seemed as if we were living at the Drury Lane. We lunched and practically slept there. The play was a difficult achievement, but Noel's calm throughout those endless days was something to admire. In addition to the overall pageantry, he had skillfully woven in a touching family story of extraordinary warmth. Mary Clare, one of England's most beloved character actresses, played the mother; Irene Browne, a long-standing friend of Noel's, was the family friend; Una O'Connor, who would be whisked to Hollywood shortly after *Cavalcade*, played the maid; and John Mills and Arthur MacRae were the sons. Indeed, the entire cast was admirable. The last scene, which represented a version of the jazz era as an ironic contrast to the nostalgia that had gone before, featured a song by Noel called "20th-Century Blues." It was sung by Binnie Barnes, who did not have an actual role but sat on a platform and belted out this single number in a clarion voice, slightly off key; however, her lack of pitch failed to discourage Hollywood scouts, and within a few weeks of the opening, she too was being signed for films.

The ensemble scenes were spectacular, making the intimate interludes, by comparison, all the more touching. My favorite moment was a scene set during the funeral of Queen Victoria. It was staged on the family balcony. The household stood quietly with lowered heads, watching the procession, which was never seen but rather visualized by the device of dead silence, only broken by the clip-clop sound of horses on the street below. The curtain line—at the off-stage passing of the queen's coffin—was delivered simply but implacably by a young boy clutching his mother's dress and saying, "Mum, she must have been a very little lady."

Rehearsals proceeded with the usual ups and downs, except that just before opening night, there was a definite "down." Inspired by a few radicals in their ranks, the three hundred extras struck for higher wages. I will never forget Cochran's behavior, which proved him the great producer that he was. Calling the entire company together, he went on stage to explain that he was aware that the salaries for the ensemble were on the small side, but that the show had been budgeted on that basis and they had all agreed on the amount. He ended by quietly but firmly stating that any wage increase would be impossible, and if they chose to insist on their demands, he would cancel the entire production, then and there. Considering that there must have been more than £100,000 already invested in the production, Cochran handled himself with aplomb. The strike was over in approximately ten minutes.

Opening night went well, except for when one of the stage elevators jammed and was out of commission for at least ten minutes. I was frantically dispatched by Noel to go backstage to ask if I could be of any help. There below, trapped in the depths of the Drury Lane, was the fifty-piece orchestra valiantly interpolating a group of reprises never planned by the composer. The time seemed endless, but the elevator eventually proved amenable and the play continued, climaxing as an unmistakable success.

It was the second night, however, that I consider my greatest personal experience in the theater. Noel had been accused of timing the opening of *Cavalcade* with the general election, which had taken place the day before. The Conservative Party had been overwhelmingly returned to power, and everything Noel inferred in the historical content of the play was interpreted as his own shrewd political timing. This was definitely untrue, as he had been at work on the play for more than a year, acquiring most of his research from back copies of the *Illustrated London News*. His only intent had been to present a pictorial chronicle of English life throughout the years. In fact, Noel never paid any attention to politics and had been so immersed in the final rehearsals during the election that it never occurred to him to vote. Nevertheless, few people were convinced of this, and our second night proved—at least to them—that their theories might have been correct.

The entire Royal Family arrived for the show: the reigning king and queen [George V and Mary], children, aunts, and uncles. News of their attendance had gotten around that afternoon, and so the house was packed. In view of the occasion, management allowed hundreds to sit on the stairs of the dress circle and the gallery, and had extra chairs placed in the aisles and stalls. The performance, of course, was electric. The reaction of the audience was even beyond the power of the play and bordered on hysteria. I don't remember too much else, as I was frankly in floods of tears the entire evening. Noel, Cochran, and the leading members of the cast were received by the Royal Family during the entr'acte. The applause at the end, both for the play and the visiting royalty—who had to return to their box for a second bow—was overwhelming. I stumbled home and had a strong drink.

Two years later, *Cavalcade* was made into a film by Twentieth-Century Fox. It was beautifully directed by Frank Lloyd and starred Diana Wynyard, Clive Brook, Ursula Jeans, and Una O'Connor duplicating her original London role. The movie was an unmistakable success, and even Noel liked it. The film also ensured that millions saw on the screen what only thousands had witnessed on stage, in spite of its long tenure at the Drury Lane Theatre. To me, *Cavalcade* ranks as Noel's greatest theatrical achievement. [Coward, in the last pages of his first autobiography, expresses his disappointment that *Cavalcade* was perceived by many as being "dashed off in a few days merely to help the General Election and snatch for myself a little timely national kudos." But he also acknowledges that the performance in front of the Royal Family was a "tremendous night for me; a gratifying theatrical flourish to my twenty-one years of theater."]

CHAPTER SEVEN

~

The Lunts

In 1932, following *Cavalcade*, Noel came up with an idea for another revue. Always changing the pace, this time he elected to have no important stars, but rather a galaxy of young people along the lines of the *Garrick Gaieties*, the show from which he might have subconsciously absorbed the idea. Titled *Words and Music*, it was presented at the Adelphi Theatre, produced by Charles Cochran, and it was a moderate success.

"Moderate success" in London is a very elastic phrase. In New York, the fatality of a not-too-successful play can be embarrassingly abrupt. It can open on Tuesday and close on Saturday night. But in London, the reaction is more subtle and gentle, and a play that fails to gain critical success can usually manage a run of several months or longer. It may have something to do with economics, including cheaper seats and operating costs, or it may simply be the relative indifference of the London public to critical comment. At any rate, it is a distinction that I have never fully comprehended. *Words and Music*, despite only amiable reviews, ran a jolly decent course. Some years later, the title was changed to *Set to Music* for the Broadway production and starred Bea Lillie.

The following autumn in New York, we embarked on a production called *Design for Living*. Written by Noel and starring Alfred Lunt, Lynn Fontanne, and himself, it was automatically a dainty dish. There was also a plan to use Alexander Woollcott in another role, which would have been perfect typecasting since Noel had written the part with Alex in mind. When Ethel Barrymore heard this, she commented in her exquisite, low tone, "What an excellent idea. That makes *four* amateurs!" As it turned out, Alex refused the part anyway.

Words and Music is a 1932 musical revue by Noel Coward that introduced two of his most popular songs: "Mad about the Boy" and "Mad Dogs and Englishmen." Coward did not appear in the show but wrote the songs and sketches, several of them praised for their acidic wit. The London cast included Joyce Barbour, Ivy St. Helier, John Mills, Romney Brent, Doris Hare, and Graham Payn. The scintillating score also included "The Party's Over Now," "Something to Do with Spring," and "The Younger Generation." *Words and Music* received favorable notices from the press and ran just shy of two years.

Alex was self-opinionated and prissy, not to mention severely overweight and magnificently ugly. By his own choice, he had few friends, and those he had he ruled with an iron hand. Edna Ferber called him the "New Jersey Nero." I can recall one particular evening at a party given by Constance Collier in New York. I left for home at about one in the morning, and the next day Alex was on the phone with Noel, telling him that he *must* get rid of me, as my manners were so appalling. It finally boiled down to the fact that Woollcott was outraged because I had left the party before he had.

Design for Living is a 1933 comedy by Noel Coward that was first produced on Broadway because it was feared that the British censor would not allow such an "adult" play on the London stage. Bohemian interior designer Gilda (Lynn Fontanne) is loved and loves both playwright Leo (Noel Coward) and painter Otto (Alfred Lunt), even while she goes through a marriage with stuffy Ernest Friedman (Campbell Gullan). In truth, they love one another and are most happy when it is a ménage à trois. Coward wrote *Design for Living* with himself and the Lunts in mind, and the three stars also produced the play, with Coward directing.

The threesome was considered to be at its peak by the press, and audiences agreed, but the comedy only ran for four and a half months because the stars had other commitments. A London production of *Design for Living* did not open until 1939, and starred Diana Wynyard, Anton Walbrook, and Rex Harrison as the free-thinking threesome. The critical and popular reaction was positive, and the comedy ran for 233 performances, cut short by the beginning of World War II. A 1933 screen version, directed by Ernest Lubitsch, with a heavily sanitized and altered script, starred Miriam Hopkins, Gary Cooper, and Fredric March. *Design for Living* showed up on British television in 1964 and 1979.

Alexander Woollcott (1887–1943) was a theater critic and author who is most remembered as the acerbic personality that inspired the main character in the comedy classic *The Man Who Came to Dinner*. Born in Phalanx, New Jersey, and educated at Hamilton College, he served as a police reporter for the *New York Times* before becoming one of its drama critics in 1914. With time off for World War I, he remained at the paper until 1922, when he wrote for the *New York Herald*, the *Sun*, and finally the *World*. He wrote paeans of praise on Mrs. Fiske and the Marx Brothers but detested many of Eugene O'Neill's best plays. Woollcott's books include theatrical criticism, biography, and reminiscences.

Even though he was a critic, he was close friends with many people in the theater and movies, and on literary scene, as witnessed by his participation in the witty Algonquin Round Table set. With George S. Kaufman he wrote two failed plays, *The Channel Road* (1929) and *The Dark Tower* (1933). In his last years he largely devoted himself to radio and writing magazine articles but also took time to appear on Broadway in *Brief Moment* (1931) and *Wine of Choice* (1938), and in 1940 he headed the road company of *The Man Who Came to Dinner*, in which he essentially played himself.

Alex had a passion for backgammon and croquet, both of which he invariably played for stakes. His method with backgammon, which was usually played for ten cents a point, was quite simple. If by chance he lost, he would suggest that the amount of his loss be "carried over" until he and his opponent played again—whereupon it would be conveniently forgotten or, if remembered, made up in the next session. He rarely lost. His croquet system, usually played for $1,000 a head, had its whimseys, too. If Alex's ball went out of bounds, it was not supposed to have done so and would be returned to the court without apology or explanation. If an opponent's ball went out of bounds, on the other hand, the usual penalty was assessed. So again, this arrangement gave Alex a considerable advantage.

He had a habit of giving Sunday morning brunches in his New York apartment, and large crowds of people flocked to attend. Alex was fully conscious that the guests were honored to be part of his inner circle. Yet, he frequently paid no attention to them whatsoever. Instead, he would select the richest man in the room, plunk him down at the backgammon table, and spend the entire party allowing his guests to wander at will while he sat fleecing his opponent. I am sure those parties paid for themselves.

Alex eventually decided that New York was too much for him and bought an island called Neshobe at Lake Bomoseen in Vermont. (He had once had a radio program and made considerable money as the Town Crier.) He was absolutely the "czar" of his island, and I always felt in a curious way that it led to his death. His egomania swelled to enormous proportions in Vermont, and old friends like Neysa McMein and Harpo Marx simply gave up going. The croquet abounded, but the players dwindled. I do not remember the date, but he died of a cerebral hemorrhage, and thus passed from the scene one of the most colorful figures of his time. [Woollcott died in New York City on January 23, 1943. He had requested that he be cremated and his ashes buried at Hamilton College in Clinton, New York. They were mistakenly sent to Colgate University in Hamilton, New York. It took some doing before Woollcott finally ended up in the right place.]

Noel gave *Design for Living* to Max Gordon to produce, which annoyed a great many managers—most notably Gilbert Miller—who had been associated with Noel in the past. But he had taken a fancy to Max and decided to let him have this obvious plum. [Max Gordon (1892–1978) was a colorful Broadway producer who presented such hits as *The Band Wagon* (1931), *The Cat and the Fiddle* (1931), *Roberta* (1933), *Dodsworth* (1934), *The Women* (1936), *My Sister Eileen* (1940), *Junior Miss* (1941), *Born Yesterday* (1946), and *The Solid Gold Cadillac* (1953).] It happened to come at a very fortuitous time in Gordon's career. Despite an impressive backlog of smash hits, Gordon was, at that exact moment, going through a bad period, as everyone in the theater invariably does. *Design for Living* pulled Gordon out of the doldrums of temporary inactivity and put him straight back as an important producer, which indeed he was. His gratitude was more than routine, as he later offered Noel share ownership in his subsequent productions.

Still being groomed for my eventual producer's role, I was general manager on *Design for Living* and, consequently, was at the theater most of the time during its run. The play was an automatic hit and even managed to survive the stock market crash and subsequent bank closings that brought ruin to many of the other shows in town. I'm not sure where our fans found their money, but the fact remains that we played to capacity throughout the crisis and emerged triumphant and unscathed.

Our stars were brilliant, of course. Lynn Fontanne isn't ordinarily given to idiosyncrasies, but she came up with one in this particular instance. In normal conditions, understudies are never engaged to back up stars as important as the Lunts. The audience may come to see the show, but they primarily come to see the stars, and in their absence, it is usually wiser not to play. In

The Lunts were the most famous and beloved acting couple of the American theater for more than thirty-five years. Alfred Lunt (1892–1977) was an actor and director who was considered by many the greatest leading man of his generation. He was born in Milwaukee and educated at Carroll College. He abandoned his early ambition to become an architect and made his theatrical debut with the Castle Square Theatre stock company in Boston in 1912, and then toured with Lillie Langtry and Margaret Anglin. Broadway first saw him in *Romance and Arabella* (1917), but it was his performance as the shy, bumbling young man in *Clarence* (1919) that brought him recognition. In 1922, Alfred married Lynn Fontanne and rarely performed without her. Three of his few noteworthy solo assignments were as Mr. Prior, the boozy, newly dead young man in *Outward Bound* (1924); flashy bootlegger Babe Callahan in *Ned McCobb's Daughter* (1926); and Marco Polo in *Marco Millions* (1928).

Lynn Fontanne (1887–1983) was one of the great ladies of the American stage. The willowy, dark-haired, sharp-eyed actress with a throaty contralto voice and regal bearing was born in London, where she studied with Ellen Terry before making her debut in 1905, in *Cinderella*. Fontanne came to the United States in 1910, appearing in *Mr. Preedy and the Countess*, but she soon returned home and did not permanently settle in the Unites States until 1916. Thereafter, she appeared in a rapid succession of plays, including *A Young Man's Fancy* (1916), in which she met her future husband. Early in her career, Fontanne enjoyed a major hit as the pushy, cliché-ridden wife in *Dulcy* (1921).

The Lunts' first great triumph together was in *The Guardsman* (1924), followed by *The Second Man* (1927) and *The Doctor's Dilemma* (1927). After creating the role of Nina Leeds in *Strange Interlude* (1928), the couple permanently reunited and was cheered for their performances in *Elizabeth the Queen* (1930), *Reunion in Vienna* (1931), *Design for Living* (1933), *The Taming of the Shrew* (1935), *Idiot's Delight* (1936), *Amphitryon 38* (1937), *The Seagull* (1938), *There Shall Be No Night* (1940), and *The Pirate* (1942). The Lunts spent the rest of the war years playing in England, returning to New York to appear in a series of competent, but often indifferent, comedies: *O Mistress Mine* (1946), *I Know My Love* (1949), *Quadrille* (1954), and *The Great Sebastians* (1956). Only with their farewell play *The Visit* (1958) did they again find a worthy drama.

Lunt occasionally directed plays, for example, *Candle in the Wind* (1941) and *Ondine* (1954). While Fontanne was often considered the more restrained of the two actors, it was their chemistry on stage that made them so unforgettable. The Lunts made only a handful of films, for instance, *The Guardsman* (1931), and a few television dramas, most memorably *The Magnificent Yankee* (1965), so there is too little evidence of their superb acting talents. But for the many theatergoers who saw them, they are indelibly remembered. In 1958, the Globe Theatre on Broadway was renamed the Lunt-Fontanne Theatre in their honor.

this case, however, Lynn made a special point that since she had two male costars, it was advisable to engage one understudy to cover either one of them in case of an emergency. In fact, she had an understudy in mind, whom she lyrically described as "experienced, talented, and full of charm." As we invariably heeded her requests, we immediately hired him. On the train trip to Cleveland for our pre-Broadway tryout, his behavior was such as to give the rest of us slight doubts about Lynn's recommendations. But he was kept on and returned to New York, where, for months, he paced up and down the aisles of the Barrymore Theatre at a considerable salary.

Then came the day when Noel fell ill and was taken to a hospital, but when the eager young man bounded onto the stage to assume his role, Lynn gave a cold, shrewd, appraising glance at her enthusiastic, determined choice and said calmly, as only she could say calmly, "But darling, nothing on earth would induce me to go on the stage with you." So we closed the play until Noel returned to complete the run, which was terminated by mutual consent. Years later, in 1939, *Design for Living* was recreated in London, with Rex Harrison, Diana Wynyard, Anton Walbrook, and Alan

The Pirate is a romantic swashbuckling comedy by S. N. Behrman that found success on Broadway because it featured the Lunts in one of their most robust performances. Serafin (Alfred Lunt) and his band of actors arrive on a West Indies island but are denied permission to perform by the mayor, Vargas (Alan Reed). Serafin recognizes Vargas as the infamous pirate Macoco, so he woos the mayor's wife (Lynn Fontanne) and ends up winning her heart and putting Vargas in jail. The press thought more of the acting and the lavish and colorful production than the play itself. The Theatre Guild and the Playwrights Company produced the comedy, with Lunt and Wilson codirecting, and it ran for 177 performances. *The Pirate* was turned into a movie musical in 1948, starring Gene Kelly and Judy Garland, and featuring a score by Cole Porter.

Webb. It was again a great success, but I regret to report that it wasn't quite as good as New York.

I have known the Lunts for so long that I can't even remember where or when I met them. They are, of course, the most remarkable team in the English-speaking theater, but I doubt that the thousands who have seen them move about the stage with such ease and grace are aware of the meticulous exactitude that they have put into rehearsals to achieve this effect. They are insatiable perfectionists, which has frequently made them the despair of directors. I was hired to stage them in a play called *The Pirate* and soon learned that directing them is as inessential as it is inadvisable. My solution was to devote myself to the rest of the cast, while the scenes played by the Lunts were worked out by the Lunts. [Wilson's direction of *The Pirate* was more effective than he gives credit. Although he was codirector with Alfred Lunt, Fontanne wrote to Coward that, "Jack has become very dear to us. He has a definite talent for directing and . . . was excellent on the script altogether, and I suppose it is a great tribute to his ability and his kindness and tact that we have come out of this long, torturous readying of the play more devoted than ever."]

The Lunts would evolve a treatment of a sequence and play it brilliantly; in normal conditions, many other actors would have settled for it as it was, but not the Lunts. They would proceed to rehearse it again in quite a different way, which would invariably turn out equally good and effective. After that, when one thought that everything was more or less set, they would try it a third way, then a fourth, and even on occasion a fifth. My presence was frankly redundant, although they insisted on my opinion after each version, to which they paid not the slightest attention. Even Noel was subjected to this on several occasions when he directed them. But he was less patient and would often walk out of the rehearsal in mild exasperation, saying, "I'm going to the movies. I expect when I come back, you'll be just where I left you."

Their precision even persisted with authors, including Noel, Robert Sherwood, Sam Behrman, and the other important playwrights who wrote for them. For instance, on the tour of *The Pirate*, which lasted for about twelve weeks, Sam made it his habit to register in a hotel under his own name and then move to another under an assumed one. He knew that the Lunts, immersed in an analysis of some scene, might ask him over at two in the morning to discuss their new ideas. One is, however, richly compensated for any difficulties. Once a play with the Lunts is set, they will continue in it for as long as it lasts—whether it be a season or years.

Behrman, under whatever name he may have registered, was a roly-poly, witty companion and a superb listener. In addition, he could top anyone conversationally without being offensive or annoying. His private life was a little bizarre. For example, he had a passion for being alone. Although he adored his wife, they maintained separate apartments during the time that I knew them. His greatest phobia was the telephone. In his early years as the personal secretary to Jed Harris, one of the theater's most eccentric and colorful producers, Jed's phone rang constantly, and he also frequently called Sam at home throughout the night. Sam developed an antipathy toward telephoning that he was never able to shake. In his work, Sam would never use an easy word if he could substitute a more difficult one. We used to joke about this and kept a large dictionary on the stage manager's table. During rehearsals, we could always look up Sam's words and find out what they meant. I think it tickled him to stump us. He also had an engaging sense of humor. At one point, Noel was making frequent visits to the White House as a guest of President Roosevelt, and Behrman quipped, "Noel thinks he's being asked down to settle the state of the nation. The truth of the matter is that he's been asked simply to play 'Mad Dogs and Englishmen.'"

One of the particular excitements of *The Pirate* was persuading the Lunts to use two comparatively unknown young men as scenic and costume designers: Lemuel Ayers and Miles White. Throughout their careers, Alfred and Lynn had been accustomed to using established, important designers, and they were somewhat reluctant to tackle newcomers. Nevertheless, Lem and Miles were graciously invited to Genesee Depot, Wisconsin—the location of the Lunts' country home, known as Ten Chimneys—where their drawings were surveyed and probably their teeth as well. They passed the test and did their jobs—superbly. [Lemuel Ayers (1915–1955) was a theater director and producer primarily remembered for his scenic and costume designs. Miles White (1914–2000) was a renowned costume designer who was active on Broadway between 1938 and 1977.] Lem and Miles' next assignment was a little number called *Oklahoma!* and they went on in their various ways—and frequently together—to subsequent important achievements. Miles became the mainstay of the Ringling Brothers' Circus, doing décor, costumes, and floats. He also found time to work on innumerable Broadway productions, including magnificent work for me on *Bloomer Girl* and *Gentlemen Prefer Blondes*. Lem also did a series of distinguished shows, climaxed by his becoming a producer, in association with Arnold Subber, of *Kiss Me, Kate*.

The Lunts were troupers in the best sense of the word. One night in Portland, Maine, Lynn fell on the ice on her way to the theater and broke her wrist. She was taken to a hospital and the curtain held for an hour, but she appeared and played. Her arm was in a splint for weeks, but she never missed a performance during the entire tour. She was incredibly devoted to her work, something other actresses would do well to emulate. Another episode bears repeating, and it occurred during the run of *Design for Living*. One Friday night, Lynn went to Noel with a particular problem. In one scene she had to take a letter out of her handbag, and she had discovered that if it came out quickly, there was a bigger laugh than if she had to dig for it. Her suggestion to Noel was to construct a sort of steel frame inside the bag with a spring system that would virtually pop the letter into her hand, ensuring the bigger laugh. Noel demurred slightly, saying, "But, darling, we're closing tomorrow." Lynn's reply was typical: "Of course, my dear, I know that. But there's still the matinee and the evening." That's what I mean by meticulous exactitude.

At Ten Chimneys, their country retreat in Wisconsin, the Lunts do a complete volte-face in personality. They are relaxed, domestic, and even agrarian. Alfred gets up in the morning long before seven and is out on the farm milking cows, tending the garden, and building walls with his own hands. He returns to the house only at odd moments to have a cup of coffee or see how dinner—which he invariably cooks—is coming along. There are actually two cooks there, but there is no mistaking the fact that he is in charge. The kitchen is a thing of beauty and the size of an ordinary house. It contains two stoves, two refrigerators, and endless shelves of china and glass, illuminated by indirect lighting. Let's face it, that kitchen is Alfred's spiritual home.

Lynn's daily routine varies from his. She goes to bed later and sleeps in later. So as to not disturb her in the mornings, Alfred leaves his farm clothes in the hallway and gets dressed silently—and even slyly—for his early, rustic rounds. Lynn's days, however, are far from idle. She runs the house with amazing efficiency. She spends hours in the gardens, cutting large bunches of flowers that she will later arrange with exquisite taste. She also makes many of her own dresses. She has a form based on her own figure on which she fits fabrics selected in Milwaukee or nearby Waukesha. The results are so effective that upon her arrival at dinner, it is almost impossible to determine whether she is wearing a Molyneux, a Dior, a Mainbocher, or an original Fontanne. Any other spare time during the day is spent on a game of solitaire, a habit that has gone on for many years and for which she keeps a meticulous running score showing whether she is ahead of herself or behind throughout time.

Life at Ten Chimneys is run on a rather special plan, starting with breakfast served on trays. There is no official lunch, but one is encouraged to forage in the capacious twin refrigerators, so that you end up eating much more than a formal lunch would include. The great event gastronomically is dinner, which is always titivated by Alfred and the two cooks throughout the day. It is invariably a fantastic meal of four or five courses, and woe betide the guest who doesn't eat them all. The preparations and care that go into the collation demands a full appetite. Although I sometimes fall short in that department, there is no question that dinners at the Lunts' would certainly do justice to any of the great restaurants of the world.

The house is a model of luxury and comfort. In the bedrooms, for instance, there are three sets of curtains: blackouts for late sleeping, organdy for elegance, and a beautiful chintz to complete the trilogy. The bathrooms are not only carpeted, but also decorated with murals. And I don't think I have ever seen such luxurious clothes closets, also fully carpeted and muraled. The big drawing room—one of three—has a painted ceiling not unlike a Venetian palazzo. Even the piano boasts Swedish baroque designs, and the rest of the furniture has been casually but carefully selected to be of no particular period but to harmonize into an enchanting entity. The predominant motif at Ten Chimneys, and also at the Lunts' house in New York, is Scandinavian. When they were less wealthy, they built a Swedish cottage at Genesee. In later years, Alfred turned the cottage over to his mother and built on the same property—at least one hundred acres—the manor house where they now live.

I had always taken for granted that Alfred was Swedish, given that his houses featured that décor and he even seemed to have a slight foreign accent. In fact, during the run of *There Shall Be No Night*, he accepted a decoration from the Finnish minister with the calm and aplomb of a Finnish native. It was not until years afterward that I learned the actual facts of his background. It turned out that he was born of solid American parentage. His father died at an early age, and his mother—one of the most remarkable women I have ever known—married a Dr. Sederholm, who was indeed an authentic Scandinavian. They lived in Milwaukee but spent summers in Sweden, which is where, I presume, Alfred picked up his association with that culture. Dr. Sederholm later moved his practice to the nearby town of Waukesha, and sometime after that moved to the village of Genesee Depot, where he set up another practice and bought land, which was the kernel of the present Lunt estate. Alfred and Lynn are now firmly—if somewhat naively—convinced that they were both born and bred on the property, in spite of the evident fact that it was the result of the peregrinations of a somewhat erratic stepfather.

Lynn rarely speaks about her own family background, but I know from occasional remarks she has made that she was born in England, and that her father, Jules Pierre Antoine Fontanne, was French. She is still unequivocally

Laurette Taylor (1884–1946) was a short, slim redhead with wide, hazel-blue eyes and high eyebrows. She was one of the greatest, yet, in a way, most tragic of all American performers. She began her theatrical career as a child in vaudeville, where she was billed as "La Belle Laurette." She later played for many years in various stock companies, also touring in plays by her first husband, Charles A. Taylor, before getting noticed as the burglar's sweetheart Rose in *Alias Jimmy Valentine* (1910). Her first major success was as Hawaiian princess Luana in *The Bird of Paradise* (1912). Even greater acclaim came with her winsome performance in the title role of *Peg O' My Heart* (1912), written by her second husband, J. Hartley Manners.

Afterward she wasted her enormous, if sometimes undisciplined, talent starring in minor vehicles that Manners wrote for her. Following his death, Taylor virtually retired from the stage, becoming a recluse and an alcoholic, but she returned for occasional revivals. The most notable was a 1938 mounting of *Outward Bound*, in which she played Mrs. Midgit. Her last Broadway appearance was generally acknowledged as not only her greatest, but also one of the most memorable performances of her generation, when she played the desperate mother Amanda Wingfield in *The Glass Menagerie* (1945). She continued in the role until shortly before her death. Taylor made only three movies, all silent, but the 1922 version of *Peg O' My Heart* reveals glimpses of her acting prowess.

one of the great beauties of the theater, which is all the more remarkable, as her exact age, to put it politely, is unrevealed. Her posture is faultless, and Alfred always says that as far as he is concerned, he looks old enough to be her father. [Fontanne was actually older than Lunt. At the time Wilson was writing, the Lunts had been retired for two years; he was sixty-eight and she seventy-three.] She began her career doing walk-ons on the London stage, where she attracted the attention of Laurette Taylor, who not only divined Lynn's histrionic talents, but also became her close friend. Laurette returned to New York, while Lynn graduated to larger and more important roles in London. Laurette eventually sent for her to come to the United States, offering her a room in her magnificent Riverside Drive home, as well as parts in her subsequent plays.

Laurette was, at the time, married to a courtly gentleman, J. Hartley Manners, who wrote many of her important plays, including the immortal *Peg O' My Heart*. He never appeared in public without a top hat, walking stick, and carnation. Laurette adored him, although their personalities seemed completely opposed. She was an Irish hoyden—volatile, witty, kind, and vindictive, and, in fact, a combination of those gregarious qualities, which made her America's greatest actress. She often hosted supper parties at Riverside Drive. But for all her star power and popularity, Laurette was so tiny at those parties compared to Lynn, who stood head and shoulders above her. It was a sight to behold. In fact, Laurette took a dim view of Alfred's courtship of Lynn and did whatever she could to stop their marriage. But married they were, although where or when has never been disclosed to me. [The Lunts were married in New York City on May 26, 1922.] They never forgave Laurette for her interference. In later years, after Hartley's death, she was forced to sell her house and move into a small apartment above the Copacabana. Neither Lynn nor Alfred ever visited her or sent her a message up to and including the day she died.

Since the day they married, whether on or off the stage, the Lunts are seemingly never separated. Theirs is an incredibly strong bond. They seldom have visitors at Ten Chimneys, but the few who have been fortunate enough to be invited always find it a wonderfully unique and pleasant experience.

CHAPTER EIGHT

~

The Royal Princess

It was during a trip to London to see Noel's *Conversation Piece* that I first met Princess Natalie Paley. I arrived on the *Aquitania* to find an invitation to dinner from noted hostess Alice Astor, who at that particular time was married to Raimund von Hofmannsthal. She had a beautiful house in Regents Park and, of course, gave a beautiful dinner for twenty or thirty people. The princess was seated next to me, and we bickered amiably throughout dinner. At the end, sitting on the terrace with coffee and liqueur, Raimund asked her how she had liked me. Her reply was, as usual, very much to the point: "I simply detested him." We have been married for twenty-three years. [In her autobiography, Carol Channing observes,

> Jack and Natasha's great bond was their sharing of impeccably fine and aristocratic taste, to the exclusion of all other kinds of good taste. I remember Jack . . . saying to me once, "You know, Carol, I can live without anything except luxury." I suppose you *better* marry the Princess Paley of all the Russias if you feel that way.

Natasha's close friend Anita Loos, in one of her autobiographies, states, "Natasha became involved in the theater through her happy marriage to Jack, but she hated the theater and branded showbiz as her own private version of *The Curse of the Romanovs.*"]

Natasha's history was as equally checkered as mine, but far more interesting, especially as it was in reverse. Her father was Grand Duke Paul of Russia, uncle of the last czar. Paul first married Alexandra, princess of Greece

Natalie Paley (1905–1981) was a notable fashion model, film actress, and socialite who was as beautiful and exotic as her royal ancestry suggests. She was born in Paris as Princess Natalia Pavlovna von Hohenfelsen, the daughter of Grand Duke Paul Alexandrovich of the royal Russian Romanov family and first cousin to the last czar, Nicholas II. The Grand Duke had left Russia in 1902, after his royal wife died during childbirth, and he married a commoner, Olga Karnovich, to the displeasure of some members of the royal family. Nicholas finally welcomed the family back to the Russian court in 1912, but six years later, during the Bolshevik Revolution, Alexandrovich was killed and thirteen-year-old Natalia escaped to Finland in the middle of the night with her nanny and sister Irina. Their mother eventually rejoined the girls, and they settled in Paris in 1920.

As an adult, Natalia was a celebrated member of Parisien high society, and her beauty opened doors for her in the fashion world. She was employed by and briefly married to fashion couture Lucien Lelong, and as Natalie Paley, her fame as a fashion model grew. (All of her friends and family called her Natasha.) Filmmakers in Europe and Hollywood pursued her, and she appeared with Katharine Hepburn in one film, *Sylvia Scarlett*, but Paley's movie career was unsatisfying and she gave it up in 1935. She married Wilson in 1937, continued her modeling career, and enjoyed celebrity as a frequent subject of New York's society columns. She became an U.S. citizen in 1941 and passed away in 1981, having outlived Wilson by twenty years.

and Denmark, and they had two children, Grand Duchess Marie and Grand Duke Dmitri. Several years after the death of his wife, Grand Duke Paul met and fell in love with a Russian commoner, Olga Valerianovna Karnovich, whom he eventually married. The Imperial family was not receptive to this idea but sufficiently relented in 1904, when the prince regent of Bavaria granted her the title of Countess von Hohenfelsen. Nonetheless, the family was unwelcome in Russia, and Grand Duke Paul moved them to Paris, to an apparently beautiful house and a life of luxury, gaiety, and social preeminence. It was there that Natasha and her older sister Irina were born and lived for some time.

The family was eventually pardoned by the Romanovs and invited on a special reprieve to build a home in St. Petersburg; in 1915, Czar Nicholas made Natasha's mother Princess Paley. The gesture turned out to be an unhappy one when the Russian Revolution broke out a few years after their arrival. Grand Duke Paul was imprisoned and later killed, and Natasha's older brother Vladimir was sent to Siberia, where he was also later killed. Only the women of the family were left. With courage and determination, they escaped one night to Finland and walked several miles through snow to safety. They later exiled to France and returned to Paris. The earlier banishment thus turned out to be a blessing, as Princess Paley and the two girls already had a house and a considerable bank account in Paris. The relatives they left behind in Russia were far less fortunate, as the Bolsheviks seized their property and belongings.

And so Natasha was brought up in Paris with care and a certain degree of luxury. She was, however, restless—as she is today—and eager to accomplish something beyond the rounds of routine social procedure. To the horror of the upper echelon of French society and at an early age, she accepted a job in the famous dressmaking establishment of Lucien Lelong and eventually married him. They worked together during a period of years and made several trips to the United States, but for reasons about which I would never enquire, as it is certainly none of my business, they were separated.

Married or separated, Natasha was unquestionably the toast of Paris and certainly never lacked attention or company. She was extremely beautiful and still is—blonde, diminutive, and with the figure of an eighteen-year-old. [The princess was more than fifty years old when Wilson was writing this.] The film studios got after her, and she became an important figure in French cinema for a period of time. As a matter of fact, on the night that we met in London, she was there on assignment for Elstree Studio with Douglas Fairbanks Sr. for the filming of *The Private Life of Don Juan*. She later went to Hollywood to play opposite Maurice Chevalier in another picture, *Folies Bergere*. She returned there once more—and I'm afraid on my advice—to play in *Sylvia Scarlett*, a film that also featured Katharine Hepburn, Cary Grant, Edmund Gwenn, and Brian Aherne. George Cukor, a fine director and good friend of Natasha's, handled the production. For some reason, in spite of the great cast and the auspices that presided over it, *Scarlett* was not a box-office success. [Today *Sylvia Scarlett* (1935), in which Hepburn plays a con woman disguised as a boy, is something of a cult favorite.]

In 1937, Natasha decided she had enough of acting, washed her hands of the business, and finally settled for marrying me. I was producing a play by Gerald Savory called *George and Margaret* at the time. We did our out-of-town tryout in Toronto, so Natasha and I decided to make it sort of a "busman's honeymoon" as well. We had been married three days prior in Connecticut, with Noel as best man. On the way to Canada, we spent forty-eight hours at Saratoga Springs, where the waters proved a little more than efficacious, but the bulk of our honeymoon was spent in Toronto, attending rehearsals and parties given by the current socialites, who were most generous and kind to the entire company. [The marriage of Wilson and Princess

Paley was one of companionship and deep friendship, if not sexual passion. It is not clear when Wilson and Coward ceased being lovers. The termination of the affair must have been amicable, as both men remained close friends and business partners. Wilson's ex-lover Coward serving as best man at his wedding to Princess Paley may strike one as ironic, but the threesome were good friends for many years. The Wilson–Paley marriage has been compared to another famous pairing of the time, that of Cole Porter and socialite Linda Lee. The two couples spent a great deal of time together, usually in Europe. Everyone in their circle understood the arrangement and welcomed the two couples into the world of high society. In fact, they were among the most attractive and charming foursomes on two continents.]

On opening night of *George and Margaret* in Toronto, Natasha and I were invited to dine with the governor general. It was a gathering of about twenty, including the top echelon of the local aristocracy. The ladies were elegant and bejeweled, and the gentlemen faultless in their tailoring, if a trifle dull in their conversation. In this setting of impeccable colonial grandeur, I managed to make two very distinct blunders in protocol. To begin, I preceded the governor into the dining room. And then, at the end of dinner, I took a sip of port before the assemblage had a chance to toast the king of England. As I was American, all was forgiven, and we went off to the theater for a pleasant evening.

George and Margaret—who, incidentally, never appear but are discussed throughout the play—was a light, even fragile, play, but in the hands of such accomplished performers as Irene Browne, Alan Webb, Gladys Henson, and Moya Nugent, it added up to an enjoyable comedy. This proved true not only in Toronto, but also subsequently at the Morosco Theatre in New York, where it ran for eleven weeks.

Conversation Piece, which takes us all the way back to my first meeting Natasha in 1934, was an elaborate period operetta. Charles Cochran, as producer, was able to persuade famous French star Yvonne Printemps to appear, and Noel selected Romney Brent to play opposite her. After a reasonable period of rehearsals, however, it was decided that Romney was wrong for the part, and an amicable arrangement was made. He resigned, and to no one's particular surprise, Noel took over the part, stipulating, as usual, that it was to be for a limited period. Also in the cast was Louis Hayward, who ended up in Hollywood, as did so many of our stars, as well as Irene Browne and a young gentleman in a relatively small part, George Sanders. Gladys Calthrop again did a superb job on the costumes and scenery, and the play was a gratifying success.

Conversation Piece is a 1934 comedy with songs by Noel Coward that, unusual for him, was based on another work, in this case the novel *The Regent and His Daughter* by Dormer Creston. Paul, the Duc de Chaucigny-Varennes (Coward), sees Mélanie (Yvonne Printemps) singing in a Paris café and brings her to England, where he makes her his ward, hoping to marry her off to someone rich, thereby securing his own future. But Mélanie falls in love with Paul, and after some struggle, he realizes the feeling is mutual. The Coward score included the future standard "I'll Follow My Secret Heart," but most critics felt the show was unsatisfying as a musical and comedy. There were more compliments for the performers, in particular French actress Printemps, who spoke no English and learned the dialogue by rote.

Despite the critics' qualms, *Conversation Piece* ran for 177 performances in London, although Coward departed from the cast after three months. The Broadway production later that same year also starred Printemps as Mélanie. Some critics applauded her performance but felt the lightweight piece was lacking and did not recommend it. Produced by Charles B. Cochran and directed by Coward, as it had been in London, the Broadway version closed after fifty-five performances.

At a given point, Noel left the cast, and his part was taken over by Pierre Fresnay, Yvonne's real-life husband. On Noel's last night, Cochran did a strange and sensitive thing. The fact that Alfred, Lynn, and Noel were planning to set me up as a producer was supposed to be a deep-died, private secret. I suspect there is no such thing in the theater, however, because Cochran presented Noel with a handsome gold cigarette case with an inscription saying how happy and proud he had been in their association throughout the years. It was a slight shock because we didn't think he knew that I would soon be producing Noel's plays, but it was a generous and touching farewell gesture.

Pierre Fresnay was excellent in the role, but Noel took a slightly malicious pleasure in the fact that business dropped off after his abdication. The following year, the play was done again in New York, still with Yvonne and Pierre. I don't know all the details, as I had no official connection with it, but apparently there were financial difficulties involving lawsuits and injunctions, and the show was definitely a failure.

CHAPTER NINE

~

Launching the Company

Having passed my course in the rudiments of theatrical chicanery, it was finally decided that I had achieved my diploma and was ready to be a full producer. Alfred and Lynn, and Noel and I, formed Transatlantic Productions, Ltd., in which we all made a token investment but produced under my name.

The play selected for our initial embarkation was *Biography* by S. N. Behrman. It had starred Ina Claire in New York and been a big hit. She finally agreed to repeat it in London, which was certainly an achievement for us, as Ina has always been independent, evanescent, and difficult to tie down to any particular assignment. She arrived from Paris, where she had been selecting a new wardrobe for the play, and was properly met at Dover by Hugh "Binkie" Beaumont and me, and escorted to Noel's nearby country house. Binkie was one of *Biography*'s main investors, and the show was eventually to be housed in the Globe Theatre, which he owns.

Binkie Beaumont is one of the outstanding theatrical figures in the world today and certainly the most successful producer in London. He makes it a rule to keep eleven shows running simultaneously, and I doubt if even Charles Cochran, Florenz Ziegfeld, or Charles Dillingham ever matched this record. I used to tease him, saying, "Why eleven?" It was a long while before he finally confessed the reason behind that setup. He explained that there were really only eleven good theaters in London and that by keeping them all occupied, no author—famous or unknown—would ever send a script to any other producer. He even achieved the distinction of being the subject

Biography is a 1932 American comedy by S. N. Behrman with a dark and disturbing subtext. Marion Froude (Ina Claire) is a celebrated artist who has had many lovers throughout the world but no husbands. One of her earliest loves, Leander Nolan (Jay Fassett), now a successful lawyer running for senator, comes to have his portrait painted. At the same time, Richard Kurt (Earle Larimore), a radical young editor, appears with an offer to publish Marion's autobiography. Although she first finds Kurt "bumptious and insufferable," she quickly develops a fondness for him, and he falls in love with her. When Nolan learns that Marion has agreed to write her life history, he is furious, for he knows it will ruin his chances of election. But the behavior of his prospective father-in-law and his fiancée makes him wonder if he really doesn't still love Marion. Marion eventually recognizes that she would be happy neither with Nolan, who has grown too conservative, nor with Kurt, who is hopelessly hate-filled. She destroys her manuscript and, receiving an offer to paint some Hollywood celebrities, tells her maid to pack; she will resume her wayfaring, wayward existence in California.

Biography is considered Behrman's finest work, and most would agree that Claire gave her greatest performance as the charming and infuriating Marion. Philip Moeller directed the Theatre Guild production, which ran for a profitable five months during the dark days of the Depression. Claire reprised her Marion in the 1935 London production directed by Noel Coward and produced by Wilson, but British audiences were not as taken with her or the play and its run was short and unprofitable. Ann Harding played Marion in the 1935 screen version titled *Biography of a Bachelor Girl*, and Gertrude Lawrence played her in a 1950 television production.

of a two-day debate in the House of Commons as to whether his theatrical interests constituted a monopoly.

When I first knew Binkie many, many years ago, he was working in a London box office. I suspect that his real name is no more Hugh Beaumont than mine is. He eventually got a job as a booking agent with the Moss Empires company, which owned most of the theaters in England, and managed to convince them that they would be wise to produce their own plays to put into their own theaters. His immediate boss was a man named Harry Tennent, who took a liking to Binkie and his ideas. They agreed to resign from Moss Empires and start their own company, H. M. Tennent, Ltd., with Harry in charge. Harry was a charming gentleman who belonged to all the right clubs. He never failed to wear a bowler hat and carry a carefully rolled umbrella. But his knowledge of the theater always struck me as being slightly

Hugh "Binkie" Beaumont (1908–1973) was a prodigious London theater producer and manager, and cofounder of the prestigious production company H. M. Tennent, Ltd. He was born Hughes Griffiths Morgan in the Hampstead section of London, the son of a barrister, and grew up in Cardiff, Wales, with his mother and stepfather, William Beaumont. When he was fifteen, Beaumont left school to work in a theater box office, and he went on to become a manager of local and touring theater. By the end of the 1920s, he was working in the West End as an assistant to theater mogul Harry Tennent. In 1936, Tennent and Beaumont formed H. M. Tennent, Ltd., which would become a powerful producing organization in Britain.

After Tennent died in 1941, Beaumont ran the company alone and, while shunning the limelight like other producers, became one of the most important men in the British theater. Beaumont produced old and new plays, musicals, and star vehicles. He was closely associated with many different artists but mostly worked with Noel Coward and John Gielgud. In his later years, Beaumont was active as a founding member of the National Theatre.

naive, although he was the nominal head of a company running theaters. Even so, it became increasingly clear that Mr. Beaumont would slowly but surely take over the reins.

Binkie's methods were as methodical as they were subtle. For example, he suggested that I move my office from Regent Street to one in his establishment above the Globe Theatre. I was naturally to pay for it during occupancy, but it would be rent-free during my considerable periods in New York. His reasons may have been utterly philanthropic, but the results were very beneficial to him. At this point in his career, he knew very few important theatrical people, and I knew nearly all of them. When they would stop by my office—whether it was Noel or John Gielgud or any other member of the top echelon—Binkie would conveniently "drop in." He slowly built up a stable of nearly every important star in London, and I must say that any actor who has ever worked for him happily goes back to work for him again. His list became formidable throughout time. In the eleven theaters that he manages to keep running, there is not a knight or a dame in the "theatrical peerage" who is not appearing under his banner. "Under his banner" is slightly inaccurate today because after Harry Tennant died in 1941, the firm continued to bear his name. It apparently amuses Binkie to have this secret power, and he still insists on giving program credit to a firm that only exists because of him.

Now back to *Biography*. On the Monday following Ina's arrival, Noel, Binkie, and I solemnly escorted her to London to begin rehearsals. Noel was the director, and we had lined up an excellent supporting cast. Ina's only objection was to the young man who played opposite her in their most intimate scenes. She said, in frankly outspoken terms, that he couldn't act, that she got no response from him, and that he was lacking in charm and very definitely talent. His name was Laurence Olivier.

The play did not repeat its American success. Ina, whom we had expected to be the toast of the town, seemed to confuse everyone. Perhaps her technique was too facile, or maybe the London audiences just didn't understand the play. But it was apparent in the early part of the first act that a liaison of some sort was missing between the audience and the other side of the footlights. Sensing this vague but unmistakable apathy, Ina elected to double her pace, literally whipping through the performance like a tornado. If I've ever seen an audience told where to get off—short of advancing to the footlights to say so directly—by inference and manner, she conveyed it in no uncertain terms. Her performance was brilliant. Of course, it would be impossible for Ina to be anything else. But the sad fact remains that our play was not well received, and sadder still, neither was she.

Ina is probably one of the greatest comediennes on the American stage. I saw her for the first time in Boston when I was at Andover and she was playing in *The Sunshine Girl*. Even today, at an age that I couldn't possibly guess, Ina continues vigorous and vital, with exquisite looks and a bubbling love for life. [At the time Wilson was writing, Claire was sixty-two years old.] Her most famous characteristic is her passion for conversation, or perhaps I should say monologues. She is vocally tireless and, although never boring and always witty, amazes her many friends by the sheer strength of her larynx. There was one lunch I remember at the Palace Hotel in San Francisco with Ina, Sam Behrman, and myself. We sat down at one o'clock, and by four were finally asked by the waiters to leave. Ina talked solidly the entire time—neither Sam nor I were able to utter a word—and it was quite amazing that she somehow managed not only to breathe, but also eat her lunch. Sam and I left together, and when we got into the taxi, he turned to me and, with his usual ironic sense of humor, said, "Jack, I must say, I've never heard you so brilliant!"

After her divorce from Jack Gilbert, Ina pursued her life independently for a while but eventually succumbed to the courtship of William Wallace, an attractive man who had apparently been a childhood sweetheart. He lived in San Francisco and was extremely rich, and his gain in marriage was the theater world's loss. Difficult as it had been for years to trap her into a contract, it became virtually impossible. But Ina is extremely happy with her husband and adored by San Francisco society, and she has what is known as "everything that money can buy." Once in a while she hints that she would like to return to the stage, but one would be well advised not to take her too seriously. She did return—oddly enough at her own request—in 1954, for one season in New York in T. S. Eliot's *The Confidential Clerk*; however, ordinarily she is far too content in that most beautiful of cities, leading her own life and, as usual, talking her head off. [Claire never returned to the Broadway stage after 1954, even though she lived for another thirty-one years.]

My second venture under the Transatlantic Productions setup was a star-studded production of a play called *Theatre Royal*. It was a brilliant satire on the Barrymores by Edna Ferber and George S. Kaufman. It had been a great success in the United States, where it was called *Royal Family*, but in London Lord Chamberlain refused to pass on the original title. After a few sleepless

The Royal Family is a 1927 American comedy by Edna Ferber and George S. Kaufman that was a thinly disguised and rather satiric portrait of the famous Barrymore–Drew family of actors. The Cavendishes are the greatest acting family in the United States, presided over by the aging Fanny Cavendish (Haidee Wright). Her daughter Julie (Ann Andrews) is the leading contemporary actress, while Julie's daughter Gwen (Sylvia Field) is a promising ingenue. Both Julie and Gwen are toying with abandoning the theater and getting married to nontheater men. Fanny's dashingly handsome son Tony (Otto Kruger) could have been the greatest performer of all, but he prefers the celebrity that comes with being a film star and wild affairs with women, so his escapades keep him on the run. Fanny's brother Herbert Dean (Orlando Daly) is a fine farceur and former matinee idol who is fighting the ravages of age and a faltering career. Hovering over the family is the great producer Oscar Wolfe (Jefferson De Angelis). For all their complaints about their lives, the call of the theater is irresistible. Thus, Julie leaves her own problems to rush off to meet a curtain, and Fanny quietly dies while planning yet another tour.

Jed Harris produced the uproarious send-up of acting families, which infuriated Ethel Barrymore but delighted the critics and audiences for 267 performances. When Wilson produced the play in London in 1936, it was titled *Theatre Royal* because Lord Chamberlain thought the original title disrespectful to the real Royal Family. The title was also changed for the 1930 Hollywood movie, which was called *The Royal Family of Broadway*. On screen, the daffy Cavendish clan included Fredric March, Ina Claire, Mary Brian, and Henrietta Crosman. Early television versions of *The Royal Family* were made in Britain in 1939 and the United States in 1948, followed by small-screen adaptations in 1950, 1951, 1952, 1954, and 1977.

nights, I came up with *Theatre Royal*, which seemed to satisfy his fastidious taste and was accepted.

Noel had been asked to take on the direction but instead elected to charter a yacht and cruise the Mediterranean with Louis Hayward. They only managed to reach Corsica, whereupon the boat promptly sank in the midst of a severe thunderstorm. Luckily, they were rescued by local fishermen and taken to Nice, where they arrived without passports, without Noel's beret, and, in fact, without anything but the clothes they were wearing. The officials were considerate in view of their dilemma. When they finally arrived in London, Noel decided to stay land-bound, at least long enough to direct *Theatre Royal*.

The cast was indeed star-studded. It featured Marie Tempest, Madge Titheradge, and Laurence Olivier in the principal roles. As the play was emphatically about stage people, I suggested that a special matinee be given for the stage stars in London. It was a fascinating afternoon, owing to the juxtaposition of the actors on stage with the actors in the audience. Among

You Can't Take It with You is an endearing 1936 farce by Moss Hart and George S. Kaufman that ranks as one of the best of all American comedies. The wacky Vanderhof family enjoys life to the fullest. Grandpa Martin (Henry Travers) gave up his job years ago to raise snakes and attend commencement exercises. His daughter Penelope (Josephine Hull) writes plays that she never finishes, while her husband Paul (Frank Wilcox) experiments with fireworks in the basement. Their grown daughter Essie (Paula Trueman) and her husband Ed (George Heller) have similarly offbeat pursuits, as do the visitors and friends that pass in and out of the household. When the "normal" daughter Alice (Margot Stevenson) brings her fiancé, Tony Kirby (Jess Barker), and his strait-laced parents (William J. Kelly and Virginia Hammond) to the house, the evening is a disaster, but nothing that can't be mended by Grandpa the next day.

The unconventional but lovable Vanderhofs were embraced by the press and the public, and the comedy was the nonmusical hit of the season, winning the Pulitzer Prize, running for more than two years, and going on to become one of the most produced American comedies. Sam H. Harris presented the original production, and coauthor Kaufman directed. The 1937 London production of *You Can't Take It with You* featured English performers who were deemed too British for such an American work, and the comedy didn't run for long. The 1938 film version, starring Lionel Barrymore as Grandpa, took many liberties with the script but won the Oscar for Best Picture all the same. There have also been television adaptations of *You Can't Take It with You*, in 1945, 1947, 1979, and 1987.

those present were Douglas Fairbanks Jr., Gertrude Lawrence, Ivor Novello, Raymond Massey, Adrianne Allen, Gladys Cooper, Edna Best, Isabel Jeans, and many more of the theatrical elite. The next day, the *London Sketch* came out with the headline, "Stage Stars Attend a Play about Stage Stars." And that aptly summed it up. Although it never equaled its New York success, *Theatre Royal* enjoyed a nice, comfortable run.

The next year, I did another Kaufman comedy in London called *You Can't Take It with You*. This had been a sensation in New York, and I remember on the first night running into Ina Claire and saying, "Do you think this would be a success in London?" She replied, "Darling, this would be a success in Shanghai!" Well, it actually *wasn't* a success in London, and the reasons are hard to define. It may have been that we had an English cast. It may have been that George Kaufman insisted on his stage manager coming to direct. Or it could have been that the London audiences did not appreciate the unmistakably whacky American quality of the play.

The transposition of American plays to London and vice versa has always been a dangerous gamble. It is rare for shows to repeat the success achieved in the originating country. The greatest producers on both continents have long been baffled as to what the formula for success could be and have never been able to determine it. For example, *You Can't Take It with You* was actually an enormous success during its tryout sessions in Manchester, even justifying the lead editorial in the *Manchester Guardian* to praise its intelligence, understanding of human nature, and wit and wisdom. On the other hand, following its London opening, a notice appeared in the *London Times*. Brief and brutal, it read, "The play seemed endless but was actually very short, which the clock surprisingly proved on its own." I think we managed three or four weeks.

A few weeks after the London opening of *Theatre Royal*, I was back in New York with Noel. But with his inevitable change of pace, he decided to do a film. He was talked into this by authors and producers Ben Hecht and Charles MacArthur, the principal bait being Charlie's wife Helen Hayes as his costar. As it turned out, she wasn't delivered, and a Miss Julie Haydon was hired for the job. She was sweet, cooperative, and absolutely terrified. I recall one day in a highly emotional scene where tears were required that it was necessary to resort to first blowing a camphor pipe into her eyes and, second, twisting her ankle off-camera to achieve the ultimate emotional result. [Julie Haydon (1910–1994) was a stage and screen actress who specialized in delicate and vulnerable characters, most memorably as Kitty in *The Time of Your Life* (1939) and the original Laura in *The Glass Menagerie* (1945).]

The film was *The Scoundrel*, and it was done on a shoestring. Noel agreed to accept a minimum wage with the understanding that he was to receive

The Scoundrel is a little known 1935 movie that arguably boasts Noel Coward's finest screen performance. Cutthroat publisher Anthony Mallare (Coward), who made many enemies as he ruthlessly clawed his way to the top, dies in a plane crash, and no one mourns him. Mallare's ghost is forced to roam the world, hoping to find someone who expresses one tear of sympathy for him. Coward's portrayal of Mallare is insightful and moving, and he gets strong support from Julie Haydon, Stanley Ridges, Lionel Stander, Martha Sleeper, and, in a rare screen appearance, Alexander Woollcott. Ben Hecht and Charles MacArthur wrote and directed the Paramount film, which was modestly successful in 1935 and, decades later, has gained something of a cult status.

enormous percentages of the "fabulous" profits that were sure to follow. The fact that such profits never followed annoyed him and his solicitors for years. It wasn't until much later that we discovered that the "boys" (Hecht and MacArthur) had made a package deal with Paramount for five movies, the profits and losses to be divided to reflect the successes or failures of all five. It was an unpredicted and perhaps unfair arrangement because *The Scoundrel* was a great box-office success, and the other four, which escape my memory and perhaps everyone else's, ate up the grosses that Noel's film had made.

I had no official connection with the picture, except that Noel liked having me around. Thus, we would travel to Astoria, Long Island, early each morning, to that same studio I had worked in years before. Hecht and MacArthur were a little remote, spending large blocks of time in a private office that happened to be decorated floor to ceiling with lithographs of full-size nudes. On the set, they were equally whimsical. During "set-ups," which everyone who knows the film industry knows are interminable, they would engage Noel in endless games of backgammon until camera and lighting were finally ready for the next take. At this point the producers would return to their nude-hung chamber, and Noel, with the consistent cooperation of Lee Garmes—one of the finest cameramen in the industry—would put together the next scene.

Although the entire picture was accomplished in three or four weeks, it was not an easy job for Noel. There were long sequences where he was neck deep in a water tank and couldn't have been very comfortable. At the end of a scene, he would emerge dripping wet; then the big brass would return, and the inevitable backgammon would be resumed. Noel maintains to this day that he was a consistent winner and, furthermore, never paid.

CHAPTER TEN

~

Gertie and Friends

Alfred and Lynn had been besieging Noel for a considerable time to write a play for them in which their reactions to one another would not be all sweetness and light, gaiety and understanding. They felt that a situation in which they were pitted against one another would be an intelligent and interesting change. The year following *Theatre Royal*, Noel eventually wrote and directed a little opus called *Point Valaine*. It was set in the South Sea Islands, and although Alfred and Lynn were ostensibly lovers, they fought continuously. In one scene, he actually spat in her face, which shocked their ever-loving public to the core. Lynn later confessed that after the first few rehearsals, she not only became accustomed to it, but frankly liked it.

Lynn's role in *Point Valaine* was that of an innkeeper, and among her guests was the late Osgood Perkins in a part admittedly modeled on Somerset Maugham. There was also a younger guest, played by Louis Hayward, for whom Lynn's interest caused serious altercations for Alfred. He played the headwaiter at the inn and also, of course, Lynn's lover. His reaction to the young man was so violent that at the end of the second act, he threw himself over the terrace and into the sea, presumably to be immediately devoured by sharks.

In Philadelphia, we had an unfortunate experience, heightened by the fact that our great friend Alexander Woollcott was in the audience that night. Alfred dutifully plunged over the terrace, and the act reached its carefully scripted climax. For some unknown reason, the curtain—having been properly lowered—was raised again a few moments later to reveal the

Point Valaine is a 1934 melodrama that Noel Coward wrote for the Lunts to perform on Broadway. For many years, Stefan (Alfred Lunt), the sensual headwaiter at the Point Valaine Hotel, has been the lover of the proprietress, Linda Valaine (Lynn Fontanne). But when Linda takes up with young English aviator Martin Welford (Louis Hayward), Stefan registers his disgust by spitting in her face, slitting his wrists so that the sharks will find him, and jumping into the sea. The cast also included Osgood Perkins, Lillian Tonge, and Fred Leslie. The press politely but firmly rejected the forced drama and even found fault with the Lunts, giving them one of their few stage disasters. Wilson produced and author Coward directed *Point Valaine*, which struggled on for seven weeks.

supposedly deceased Alfred clambering over the wall en route to his dressing room. This upset him so unbelievably that he stormed out of the theater in full makeup. Lynn, Noel, Alex, and I later went back to the Warwick Hotel, expecting to find him, but he wasn't there. We sat apprehensively waiting until finally, at four a.m., he returned, exhausted and bedraggled. He had been walking the streets of Philadelphia in an effort to efface the shame and humiliation or, as he termed it that night, "the *end* of my career."

The play was not very successful in New York. Lynn and Alfred may have wanted an antipathetic situation, but their admirers—and they had thousands of fans worldwide—did not and resented any relationship in which their favorite stars were not cozily and happily in love. The Broadway run lasted for only fifty-five performances, and we shut down.

Another idea that the Lunts had for a long time was to take on a Shakespearian repertory, which frightened me as a manager because of the enormous expense of a series of such plays, with their incumbent sets and costumes. But they were firm in their decision, and we went ahead anyway, starting out with *The Taming of the Shrew*. Based solely on my financial concerns, we agreed to coproduce with their former employers, the Theatre Guild. In fact, I made a grave mistake because in spite of the cost of the production, it turned out to be a great success. The cast was enormous, including such important actors as Richard Whorf and Sydney Greenstreet, and they all rollicked, frolicked, and camped it into an exciting production. Offbeat though it may have been in certain circumstances, it was probably the best and most intriguing rendition of *The Shrew* ever performed up to that time; however, neither the Theatre Guild nor I should claim too much credit, as Alfred and Lynn supervised the staging, costumes, scenery, everything. It was, in every sense, their personal project.

Somewhere in Texas, with their incorrigible enthusiasm, the Lunts had taken a fancy to Jean Giraudoux's play *Amphitryon 38*, so called because it was the thirty-eighth version of the Greek legend of Amphitryon. [Jupiter is so taken with the beautiful mortal Alkmena that he assumes the appearance of her husband Amphitryon so that he can bed her for one night. The offspring of their dalliance is the part-mortal Hercules.] Alfred and Lynn liked it so much, they wanted it in the repertory as soon as possible. Despite the enormous work involved in playing the *Shrew*, they rehearsed every day, and several key members of the cast—particularly Richard Whorf, who played the character Mercury—were incorporated in the new production. Alfred, being on the premises, was director, but the clothing and sets presented more of a problem, as the company was roughly 3,000 miles from New York, where they were made. I don't know how many weeks it took to rehearse it, but by the time they finished their various engagements with the *Shrew*, they were ready to open in San Francisco in the new play. Natasha and I crossed the continent for the occasion, arriving just in time to witness Dickie Whorf and Alfred shaving one another's legs in the Lunts' hotel room. In the play, they were virtually naked from the waist down and felt that the depilatory job would enhance their costumes and general appearance.

In any case, *Amphitryon 38* opened, and Alfred (shaven) and Lynn (unshaven) were both captivating. As Alkmena, Lynn was arch and flirtatious, one minute retreating from Jupiter's (Alfred's) advances, intimating that at any moment she might submit. Alfred was never anything but sure of himself, and it was perfectly obvious that his seduction would not fail. The play was a great success and went on to a season in New York. Never has a razor been put to a better purpose. [*Amphitryon 38*, adapted from the French original by S. N. Behrman, ran for 153 performances on Broadway.]

After a well-earned rest following *Amphitryon*, the Lunts elected to do *Idiot's Delight*, which was produced by the Theatre Guild, in association with me. This was one of the late Robert Sherwood's most important plays. It dealt with a strange conglomeration of international characters trapped in a Swiss hotel on the eve of World War II and provided Lynn with the opportunity to play a Russian tart in a blonde wig and a not too authentic accent, kept by a German munitions tycoon. It also allowed Alfred the pleasure of staging an impromptu musical number with six traveling chorus girls, where he sang, kicked up his heels, and did a pure Harry Richman. [Harry Richman (1895–1972) was a popular American song-and-dance performer of stage, film, and radio who was at the peak of his popularity in the 1930s.] *Idiot's Delight* ran for fifty-two weeks in New York, and in consequence we could hardly complain. [Natalie Paley, who was seeing but not yet married

Idiot's Delight is a 1936 dark comedy by Robert E. Sherwood that starred the Lunts and won the Pulitzer Prize. At a hotel in the Austrian Alps, visitors from different nations vacation as the shadow of a world war looms. American song-and-dance man Harry Van (Alfred Lunt) is touring Europe with a second-rate nightclub act and meets up with phony Russian countess Irene (Lynn Fontanne), whom Harry remembers as a Cockney chorine he had a fling with years earlier. The two fall into a careless romance and, in the last scene, are sipping champagne as bombs start to drop outside.

The large and impressive cast included Sydney Greenstreet, Francis Compton, George Meader, Bretaigne Windust, Richard Whorf, and Le Roi Operti. The dark, amusing comedy was as well received by the press as were the luminous Lunts, and the play ran for ten months, returning the next fall for another three months. Bretaigne Windust directed the Wilson–Theatre Guild production. The 1938 London production featured Raymond Massey and Tamara Geva as Harry and the countess. The 1939 Hollywood version of *Idiot's Delight* stars Clark Gable and Norma Shearer, with strong support from Charles Coburn, Edward Arnold, Laura Hope Crews, Burgess Meredith, and Joseph Schildkraut.

to Wilson in 1936, actually coached Fontanne on her Russian dialect for *Idiot's Delight.*]

However, our stars refused to play it in London, so it was leased to Raymond Massey. He engaged Tamara Geva, the Russian ballerina, for Lynn's role and naturally played Alfred's himself. There were two interesting points involved in this switch. First, the Lunts were in London at the time and refused to see a performance, with Alfred remarking, "To watch another actor play a part that I originated is like having a stranger use my toothbrush." Second, Madame Geva, on stage or off, or both, managed to disrupt Ray's marriage to Adrianne Allen.

To the credit of Robert Sherwood, his play received an equally enthusiastic critical reaction on both continents, and to this day *Idiot's Delight* remains an exciting play. Bob was probably one of the most distinguished playwrights of his day, and his work will undoubtedly be performed for a long time to come. He was thin and nearly seven feet tall, with a drawling voice and a wicked sense of humor. He was the life of every party he attended—there were only a few he didn't—and our cue to when he was around the bend was unmistakable. He would burst into a rendition of "When the Red, Red Robin Goes Bob, Bob Bobbin' Along" and resume it at intervals throughout the evening.

Robert E. Sherwood (1896–1955) was a respected American playwright known for his powerful plays with strong sociopolitical themes. He attended Harvard, where he was active with the journal *Lampoon* (which his father had cofounded), worked with the theatrical group the Hasty Pudding Club, and studied theater history under George Pierce Baker. After spending World War I with the Canadian Black Watch, Sherwood returned home disillusioned with the governments that had started the conflict. After serving in various capacities at *Vanity Fair*, *Life*, and *Scribner's Magazine*, and earning a reputation as one of the earliest serious critics of film, he found success with his first play, the antiwar comedy *The Road to Rome* (1927). His wartime romance *Waterloo Bridge* (1930) found a better reception in London than in New York. Nevertheless, the rest of the 1930s proved his heyday, with such memorable works as *Reunion in Vienna* (1931), *The Petrified Forest* (1935), *Idiot's Delight* (1936), *Abe Lincoln in Illinois* (1938), *Tovarich* (1936), and *There Shall Be No Night* (1940).

Most of Sherwood's plays were turned into films, and he contributed original screenplays for such movies as *Rasputin and the Empress* (1932), *The Scarlet Pimpernel* (1934), *The Adventures of Marco Polo* (1938), *Northwest Passage* (1940), *Rebecca* (1940), *The Best Years of Our Lives* (1946), *The Bishop's Wife* (1947), and *Man on a Tightrope* (1953). One of the founders of the Playwrights Company, he turned to politics in his later active years, serving as a speechwriter for Franklin Roosevelt and writing history articles and books. He won the Pulitzer Prize three times: for *Idiot's Delight*, *Abe Lincoln in Illinois*, and *There Shall Be No Night*.

He was first married to the smartest woman I have ever known, Mary Brandon. After their divorce, he eventually married Madeline Connelly, whose first husband had been another prominent playwright, Marc Connelly. Madeline and Bob spent many weekends with Natasha and me at our home in Connecticut. Madeline would giggle and gossip about fashions and friends, while Bob drawled on about politics and the state of the world at large. He had spent many years with Roosevelt at the White House, and it was generally acknowledged that he was responsible for most of the president's speeches. Important intellectual figure that he was, however, Bob often succumbed to the Lunts' verve during rehearsals of the many plays he wrote for them, gently accepting their suggestions or even drastic alterations.

Bob was not an easy man to know because of his shyness, but he was always unassuming and loyal to his friends. He died in New York after a short illness, and I will never forget the torrential rain on the morning of his funeral. Alfred, Howard Lindsay, Russel Crouse, and I were honorary pallbearers; and there were so many of Bob's other theater colleagues there. It was a sad morning for all of us.

Sometime in 1936, Noel had an idea for still another change of pace. This could have been an escape from boredom—as he always hated playing the same play eight times a week—and consequently evolved on a splendiferous scale. There would be ten separate one-act plays, to be performed in rotation for three nights, the playlets running the gamut of everything from musical to comedy to tragedy. It was an ambitious and, under normal circumstances, dangerous project, but since it starred Gertrude Lawrence and Noel himself, both of whom appeared in all of the plays, it was an inescapable success.

I had the honor of presenting it. In Manchester, it played under the title *Tonight at 7:30*—that being the local curtain time—and subsequently transferred to London (and later New York) as *Tonight at 8:30*. Gertie and Noel were, of course, wonderful, and the supporting cast was capable to the point of excellence. It could have run forever if the stars had not decided to shut it down after a given period.

Tonight at 8:30 was a 1936 series of short plays and musicals by Noel Coward that was first a success in London and then New York. The British version consisted of three different bills of ten short pieces that alternated during a period of four months, allowing Coward and Gertrude Lawrence to play a variety of roles in brief comedies, dramas, and musicals. Among the most memorable playlets were *Fumed Oak*, about a hen-pecked husband who finally rebels against his nagging family; the backstage comedy *Red Peppers*, about a quarreling musical hall couple; the mini-musical *We Were Dancing*, in which a couple quickly falls hopelessly in and out of love; and *Still Life*, in which two people married to others have "brief encounters" in a lunchroom where they change trains. (This last playlet was turned into the British film classic *Brief Encounter* in 1945.)

Coward's score for *Tonight at 8:30* included such favorites as "You Were There," "Has Anyone Seen Our Ship?," and "We Were Dancing." Reviewers felt the versatility of the two stars made the program special and also had compliments about some of the writing. Wilson produced the show (which was billed as *Today at 2:30* for matinees), and Coward directed. The Broadway version later in 1936 was made up of nine playlets, presented in two different bills. Coward and Lawrence reprised their performances and were roundly praised by the press and applauded by audiences for 118 performances.

Graham Payn (1918–2005) was a British actor and singer most remembered for his roles in musicals by Noel Coward, who was his longtime romantic partner. He was born in Pietermaritzburg, South Africa, but when his parents divorced, he moved to England, where he was a child actor. At the age of thirteen, Payn made his London debut as one of the lost boys in *Peter Pan* and sang on BBC radio. The next year, he auditioned for Coward's revue *Words and Music* (1932) and was featured in two numbers. The boy soprano was then hired to go on tour and sing in movie houses throughout Britain, but his voice broke. Out of work, he returned to South Africa, where he taught in various dance schools.

In 1936, Payn returned to England and performed on radio and then in stage revues and pantomimes. Reunited with Coward in the late 1930s, the two became lovers, and the playwright promoted Payn's career by casting him in *Pacific 1860* (1946), *Tonight at 8:30* (1948), *Ace of Clubs* (1949), *After the Ball* (1953), *Waiting in the Wings* (1960), and *Present Laughter* (1965). Payn also appeared in a handful of stage works by others and a few films. He remained with Coward until the playwright's death in 1973 and administered Coward's estate until his own death in 2005. Payn wrote his autobiography, *My Life with Noel Coward*, in 1994.

Many years later, at the insistence of Fanny Holtzmann, a well-known theatrical lawyer, *Tonight at 8:30* was catastrophically revived in New York—fortunately under other management—with Gertie in the original roles and Graham Payn taking over for Noel. It lasted about four weeks. [The 1948 production featured six of the original playlets, and it only ran for twenty-six performances.] Gertie Lawrence was an extravagant woman, and Fanny Holtzmann, out of kindness, plus a sizable percentage, firmly managed her affairs. In the late 1940s, Gertie found herself without a stage vehicle—a situation that was very rare—and so Fanny decided to do something about it. She hit upon the idea that Noel and her client should do a revival of *Tonight at 8:30*, but Noel indignantly refused. Fanny persisted, however, and I was selected as director as second choice to Noel.

It was at this point that Noel took matters into his own hands. He set up a meeting of himself, Fanny, Gertie, and me. Fanny and I sat there saying nothing, while Noel and Gertie discussed the inadvisability of the idea. I was against it myself but thought it better to let them thrash it out. By the end of the meeting, it was generally accepted that the project should be dropped. But Fanny hadn't finished. The next day, she called me at my office and asked, "Well, Jack, when do we start rehearsals?" Somewhat taken aback, I reminded her that just the day before we had agreed to drop the revival. But she simply replied, "Not at all," and went on to explain her plan. She had decided that Noel's pet protégé at the time, Graham Payn, should take over Noel's parts, that the production should be reduced to six plays to cut the overhead, and that, as far as Gertie was concerned, there was no problem there, since she, Fanny, could "make Miss Contrary do exactly what I want." By this she meant Noel, and in that regard she was right.

Noel was won over by the suggestion of Graham following him in his roles, and Fanny, after all her scheming machinations and hard work, successfully achieved one of New York's greatest flops. [The only reason Coward agreed to the project was probably to promote the acting career of his new lover Payn, who for years disliked the fact that Coward remained loyal to Wilson and went on working with him even though they were no longer lovers. In the end, Payn needn't have been so concerned. He outlived Wilson by more than forty years and edited both Coward's letters and diary, as well as wrote his own autobiography. It is telling that in 1979, when Payn cowrote the illustrated book *Noel Coward and His Friends*, he failed to include even one photograph of Wilson.]

Then, back again in 1936, I returned to London to do a play adapted from the French of Jacques Deval called *Mademoiselle*. It starred sterling actress Madge Titheradge and was directed by Noel. [*Mademoiselle*, about a spinster chaperone who helps her unmarried pregnant ward by adopting her baby, was a success in New York in 1932, in an adaptation by its star, Grace George. The 1936 London production ran for thirteen weeks.] A much lesser-known young lady, Greer Garson, had a small role, and it turned out fairly well for her. She was noticed and immediately picked up by Hollywood talent scouts and would go on to fame and fortune in *Mrs. Miniver* and other roles. [Greer Garson (1904–1996) was a beautiful, stately British actress who was one of Hollywood's top stars in the 1940s and 1950s. In addition to *Mrs. Miniver* (1942), her other memorable films include *Goodbye, Mr. Chips* (1939), *Pride and Prejudice* (1940), *Madame Curie* (1943), and *Sunrise at Campobello* (1960).] There had always been a mythical *queen* at MGM, and for many years—following in the footsteps of Norma Shearer, Marion Davies, and Greta Garbo—Greer Garson held the scepter with dignity, slightly tempered by obvious enthusiasm. Since our nascent experience in *Mademoiselle*, I have frequently run into Greer on the MGM lot and at elegant private parties. Given her elevated position, I never fail to do a royal bow—which she accepts and, I imagine, expects.

CHAPTER ELEVEN

~

Lillian and Bea

My first independent American production was a play called *Excursion* by Victor Wolfson. Gladys Calthrop did an extraordinary set of a ship that folded and unfolded like a pack of cards during the many scene changes. Worthington Miner directed a large cast that included some interesting people. There was young Joseph Olney, who would later become Joseph Cotten; and Whitford Kane, who remained Whitford Kane. And there were Marilyn Erskine, Anthony Ross, Frances Fuller—who was Tony Miner's wife—and particularly a budding young actress named Shirley Booth. Richard Maney was our press agent, and typical of his promotional feats, he induced the clergyman who had married the Duke and Duchess of Windsor to attend a performance. Those newsworthy nuptials had made the little minister the hottest item in town, and he entered the theater flanked by photographers whose presence had obviously been arranged in advance by Maney.

Excursion was a critical success in New York and was subsequently sold to MGM for $100,000. The script dealt with a Coney Island ferry boat captain, played by Whitford Kane. Looking over some of his bedraggled passengers, the captain decided that what they needed most was freedom from the drudgery of their daily existence. Thus, he changes the boat's course and heads out to the open sea. Some audiences may have been confused by—or indifferent to—the philosophical differences, because business at the box office began to fall off after a few months. But I kept it going—philanthropic as it may have been—until the movie-rights bonanza was finally exhausted. This added some months to its run. As far as I know,

> **Excursion** is a 1937 comedy by Victor Wolfson that was the first New
> York hit for beginning producer Wilson. On the last day that the old tub
> *S. S. Happiness* is to ferry between New Bedford and Coney Island, crusty
> old Captain Obediah Rich (Whitford Kane) and his brother Jonathan (J.
> Hammond Dailey) decide to set out to sea with the passengers aboard
> and head for an idyllic island in the West Indies. At first the passengers
> are alarmed and outraged, but the prospect soon brings them happiness
> and all are disappointed when the Coast Guard rescues them. The press
> cheered the merry, life-affirming comedy, and audiences agreed for nearly
> four months. Worthington Miner directed the complicated production,
> which called for a large cast and many sets.

the script is still reclining in MGM's files. [No movie version of Wolfson's
play has ever been made.]

I have been blessed with a remarkable staff throughout the years. There is
Ward Bishop, who has stage-managed most of my productions for some thirty
years, beginning with *Excursion*. He is a frail, gentle man, but his strength
and authority in handling a stage definitely belie his cadaverous appearance.
He has certainly been a comfort to me during these many years.

Then there is my general manager, C. Edwin "Eddie" Knill, who came to
me more than twenty-five years ago as an office boy and has since become
an important figure on the Broadway scene. He has managed dozens of my
shows and is frequently engaged by other producers eager for his services
when I am not actively involved. He has been known to manage six shows simultaneously. But with whatever management he happens to be ensconced,
we remain loyal and devoted friends.

Last but certainly not least is my wonderful Mrs. [Gertrude] Bent. She,
too, came to me more than twenty-five years ago, but with considerable
reluctance. She had been secretary to the president of a New York bank
and thus felt that the world of the theater was too far removed from her
experience. We compromised on the idea of her taking the job with me for
one month. The idea was that at the end of the month, we would mutually
decide if she should stay on. Mrs. Bent has been an essential part of my life
ever since—advisor, nanny, nurse, and practically my mother. She has been
as invaluable to my wife Natasha as to me, and I don't know how we could
live without her. She is beloved by everyone in the New York theater and,
contrary to her nascent apprehensions, knows as much about the business as
the Shuberts themselves.

Following *Excursion*, Noel and I left for Berlin for some unknown reason. We lived in elegance at the Adlon Hotel. The reigning musical star of the German theater for countless years had been Fritzi Massary, and shortly after our arrival, a party was arranged so that Noel could meet her. [Fritzi Massary (1882–1969) was a popular star of German and Austrian operettas, creating leading roles in six musicals by Oscar Straus.] She snubbed him to the point of rudeness, and the entire evening was frankly very painful. But some months later, when both of them were staying in Alice Astor's castle in Salzburg, love suddenly began to bloom. Noel played the piano, and Fritzi sang her old German numbers, and by the end of the session—helped along, perhaps, by Alice's champagne—he offered to write a show for her. And so, out of this musical affiance, *Operette* was born.

The first problem was to write it, which Noel meticulously and laboriously achieved, stubborn in his promise to Fritzi. The next was to cast it. Massary, for all her enchantment and talent, was not exactly a debutante. Hence, it was necessary to sprinkle the cast with a few younger, more romantic personalities. Thus, we engaged Richard Haydn and a handsome young actor named Griffith Jones. It was at this point that Noel recalled the brilliance of Peggy Wood's performance in *Bitter Sweet*. Cables began to flow across the Atlantic, and Peggy eventually accepted and appeared. When Noel and I met her at Southampton, he remarked, "But she's gotten so much older." And I replied, "But so have we."

In spite of Mrs. Calthrop's excellent production, some beautiful scenes by Peggy and Fritzi, and Noel's punctilious direction, it was a rather apathetic success. Without question, Madame Massary more than justified her position in the Berlin theater. But perhaps it might have been better for all of us if Noel had never gone to Salzburg. [*Operette*, an operetta about the star of an operetta, managed to run for 133 performances. The show is only remembered as the source of the Coward song standard "The Stately Homes of England."]

Another production from that time was *Dear Octopus* by Dodie Smith. I bought the play in London, where it had been a fabulous success. As it was still running there, it had to be completely recast for Broadway. I was able to get Jack Hawkins for the John Gielgud role, and the distinguished ensemble also included Lucile Watson, Lillian Gish, Rose Hobart, Phyllis Povah, and Reginald Mason. I brought over the London director, Glen Byam Shaw, and we started rehearsals. While we were still casting, I had tried to persuade Miss Gish to play the part that was eventually assigned to Rose Hobart. It was a much smaller role than the one she selected, however, I thought, infinitely more effective. We went to Boston for the tryout, where I again commuted across the street to check on Bea Lillie, who was there playing under my management in Noel's

Dear Octopus is a 1938 British comedy by Dodie Smith that found success in London but failed to please New York audiences. Charles (Leon Quartermaine) and Dora Randolph (Marie Tempest) celebrate their golden anniversary in their North Essex home and receive two pieces of information as an anniversary present: their son Nicholas (John Gielgud) has fallen in love with Dora's faithful companion Fenny (Angela Baddeley), and their daughter Cynthia (Valerie Taylor) is returning home for good after living in sin with a married man in Paris. The 1939 Broadway production, produced by Wilson, featured a top-notch cast led by Jack Hawkins, Lillian Gish, and Lucile Watson. While the players and the lavish production were praised, the play was not, and Dear Octopus had to settle for less than seven weeks on Broadway. The 1943 British film version starred Margaret Lockwood, Michael Wilding, Celia Johnson, and Roland Culver. There were also British television versions in 1960 and 1972.

revue *Set to Music*. The strain of the two productions was a bit heavy, so after a couple of weeks I decided to take a few days off and go to our country house in Connecticut, taking Natasha and Glen Byam Shaw with me.

During this time, it must have crossed Miss Gish's mind that she had—against my advice—chosen the wrong role. In our absence, she sent for Jed Harris, a not-unknown Broadway figure, to restage and relight her in her scenes. [Jed Harris (1900–1979) was a successful but ruthless Broadway producer and director from the 1920s into the 1950s.] When I found out about it, I was naturally livid; and Noel, who was across the street with his revue, was even more so. I remember a joint attack on the subject in Lillian's dressing room. No words were spared, but she remained calmer than in any of her early silent films. She maintained that there was no reason why she shouldn't "ask a friend up to help her" and blandly refused to acknowledge the fact that she had insulted us all. Of course, this behavior was unethical and outrageous, but her studied wistfulness saved her from being hauled up before Equity for what she had done.

In the end, *Dear Octopus* was one of the most magnificent productions I have ever done. There were five sets by the inevitable Gladys, including a dinner-party scene where, wisely or unwisely, I elected to use real silver and real Chippendale furniture. It was indeed a gilt-edge show, but the critical reception was mild at best. There were many people who loved it but far too many others who didn't. I was about to close when the *New York Post*, whose critical and editorial staffs had adored it, urged me to keep it running and promised its own promotion campaign that would ensure its success. Despite

Lillian Gish (1896–1993) was the first great actress of the silent screen, but she started in theater and often returned to the stage during her remarkable eight-decade career. Her oft-unemployed family struggled as they moved from place to place and job to job. Her mother started to get acting work and, in 1902, was persuaded to put Lillian and her younger sister Dorothy (1898–1968) on the stage to earn money. Lillian made her Broadway debut in 1913, but she soon began working in movies and did not return to the theater until 1930. The Gish sisters were featured in several classic films, including *Broken Blossoms* (1919), *Way Down East* (1920), and *Orphans of the Storm* (1921).

Of the two sisters, Lillian was considered the more gifted actress and featured in many movies without her sibling, for instance, *The Birth of a Nation* (1915), *Intolerance* (1916), and *The Scarlet Letter* (1926). Gish proved to be just as accomplished in talkies, but disagreements with the studio led to her abandoning films and returning to the theater in the 1930s. Among her memorable Broadway credits are *Camille* (1932), John Gielgud's *Hamlet* (1936), *Crime and Punishment* (1947), *The Trip to Bountiful* (1953), *All the Way Home* (1960), and *Uncle Vanya* (1973). She returned to Hollywood on occasion, appearing in such films as *Duel in the Sun* (1946), *The Night of the Hunter* (1955), *The Comedians* (1967), *A Wedding* (1978), and *The Whales of August* (1987). Moreover, Gish acted in several television series and dramas. Dubbed the "first lady of the American cinema," she was a small woman with petite features and expressive eyes.

the power of the *Post*, their stimulation failed to do the trick, and after a month or two, it became obvious that we really would have to close. It was tragic for me because *Dear Octopus* has always been one of my favorite plays.

At the same time, *Set to Music* had arrived in New York to relatively good notices and absolute raves for Bea Lillie. It was Noel's whimsy in this show, however, not to include any choreography on the grounds that his lyrics and music would be sufficient entertainment. A few days after it opened, he went off on yet another of his around-the-world excursions. I telegraphed him in San Francisco to ask his permission to insert some dancing, as the audiences were clamoring for it and even demanding it. His reply was quite typical: "Tell them to turn around and look at the *standees*."

Alas, by that time there weren't any "standees," and the play was, in spite of Bea, unmistakably fading. In the end, it survived four or five months. [*Set to Music* was the 1939 Broadway version of Coward's 1932 London revue *Words and Music*. The musical ran for 129 performances in New York.]

John C. Wilson, age four, strikes a confident and charming pose, the same look that would later endear him to many as an adult. This photograph was taken at Sharp's Studio in Trenton, New Jersey, in 1903.

Wilson's senior year portrait at Yale University shows a studious young man about to begin a career as a broker on Wall Street. But fate had other plans, and he didn't stay there long. The portrait was taken at the Roger Sherman Studio in New Haven, Connecticut, in 1922.

The green-eyed comic singer Genevieve Tobin was the first celebrity with whom Wilson worked. He played a small role in her California engagement of the stage comedy *Polly Preferred* in 1923, the year she inscribed this photo to him.

Wilson joined the legions of friends and admirers of British star Gertrude Lawrence when she appeared on Broadway in 1925, in the popular musical *Charlot's Revue*, from London. Years later he would direct her in summer theater in Massachusetts.

Songwriter Cole Porter was a social acquaintance of Wilson's for more than twenty years before Wilson directed Porter's greatest hit, *Kiss Me, Kate*. In 1926, Porter (far right) and his wife Linda hosted Wilson (left) and Noel Coward (center) at the Porters' palazzo in Venice, where this photo was taken on the beach of the Lido. Courtesy Photofest, Inc.

Although Wilson's Hollywood career was sporadic, he was always part of the social set when he was there. Tinseltown photographer Bert Longworth took this candid picture of Wilson (far right) in 1931, with Noel Coward (far left), Harpo Marx, and Tallulah Bankhead.

In 1932, Wilson formed Transatlantic Productions with three of the biggest stars of Broadway and the London theater: Alfred Lunt (far left in the photo within the photo), Lynn Fontanne, and Noel Coward. In his London office, Wilson gazes at a picture of his theatrical partners.

Few people who worked with British comic Beatrice Lillie failed to fall in love with her, including Wilson, who presented her on Broadway in *Set to Music* in 1939. She is pictured here aboard the SS *Europa*, sailing to New York City in 1934, to appear in the Broadway revue *At Home Abroad*.

Renowned acting couple Alfred Lunt and Lynn Fontanne were frequent visitors to Wilson's estate Pebbles in Fairfield, Connecticut, as was Noel Coward. This snapshot of them was taken at Pebbles in 1934, when the threesome was appearing on Broadway in Coward's *Design for Living*. Joining Coward (far left), Fontanne, and Lunt is veteran stage actor Osgood Perkins, father of Anthony Perkins.

Cecil Beaton, celebrated photographer and designer of clothes and scenery, was another frequent guest at Pebbles. In this somewhat unique snapshot from 1935, he is photographed taking a photograph there.

Russian princess and international socialite Natalie Paley was a top model for *Vogue* and other fashion magazines in the 1930s. This 1936 glamour portrait of her is inscribed to Wilson, who she married the next year.

Prior to their wedding in 1937, eminent photographer Horst P. Horst took this formal engagement portrait of Wilson and Natalie Paley, who was called Natasha by her friends.

Wilson and Natasha were married at Pebbles in the fall of 1937. Noel Coward (center) was the best man. Also pictured are Wilson's mother (second from the right) and an unidentified guest.

Pictured at Pebbles on a chilly spring day in 1938 are Wilson and his sister Dorothy Wilson Cart, as well as the family pet Wilton. Wilson's estate, located next door to the exclusive Fairfield Country Club, hosted the elite of Hollywood and Broadway.

The Wilsons were frequent transatlantic travelers from New York to England and France. This photo from the late 1930s shows the couple on board an ocean liner before World War II halted such transatlantic crossings.

Natasha Wilson was close friends with many of the leading designers in Europe and the United States. She is pictured here at Fairfield in 1939, with famous jewelry designer Fulco di Verdura, who would often ask her to model his newest creations.

Richard Rodgers, dean of American theater composers, relaxes at Pebbles in May 1939, with his wife Dorothy (center). On the far left is Adrianne Massey, who was in the process of getting a divorce from actor Raymond Massey. Oddly, both Masseys ended up marrying their divorce lawyers.

Months before the world knew about the passionate romance between Laurence Olivier and Vivien Leigh, the couple found a safe haven at Pebbles, away from the press. (Both were still married to others.) This photo was taken in July 1939. His Hollywood stardom had been assured three months earlier, when *Wuthering Heights* was released. Her fame would not come until that December, when *Gone with the Wind* opened.

The Wilsons (center) joined family members for Easter 1940, at Cartwheel Farm, the home of his sister, Dorothy Cart (seated far right), in Harbourton, New Jersey. Also pictured are Dorothy's husband Theodore (standing far left), their children Theodore W. and Barbara (seated), Wilson's mother (with pearls), his brother "Bus" Wilson (obscured), and Bus' wife Jane (standing far right).

Distinctive and classy comedienne Ina Claire was featured in Broadway shows from 1911 to 1954, a remarkably durable career. This snapshot of her was taken at the pool at Pebbles in the summer of 1940.

As striking off screen as on, Hollywood star Tyrone Power and his actress-wife Annabella visited Pebbles while doing summer theater in the area. They are pictured here in the summer of 1940, in a candid yet classic Hollywood pose.

Wilson takes a Coca-Cola break with Gertrude Lawrence during the summer of 1940 on Cape Cod. He was directing her in a revival of Noel Coward's *Private Lives* at a summer theater in Dennis, Massachusetts.

Wilson's long association with the Westport Country Playhouse in Connecticut began in the summer of 1941, when this picture was taken backstage. Leona Corbett (right) and Clifton Webb were rehearsing *Blithe Spirit* with Wilson in Manhattan but traveled to Westport with social maverick Elsa Maxwell for one of the summer offerings there.

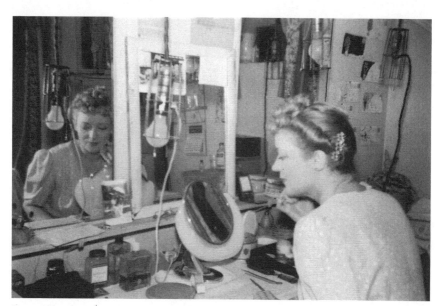

Peggy Wood, a favorite in operettas in the 1910s and 1920s, matured into an adept comedienne later in her career, as with her droll performance as Ruth in the original Broadway production of *Blithe Spirit* in 1941. Wilson, director of the show, took this snapshot of Wood in her dressing room at the Morosco Theatre.

The raucous comedy *The Pirate* (1942) allowed Alfred Lunt (leaning on piano) and Lynn Fontanne to do a bit of singing. Helping them out backstage is Herbert Fields at the piano, with producer and codirector Wilson looking on.

Brilliant lyricist Lorenz Hart (with cigar) was at the end of his career and too-short life in 1943, when his partner-composer Richard Rodgers (far left) suggested a revival of their 1927 hit *A Connecticut Yankee*. Herbert Fields (with flashy tie) revised his original book and Wilson (far right) directed, and the show was again a success. But five days after the opening night, Hart was dead of alcoholism and exposure.

Bloomer Girl (1944) is about war, slavery, and women's rights, in the form of a hit Broadway musical comedy. Wilson (center) directed, and the delectable score was by lyricist E. Y. Harburg (left) and composer Harold Arlen, seen here during a rehearsal in the Shubert Theatre.

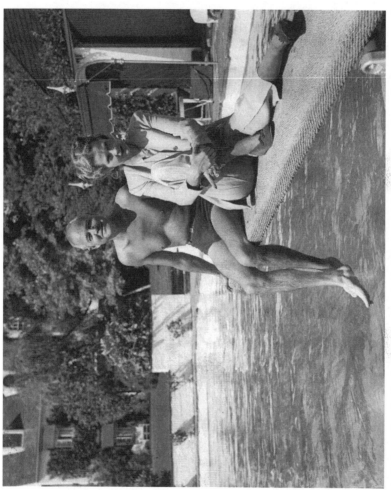

A photographer for the local newspaper took this picture of the Wilsons at home in the summer of 1946 for a feature story about them. They were not the only celebrities living in Fairfield County after the war, but Pebbles drew more famous faces than anywhere else.

Hollywood star Olivia de Havilland starred in three films released in the spring of 1946. After having undergone the premieres of *To Each His Own*, *Devotion*, and *The Well-Groomed Bride*, she escaped to Pebbles, where this snapshot was taken in August 1946.

Wilson produced and/or directed the eccentric, unpredictable Tallulah Bankhead more than any other actress, in seven Broadway, touring, and summer productions. Even more remarkable, the two remained friends. This snapshot shows her at Pebbles during the summer of 1947.

The Wilsons enjoying fall at Pebbles in 1947, lounging by the pool with former baron and fashion magazine editor Niki de Gunzburg (far right). A frequent guest at Pebbles, his name appears in the guestbook more than 100 times.

During the preparation of *Gentlemen Prefer Blondes*, director Wilson invited newcomer Carol Channing to Pebbles, where she rubbed elbows with the Lunts, Anita Loos, and Actors Studio director Robert Lewis (in white suit). This snapshot was taken in August 1949, just before rehearsals for *Gentlemen Prefer Blondes* began. Three months later, Channing was a Broadway star.

By the winter of 1950, when this picture was taken, Noel Coward (right) was a permanent resident of Jamaica to avoid exorbitant British taxes. The Wilsons were frequent visitors. In fact, Natasha Wilson continued to visit Coward there even after Wilson's death.

The Westport Country Playhouse celebrated its twentieth anniversary in 1951. For the June festivities, cofounder Lawrence Langner (center) and business manager Wilson were joined by authoress Anita Loos.

Among the many Hollywood stars that Wilson brought to the Westport Country Playhouse was the luminous Claudette Colbert. Wilson is seen with her in this publicity photo taken when Colbert appeared at the summer theater in August 1951.

Wilson's only foray into television was the NBC network variety program *The Buick Circus Hour* in 1952 and 1953. Wilson (far right) was able to line up such stars as Bert Lahr, Dolores Gray, Joe E. Brown, and John Raitt (in riding outfit), who headlined. On the left are famed circus choreographer Edith Barstow and the program's assistant director, Frank Burns.

Throughout the years, one of Wilson's closest friends was writer Anita Loos, pictured here with him in 1953. After Wilson's death, Loos was one of the handful of nonfamily members Natasha Wilson remained close to.

One might suspect that Wilson's former lover Noel Coward (right) and his wife Natasha might have been rivals of sorts. In reality, Coward and Mrs. Wilson were equally devoted to Wilson and also dear friends. They are pictured here together at the Stork Club in Manhattan in 1954.

A favorite night spot in Manhattan in the 1940s and 1950s was the Latin Quarter, in which patrons descended twenty-two steps in the heart of Times Square into the atmosphere of a speakeasy. This 1954 photograph shows a good time had by (left to right) Anita Loos, Wilson, producer-artist Gant Gaither, Cecil Beaton, and Natasha Wilson.

Pictured comfortably surf side is Noel Coward in Jamaica in 1958, the year Wilson began writing his autobiography. In dedicating the memoir to Coward, Wilson recognized their lasting friendship and the influence Coward had on his life and career.

CHAPTER TWELVE

~

Westport and the Theatre Guild

It was in 1940 that my induction as a director really evolved and under rather peculiar circumstances. Richard Aldrich called to ask if I could come to his theater at Dennis on Cape Cod to direct Gertrude Lawrence in *Private Lives*. The salary was nil, as was Gertie's, since the show was for the benefit of British War Relief, and they also asked me to settle for expenses. I refused and told Noel, who was staying with us at the house in Fairfield at the time. He made no immediate comment but some hours later lashed out—as only Noel can—accusing me of lacking ambition, being unwilling to take over new responsibilities, and being complacent and self-satisfied with being the number-one man in his personal entourage. The blast shattered me so much that I phoned Dick Aldrich at midnight and accepted his assignment. The next morning, filled with trepidation, I got into my little roadster and drove to the Cape. Rehearsals for *Private Lives* started the following day, and with butterflies in my stomach, I took charge. To my amazement—which lasts to this day—the cast not only did what I told them, but I also found that what I told them was generally right. Richard Haydn, whom we had earlier imported for *Set to Music*, played the part originally done by Noel, and Gertie reclaimed the role of Amanda.

Miss Lawrence was a remarkable person but difficult to define. She took direction like a dream and invariably gave an impeccable performance on the first night; however, in spite of her unmistakable talent, she had one fault: She would seldom stick to her original performance, but would alter it—or as she phrased it—"improve it" in subsequent renditions. There is a sequence in

Private Lives where to annoy her husband, Amanda turns on a gramophone and waltzes around the room. Two days after the opening at Dennis, I appeared at the theater to find that Gertie had supplanted the waltz with a bump-and-grind routine that would have shamed Gypsy Rose Lee. When I spoke to her about it, she said, with her ineffable sweetness, "But darling, it gets a bigger laugh that way." The only director who could ever really handle her was Noel, and then only when he was actually on stage with her himself. When she would bring in a few new "improvements," he would quietly say under his breath in the middle of a performance, "If you do that again, I'll walk off stage and have the curtain brought down." Her changed approach would invariably vanish.

But altogether it was a happy two weeks at Dennis. Gertie had a charming house and was being courted by Dick Aldrich. He subsequently wrote a successful book on his achievement—or was it Fanny Holtzmann? In any case, we spent many pleasant hours not only in the theater, but also on the beach. [Richard Aldrich (1902–1986) was a stage, television, and movie producer. He was married to Gertrude Lawrence from 1940 until her death in 1952. Fanny Holtzmann (1902–1980) was an early influential lawyer and agent in theater and film. The book authored by Aldrich, *Gertrude Lawrence as Mrs. A*, was published in 1954.]

Among her other charms, Gertie had a slight malaprop quality that was especially endearing. For instance, I was given an autograph book to sign by a half-witted housemaid, and on the preceding page was an enlightening statement signed by Miss Lawrence that read, "Be of good cheer. Great elms from little acorns grow." And on another occasion, she escorted the Gilbert Millers and myself down to the beach where her house was located, and with the water virtually lapping our toes, she sighed, "Isn't this air divine? Of course you know what it is—it's the altitude."

It was a lovely and potentially important experience: the pleasure of being with Gertie; the pleasure of working with her, plus, naturally, the excitement of becoming a director. Then—as an added plum—being invited to Dick and Gertie's famous wedding. I've already included my radio broadcast at the time of her death, but I will repeat my last line: "I'm still in love with Gertrude Lawrence."

My association with the Westport Country Playhouse began in the summer of 1941. The Connecticut theater—still going today—was owned and built by Lawrence Langner. The arrangement we agreed upon, which continued for many years, was that he would lease the theater every season to a group comprising himself, his wife Armina Marshall, and me. There was a rental charge on this, but as he bore a third of the responsibility for each season—or,

Westport Country Playhouse is one of the oldest and well-liked theaters in the United States, bringing new and old plays to the countryside since 1931. The Westport, Connecticut, theater organization was founded by Broadway producer Lawrence Langner as a summer stock theater housed in an old tannery factory. The stage was designed and built to the same specifications as the Times Square Theatre in New York, the idea being that plays could have a tryout in Connecticut and then be transferred to Broadway. The plan was successful enough that thirty-six original Westport productions went on to New York throughout the decades. During Wilson's years as manager, as he relates in this chapter, the playhouse also attracted Hollywood stars who did not have the time or courage to go to Broadway but wanted to return to the stage during a summer hiatus. Except for four years during World War II, the Westport Country Playhouse has been in continuous operation and is still a respected and favored theater venue.

I presume, maritally two-thirds—it was a fair arrangement. The theater itself, however, remained his personal possession. Contrary to general belief at the time, the third partner of the Theatre Guild, Theresa Helburn, had no active connection with his Westport enterprise. The Langners felt (and I know Terry felt) that as they spent the long winters together at the guild, the summer would be a welcome respite. Hence, the three of us ran it together.

For that first summer, I journeyed to Hollywood, where I collected Tyrone Power, Annabella, and several other stars for the Hungarian drama *Liliom*, while my partners were sedulously signing others on the East Coast. [Four years later,

Lawrence Langner (1890–1962) was a distinguished American producer-manager who ran some of the most acclaimed theater organizations of the twentieth century. He was born in Wales and drifted into theatrical work in London before immigrating to the United States. In 1914, Langner was one of the founders of the ambitious Washington Square Players. After that troupe disbanded, he was an organizer of the Theatre Guild, which he was to run with Theresa Helburn for its greatest years, supervising more than two hundred productions. Langner also built the Westport (Connecticut) Country Playhouse and was founder and president of the American Shakespeare Festival in Stratford, Connecticut. Alone or with his wife, Armina Marshall, he wrote several plays, the most notable of which was *The Pursuit of Happiness* (1933). Langner writes about these notable theater groups in his 1951 autobiography *The Magic Curtain*.

The **Theatre Guild** was the most exciting and prestigious producing organization of the American theater, presenting a wide variety of productions in New York from 1919 into the 1970s. The group began as an outgrowth of the defunct Washington Square Players. It was formally organized in 1919, with a board consisting of, among others, Lawrence Langner, Philip Moeller, Rollo Peters, Lee Simonson, and Helen Westley. Later important additions to the board were Dudley Digges and Theresa Helburn. The first production was *Bonds of Interest* (1919), but the group's success was signaled by its second mounting, *John Ferguson* (1919). Other notable early productions included *Jane Clegg* (1920), *Heartbreak House* (1920), *Mr. Pim Passes By* (1921), *Liliom* (1921), *He Who Gets Slapped* (1922), *Back to Methuselah* (1922), and *R. U. R.* (1922), all of which were foreign works. It wasn't until its production of Elmer Rice's *The Adding Machine* (1923) that the group began to mount American works as aggressively as imported ones.

Among its subsequent productions of note, both American and European, were *Saint Joan* (1923), *The Guardsman* (1924), *They Knew What They Wanted* (1924), *The Garrick Gaieties* (1925), *Ned McCobb's Daughter* (1926), *The Silver Cord* (1926), *The Second Man* (1927), *Porgy* (1927), *Marco Millions* (1928), *Strange Interlude* (1928), *Hotel Universe* (1930), *Elizabeth the Queen* (1930), *Mourning Becomes Electra* (1931), *Reunion in Vienna* (1931), *Biography* (1932), *Both Your Houses* (1933), *Ah, Wilderness!* (1933), *Mary of Scotland* (1933), *Valley Forge* (1934), *Porgy and Bess* (1935), *End of Summer* (1936), and *Idiot's Delight* (1936).

By the mid-1930s political, artistic, and financial disagreements had resulted in the formation of two major breakaway organizations, the Group Theatre and the Playwrights' Company. Thereafter, both the guild's daring and success waned, although during the next few years it produced such memorable hits as *The Philadelphia Story* (1939), *The Time of Your Life* (1939), *There Shall Be No Night* (1940), and *The Pirate* (1942). It was on the verge of financial collapse when the success of *Oklahoma!* (1943) saved it, but it was never again so important a producer. Its later offerings included the Paul Robeson-José-Ferrer *Othello* (1943), *Carousel* (1945), *The Iceman Cometh* (1946), *Allegro* (1947), *Come Back, Little Sheba* (1950), *Bells Are Ringing* (1956), *Sunrise at Campobello* (1958), and *The Unsinkable Molly Brown* (1960).

By the 1970s, the guild only existed on paper, its productions so infrequent that most thought the group was gone. Its last official offering was as coproducer of the Broadway musical version of *State Fair* (1996). In its heyday, the guild was the principal producer of such playwrights as George Bernard Shaw, Eugene O'Neill, Maxwell Anderson, S. N. Behrman, and Robert Sherwood, and it greatly advanced the careers of such players as Alfred Lunt and Lynn Fontanne. Its pioneering subscription plan guaranteed audiences in New York and elsewhere the best in modern theater and, in turn, assured the guild a loyal, knowledgeable group of playgoers.

Rodgers and Hammerstein turned *Liliom* into the musical *Carousel*.] We had a banner season and made, at least for a "Straw Hat" theater, a considerable profit. [Other stars booked for that 1941 summer season included Dennis King, Ilka Chase, Walter Slezak, Constance Collier, Grace George, Mary Boland, and Tallulah Bankhead. As Langner points out in his autobiography, "Jack Wilson not only brought an air of distinction to our theater, but his friends also gave our playhouse a cachet enjoyed by no other summer theater of its kind."]

It seems odd that I have never had the opportunity of working with Gilbert Miller, as he is one of the most outstanding producers in New York and London, owns theaters in both cities, and has been actively engaged in our trade for close to fifty years. I recall many of Noel's stories when he, appearing in Manchester or Birmingham as a child actor, would be button-holed by Gilbert—who happened to be there on some project of his own—and instructed at great length on the nuances of the theater. It is a practice that Gilbert continues to this day to anyone within hearing distance, and I must say that his advice is usually sound.

By his own admission, but for reasons he prefers not to discuss, Gilbert was disliked by his father Henry Miller, a matinee idol of the turn of the century. His father built the Henry Miller Theatre, but Gilbert did not manage to acquire it until he bought it himself a few years later. Thus, with the St. James

Theresa Helburn (1887–1959) was a distinguished producer who helped further the scope of the American theater. Born in New York City, she became interested in professional theater while studying at Bryn Mawr. After continuing her studies at Radcliffe, the Sorbonne, and with Professor George Pierce Baker at Harvard, she briefly tried her hand at acting and also served as drama critic for the *Nation*. Helburn then joined the acclaimed Theatre Guild and soon became its executive director, a post she held for the rest of her career. Helburn wrote about her fascinating career in her autobiography *A Wayward Quest* (1960).

Gilbert Miller (1884–1969) was an important producer on the New York and London stages from the 1920s into the 1950s. The son of actor-manager Henry Miller, he worked for some years as an actor before presenting his first productions in London. Miller soon became equally active in Britain and eventually made his way to New York. Curiously, with a few exceptions, he rarely produced the same plays in both theater centers. His New York offerings included *The Constant Wife* (1926), *Journey's End* (1929), *Berkeley Square* (1929), *The Animal Kingdom* (1932), *The Petrified Forest* (1935), *Victoria Regina* (1935), *Tovarich* (1936), *The Cocktail Party* (1950), the 1951 Laurence Olivier–Vivien Leigh double bill of *Antony and Cleopatra* and *Caesar and Cleopatra*, and *Witness for the Prosecution* (1954).

in London also in his possession, Gilbert's productions are assured a haven in either country at all times. He has collectively produced approximately seventy or eighty shows, including such diverse offerings as *Victoria Regina*, *The Cocktail Party*, and *Witness for the Prosecution*.

Gilbert is married to Kathryn Bache, the daughter of Jules Bache, late head of one of the most important banking and brokerage firms on Wall Street. It was in the Bache house on Fifth Avenue that the Millers lived for many years when they were in New York, elegantly surrounded by gold bathroom fixtures and a famous picture collection. Since Mr. Bache's death, the latter adorns the walls of the Metropolitan Museum. Now the Millers "somehow manage"—since the Bache house was eventually sold—to live in twenty-odd rooms on Park Avenue during the five or six months spent each year in New York. They openly prefer living in England, where they maintain two residences and constantly surround themselves with the peerage. It's amazing how Gilbert can pursue his theatrical activities through this miasma of dukes and earls, but by taking a group of them to rehearsals, he's able to kill two birds with one stone. In New York, the Millers are always giving large dinner parties, meticulously arranged, and there are invariably enough visiting Englishmen in town to create the preferred atmosphere. These parties are further populated by local social figures, plus a handpicked crop of the crème de la crème of the theater, which injects a certain carefully controlled note of Bohemianism into the gathering.

Gilbert, despite his age and engagement book, also manages to serve on innumerable theatrical committees and, whenever the enthusiasm arises, still produces plays to add to his already astounding list. Like all of us who toil in this vineyard, he has had his flops, but his overall batting average would be the envy of any big-league baseball player.

Back at Westport, intoxicated by my recent initiation, I resumed the routine normalcy of sharing chores with Armina and Lawrence. We came to the conclusion that perhaps it would be wiser for them to run the business end of the theater and leave to me, as my contribution to the triumvirate, the direction of two or three plays each summer.

A change had come to the format of the "Straw Hat" circuit. It was no longer dominated by stock companies playing on a week-to-week basis. It became a question of important plays—sometimes revivals, but frequently new ones intended to have a tryout for Broadway—peopled with important stars who refused to rehearse in Westport. This necessitated my spending most summers in New York, where the stars preferred to rehearse. It was hardly wasted time, to say the least, as during the seasons that followed I had the opportunity of working on the plays of such authors as William Inge, Thornton Wilder, Tennessee Williams, and two other fairly well-known playwrights, George Bernard Shaw and Noel Coward. In addition, there was the privilege of directing important personalities like Josephine Hull, Tom Ewell, Roddy McDowell, Mildred Dunnock, Christopher Plummer, David Wayne, Shirley Booth, and many others.

[In his autobiography, Langner tells a story that reveals Wilson's savvy way of handling production problems. Soon after Tyrone Power began rehearsals for *Liliom*, Hollywood called and ordered him to return to the West Coast for some retakes. It would have meant canceling the Westport production. But Wilson found an old law on the books that stated a person could not leave the state of Connecticut if it meant breaking a contract of any kind. Since Power had an Equity contract with Wilson, the star happily informed Hollywood that he was forced by law to remain in Westport and fulfill the contract.]

One particular incident that has always amused me occurred when I directed Grace George in *Mis' Nelly o' N'Orleans*. She swept onto the stage for the first rehearsal as the great lady she was and proceeded to introduce *me* to the rest of the company—which was unnecessary, as I had known them for years—and then said, "I'll stand here and Mr. Wilson will tell the rest of you what to do." I immediately got the point and never interfered with her personally again. She was charming and gracious but knew what she wanted and got it. [Grace George (1879–1961) was a versatile American actress who was active on the Broadway stage from 1894 to 1951, playing in comedies, melodramas, and classics. She was also a producer and wrote several adaptations of foreign plays, in which she performed.]

Gypsy Rose Lee was one of the more interesting stars who I directed for Westport. She did a play adapted by Anita Loos from the French hit *Ami*,

> **Gypsy Rose Lee** (1913–1970) was probably the most famous of all American "stripteasers," but she was also successful in the legitimate theater and films. She was born Rose Louise Hovick and, under the guidance of her pushy stage mother, began her career in a children's act in vaudeville. When variety circuits began to fade, she moved into burlesque, quickly becoming one of its greatest stars, her restraint and elegance separating her from the vulgar run-of-the-mill strippers. Lee played small roles in such Broadway musicals as *Hot-Cha!* (1932), *Strike Me Pink* (1933), *Ziegfeld Follies of 1936*, and *Star and Garter* (1942). She acted in eleven movies, usually in supporting roles, and appeared in many television programs in the 1950s and 1960s. She wrote the semiautobiographical comedy *The Naked Genius* (1943), as well as several novels, some of which were filmed. Her 1957 autobiography *Gypsy* provided the basis for the 1959 Broadway musical and 1962 movie of the same name.

Ami, which we called *Darling, Darling*. Gypsy played a fashionable magazine writer who adored her husband and tried to keep both careers going at the same time through a series of light comedic ups and downs.

In New York, Gypsy had a large house on 63rd Street, which she had bought from the Vanderbilts. It contained her famous art collection and—among other innumerable salons—a drawing room as large as any New York stage. It was at her suggestion that the company began to hold rehearsals there. It was not until many days later that I realized that her *gesture* was prompted by the fact that she would rather have the company come to her than journey to some Broadway theater for the same purpose. Gypsy, for all her stripteasing, was essentially a *housefrau*—a quality that I assume she inherited from her mother, about whom she writes so brilliantly in her autobiography. Only too frequently, we would arrive at Gypsy's to find her pushing a vacuum cleaner around those vast rooms. She would shut it off, stand it in a corner, and get to work—and good work she did.

It was always made clear, although nothing was ever said, that lunch was not to be served to the company. When I called for lunch break, she would climb into her private elevator, en route to her rooms upstairs, which I never saw. The rest of us—Anita Loos, Richard Derr, Florence Sundstrom, and Tom Tryon—would amble down the street to the nearest bistro, only to return an hour later to find Gypsy back at her vacuum cleaner.

Lawrence Langner was reluctant to allow Gypsy to play in our theater on account, of course, of her striptease background. But as there was no shadow of stripping in this production—which she played absolutely straight and extremely well—I stuck to my point and she was booked. I also reminded Lawrence that only a month before, he had starred one of *his* favorite actresses and special pets, June Havoc—known to the world as "Baby June" and, after all, Gypsy's sister.

So we opened at Westport to moderate success and went on to Mountainside, Pennsylvania, to even less moderate success, and finally decided to call the whole thing off and not go to Broadway. In any case, the weeks of rehearsals and playing gave me an opportunity to get to know an interesting, multifaceted woman and a hell of a girl.

During the summer of 1951, I convinced Noel to allow me to stage his comedy *Island Fling*, which had never been produced. I also managed to induce Miss Claudette Colbert to come from Hollywood to play it at Westport. Although her performance certainly made the trip worthwhile, she presented a few rather distressing domestic difficulties.

Since there were no hotels in Westport proper in those days, Natasha and I invited her to stay with us in nearby Fairfield, while Claudette and I

Claudette Colbert (1903–1996) was a petite, dark-haired pixie who starred in film comedies in the 1930s and 1940s. She also had a successful stage career as an ingenue and returned to Broadway years later as a classy matron. Born in Paris, she came to New York City when she was six years old and later studied at the Art Students League to become a fashion designer. But a chance encounter with a theatrical producer at a party started Colbert's acting career, and she made her Broadway debut at the age of twenty in the short-lived comedy *The Wild Westcotts* (1923). A series of ingenue roles followed, both in New York and London, but Colbert never attained star status on stage.

Although she had made a silent film in 1927, it wasn't until the talkies were firmly established that Colbert left the stage for Hollywood and a celebrated career on screen. Her many memorable films include *It Happened One Night* (1934), *Imitation of Life* (1934), *Cleopatra* (1934), *Bluebeard's Eighth Wife* (1938), *Midnight* (1939), *Drums Along the Mohawk* (1939), *Skylark* (1941), *The Palm Beach Story* (1942), *Since You Went Away* (1944), *The Egg and I* (1947), and *The Secret Fury* (1950). She returned to Broadway on a few occasions in the 1970s and 1980s, most memorably in *The Kingfisher* (1978) and *Aren't We All?* (1985). Colbert continued to act into her eighties, appearing in television movies and series until 1987. Throughout her screen and stage career, Colbert was expert at roles that called for sophisticated comedy and characters who were wealthy, intelligent, and possessed a certain foreign mystique.

scoured the surrounding vicinity for a satisfactory place for her to live. I first took her to the Longshore Country Club, an elaborate establishment with an eighteen-hole golf course and cottages facing Long Island Sound. Constance Collier had happily stayed there in the past, but Claudette had certain objections and decided against it. We then drove a considerable distance to the Cobbs Mill Inn near Weston, where Tyrone Power and Annabella—during their then-sentimental union—had been cozily ensconced during the run of *Liliom*. I forget her reason, but Claudette was again dissatisfied, and so we pushed on another twenty miles to Stonehenge, a luxurious hotel in Ridgefield, again with private cottages. To my delight and relief, she at last seemed to be content. Unfortunately, a lady sunning herself on the lawn asked her for her autograph. That did it, and off we went again. [The three inns Wilson and Colbert considered are still in operation as of 2015: the renamed Inn at Longshore, the Cobbs Mill Inn, and Stonehenge.]

In desperation, I remembered that a friend of ours, a well-known radio and television writer named Robert Shaw, had phoned a few days earlier about the guest wing of his house. It was fully equipped and unoccupied, and if Claudette cared to, he would be happy to rent it to her. I had politely refused on the phone, thinking that a private house with strangers would be the last place I would expect her to want to stay, but after her disappointment with the local hotels, and in consequent despair, I decided to take a chance on Bob's offer and drove her right up to his door. My earlier misgivings were unfounded. She loved the house on sight and even went so far as to say, "Jack, you should have brought me up here in the first place!" After completing rehearsals in New York, she moved in and took over.

[It is surprising that Wilson does not go into any detail about his own palatial country home in Fairfield, Connecticut, as it was Natasha and his pride and joy, and the setting for many memorable gatherings, including their wedding in 1937. The estate was called Pebbles, and it was built in 1927, as a Georgian Revival–style mansion overlooking Long Island Sound. Wilson bought it in 1933 by himself, not with Noel Coward, as stated in different Coward biographies. Wilson turned Pebbles into a showplace for entertaining. With its seven bedrooms and seven baths, it was also ideal for overnight guests, some of whom would stay for two to three weeks at a time. Many of the stars performing at Westport stayed there (the house is about a fifteen-minute drive from the theater), while others were frequent house guests, none more so than Coward. The guest book for Pebbles survives and reads like a who's who in the performing arts for the 1930s, 1940s, and 1950s (see appendix C). After a series of unsuccessful Broadway ventures and financial setbacks in the 1950s, the Wilsons sold Pebbles in 1957 and lived in a well-appointed apartment on Park Avenue. The pool at Pebbles was later featured in the 1968 movie *The Swimmer*, and the estate remains under private ownership, looking much like it did during Wilson's tenure.]

Claudette is a managerial girl, and during the two weeks of her stay she managed the entire Shaw household with terrifying efficiency. She promptly got rid of the servant that Bob had employed for years and engaged another from a local agency whose qualifications were more to her liking. She also organized the menus and gave definite instructions that butter and cheese were never to be kept in the same refrigerator. But Bob Shaw adored her. When Claudette's husband, Dr. Joel Pressman, Hollywood's leading sinus specialist, arrived in his private plane to join her, Bob refused to accept any rent for their visit.

She sold out in *Island Fling* for the entire engagement and then, by previous arrangement, flew to the Dennis Playhouse on Cape Cod with her husband—arriving twenty hours late because of bad weather—to repeat it there for a week. Her success at Westport had been so fabulous that after Dennis, we persuaded her to return for another week. [It is curious that *Island Fling* did not make it to Broadway. When Colbert refused to appear in the play in New York, efforts were made to bring it to Broadway anyway, but they never materialized. In 1956, under the title *South Sea Bubble*, the Coward comedy opened in London with Vivien Leigh in Colbert's role and ran for a profitable 276 performances.]

By this time, it was necessary for Dr. Pressman to return to California for his nasal practices, and he chose to take his recent host and Bob Shaw's best friend, Tom Rose, with him to be his guests in Hollywood. Claudette stayed with us this time. She was as bossy as ever and antagonized our servants to no uncertain point, but when she finally left, they felt nothing but amiability and stood mumbling fond farewells. I could only assume that she overtipped them like mad.

A year later, in 1952, we were to run into Claudette a great deal in Europe. Like so many others, she had gone there to take advantage of a U.S. government ruling that money earned during eighteen months outside the country was nontaxable; however, her scheme fell through. In her seventeenth month, just as she was approaching the finish line, the government rescinded the law. Although she was actually a resident of Paris during her stay abroad, she made frequent trips to London to see Noel, to whom she had taken a firm fancy. She even made the trek to Manchester for the opening of *Quadrille*, starring the Lunts. Being a visiting Hollywood star, she was a sensational success with the local press and the public. There were photographs, interviews, and requests for autographs on the street, and she was constantly besieged by patrons in the lobby of the Midland Hotel. She eclipsed even the Lunts in popularity, although they were far too busy with Noel's new play to care.

Natasha was with me, and naturally we all went to the first night of *Quadrille* together. It was always Noel's custom to appear in the royal box just before the rise of the curtain to accept the accolades of the audience. He was particularly shrewd on this occasion, as the celebrated Miss Colbert was in the box ahead of him and represented clear competition. Somehow he forced her into the ante-room behind the box and strode out for his personal ovation. Then, with a gracious bow in her direction, he motioned Claudette on for *her* reception, which, I'm afraid, was equally enthusiastic. All having received their wont, we settled in to watch the play, which, after all, merely starred the Lunts.

Noel and Claudette's association resumed and subsequently dissolved some years later, when he engaged her for the television production of *Blithe Spirit* in Hollywood. During rehearsals, their natural coziness definitely cooled. I don't know her side of the story, except that she was quoted as claiming that she had to buy her own wardrobe to sustain Noel's stupendous salary. According to Noel, she wasn't very cooperative and also had a fixation about which side of her face ought to be photographed. I'm inclined to believe the latter because when I directed her at Westport, she was constantly reiterating which profile she should expose to the audience—and, in that instance, there wasn't a camera within miles. Since then—as can only happen among actors—they have been rapturously reconciled. [The 1956 CBS-TV version of *Blithe Spirit* was codirected by Coward, who also played the male lead. In addition to Colbert, the dazzling cast included Lauren Bacall, Marion Ross, Philip Tonge, and Mildred Natwick reprising her wacky Madame Arcati.]

Also at Westport, I had the pleasure of directing Maureen Stapleton, certainly one of the theater's finest actresses, when she costarred with Macdonald Carey in a play called *Tin Wedding*, which, alas, never reached its predestined haven on Broadway. One of my most exciting Westport Playhouse experiences was our revival of *The Skin of Our Teeth*, which starred Betty Field in the part originally done in New York by Miss Bankhead, and also Armina Marshall, who rather reluctantly agreed to play the mother, which she did with warmth and compassion. The most notable feature of that production, however, was the appearance of its author, Thornton Wilder, who played the narrator with skill and charm.

Thornton presents an extraordinary contradiction in terms. He was essentially a scholar and a brilliant one indeed. He speaks practically every language and has a solid knowledge of world literature, which he often reads in the original. I initially knew Thornton as a young man at Yale when we were fellow members of the Elizabethan Club. He would go on to become professor emeritus at the same university. When he's there to teach, he lives with his sister in sedulous quietude in the suburbs of New Haven, but once in the theater, he is an absolute ham. At the drop of a makeup kit, he'll rush onto a stage with vim and enthusiasm, burning to perform. Nonetheless, Thornton is primarily a writer, and his rare excursions into acting are whimsically sporadic. In *The Skin of Our Teeth*, he was a delight to the Westport audiences, and to my wife as well. Natasha considered him one of the most intellectually exciting men she ever met, and I thoroughly agree.

Taken all in all, my twelve summers spent at Westport have proved a valuable and rewarding experience, as has my subsequent association with the Langners—who are, of course, the Theatre Guild—in many productions in New York. [See appendix A for a detailed listing of the Westport productions during Wilson's tenure there.]

It is hardly necessary to say that the guild is one of the most important producing firms on Broadway. For forty years, they batted it out, starting as the Washington Square Players at the Band Box Theatre on 75th Street and moving downtown to the Garrick Theatre, where they did many important experimental plays. These included several by St. John Ervine; *The Guardsman*, featuring the Lunts; and the famous *Garrick Gaieties*, the breakout show for Rodgers and Hart.

It was during this period, through their indomitable determination, that audiences were solicited to buy bonds so that the Langners could finance a theater building of their own. The frightened young ladies who volunteered to circulate with baskets during the entr'actes must have succeeded, because the Guild Theatre eventually materialized and became reality. I clearly remember its opening night and a remark by Alexander Woollcott. Recalling their modest beginnings and observing their present, tapestry-hung elegance, Woollcott famously wrote, "The Goblins will get them if they don't watch out." He wasn't far from wrong, as many years later they were forced to sell it, and it became known as the ANTA Theatre. [The American National Theatre and Academy (ANTA) ran the playhouse from 1950 to 1981, when it was bought by the Jujamcyn corporation. Today it is called the August Wilson Theatre.]

At the time, the guild was run by a board of six to eight people, and I gather that a reasonable amount of chaos resulted in an effort to arrive at a decision about any given script or cast. Lawrence and Terry Helburn eventually bought out the other board members and took over the running of the theater. Lawrence and Terry are a formidable team, famous for their hard work and love for the theater, and also for their sometimes difficult personalities. Noel Coward, for example, will not give them a play to this day. In the early 1920s, Noel had forwarded them a script, which they neither refused nor returned, but rather simply ignored. Noel has never forgotten this. I do know that in my own early relations with them—and this was very much "pre-Westport"—I was invariably treated like a part-time office boy, and there are many people in the New York theatrical profession who will only too enthusiastically agree with me. Now that I have gotten to know them so well and gotten beneath the shell, I find them friendly, kind, and courteous. They do not, however, give that impression to newcomers.

Lawrence, who is the titular head of the organization, is fanatically stage-struck. He is fortunately the senior partner of one of the most successful patent law firms in New York, but every penny he receives from that source is poured into the theater with frenetic abandon. Lawrence's methods may sometimes be a little heavy-handed, but his incredible drive and determination can never be questioned. His creation of the American Shakespeare Theatre in Stratford, Connecticut, represented two years of dedicated, hard work. He had visited Stratford-on-Avon in England and then and there decided that we should have a similar institution in the United States. He hustled around looking for sites and money—and a great deal was needed—and finally managed to achieve that very handsome theater, which is still successfully functioning today. He also put in a school at Stratford for young Shakespearean actors. [The American Shakespeare Theatre was founded in 1955, and for two decades offered outstanding classical productions, with top performers and directors. The organization struggled in the late 1970s and ceased operation in the 1980s. The school reopened as the Shakespeare Academy at Stratford in 2014, conducting a summer study program in buildings adjacent to the theater, which still stands.]

Lawrence's wife, Armina Marshall, has grown into an important position at the guild, and there is no question that she is their official troubleshooter. When Lawrence or Terry have been rude—and I don't think it is necessarily rudeness as much as exasperation caused by overwork—Armina is sent out to track down the indignant victims and cajole them back into the fold. She has such innate sweetness and niceness that seldom, if ever, has she been known to fail. Together, the Langners and Terry comprise an extraordinary trio. They may be fiends to outsiders, but to me—although it took some years—they are cozy, amiable, and loyal friends.

Cheryl Crawford, another of New York's leading-lady producers, came upon the plan that a periodic group meeting of summer-theater managers might be a good idea to promote our mutual interests and diminish any difficulties that had arisen among us. These meetings took place in the office of her lawyer, a Mr. Wildberg, and as there were a great many of us, seats were at a premium and a lot of us sat on the floor. At most of these meetings, I found myself seated next to an amiable, blond young man who proffered me cigarettes, giggled appropriately at some of the more ridiculous discussions, and generally made himself most agreeable. I was, of course, representing Westport, and he the Bass Rocks Theatre near Gloucester, Massachusetts. But the meetings would end as most meetings do—having accomplished absolutely nothing—and we would all return to our respective theaters and get back to work.

Some weeks after our first session, I received a letter asking me to come up to Bass Rocks to direct Elsa Maxwell in Somerset Maugham's *Our Betters*. It was meticulously explained to me that this was at the special request of Elsa herself, as we were old friends, and that she had "enormous respect" for me as a director. So for the second time, I journeyed north and eventually drew up in front of an old-fashioned, wooden hotel to find Elsa relaxing on the porch in a rocking chair, surveying the view. She greeted me enthusiastically, but her actual words were surprising: "Darling, how wonderful to see you. I couldn't be more pleased, but what on earth are you doing here?"

I had been trapped, of course, but as the blond young man's name was Martin Manulis, I shouldn't have been entirely surprised. The Bass Rocks Theatre, compared to Westport's semi-Broadway atmosphere, was a shambles. An indoor tennis court with folding chairs could scarcely be called impressive. It was managed by Henry Levin—who has since become an important Hollywood director—and Martin himself, whose duties seemed unending. He would sell tickets at the box office during the day, retrieve them at the door before each performance, usher people to their seats, and then miraculously whip backstage to give an excellent performance in the play.

Elsa Maxwell (1883–1963) was an internationally known gossip columnist, professional hostess, author, and sometimes actress. She was born in Keokuk, Iowa, and raised in San Francisco, where she got involved in arranging parties for the rich. Maxwell's fame grew when she came up with clever themes for her gatherings, including the idea of a scavenger hunt and a "come-as-your-opposite" costume ball. By the 1920s, she was world famous for her sensational parties in Paris, Venice, and other gathering places of the wealthy. When such activities dried up during the Depression, Maxwell worked in movies, writing scripts and making screen appearances, usually as herself. She also wrote songs, a popular gossip column, and four autobiographical books.

His wife, Katherine Bard, was also in the cast, and the production had an exceptionally successful week considering the venue. Elsa played Elsa to the general satisfaction of the local gentry, and it was not until the end of the engagement that I found out why the trap had been laid: Martin wanted to work for me in New York as my assistant. After several subtle overtures, followed by open requests, he got the job. His determination proved to be my good fortune, as he was invaluable in the office and even more so as my assistant director—particularly with *Blithe Spirit*. I later assigned him full director for Tallulah in *Private Lives*.

I don't know how many years have passed, but people in the business no longer need to be told about the reputation of Martin Manulis. He went on to become producer of television's *Playhouse 90* and an important executive at CBS, has a house in Bel Air, has begot three offspring (most of whom are my godchildren), and is well set for a future that he has earned and deserves. Nevertheless. I still remember that tentative first week at Bass Rocks and his brash method of luring me there, and I recall with pride our subsequent association. It turned out to be a good idea for both of us. [After serving as an employee and close associate of Wilson's, Martin Manulis (1915–2007) was a successful theater, television, and film producer who, in addition to *Playhouse 90*, presented such notable 1950s television programs as *Studio One* and *Suspense*.]

Elsa Maxwell is probably one of the most publicized figures of our time. She has many of the qualities of a female Robin Hood, having removed endless amounts of money from the rich and redistributed it for their own enjoyment during her career. Elsa was raised just outside San Francisco and is, by her own declaration, some seventy-odd years old. Much of her early life is still shrouded in mystery, but there is a rumor that, as a young woman, she toured a vaudeville circuit in South Africa as the piano accompanist to a lady bass. She entered the limelight in New York during World War I, when she organized nearly every charity ball in the city. This, of course, led to many important social contacts with New York's most prominent families. She remained in the United States until the Armistice and then took off for Paris, which was her home for years.

It was there—in Paris—that I first met Elsa. Almost immediately, an incident occurred that was typical of her sense of humor and bravado. She and her close girlfriend, Dickie Fellowes-Gordon, shared a small and rather rickety apartment on the Left Bank and had gone off for an extended visit with rich friends in Biarritz and Venice, but the girls neglected to pay their Paris rent while they were away and, upon their return, found themselves literally dispossessed, with their furniture scattered on the sidewalk in front of the house. Undismayed, Elsa pulled a chair up to the grand piano, which was occupying most of the street, and came forth with a rendition of *Aida* that shook the entire neighborhood.

Lacking in personal funds though she may have been, Elsa soon began giving parties of her own, sponsored by wealthy Paris friends who were only too willing to see their money used for pleasurable purposes under expert guidance. I shall always remember Elsa's kindness to me at that time. It was during my unsuccessful writing period, and I was scarcely a social asset to any of her gatherings. But she seldom failed to invite me, and I'll long be grateful for what it did for my budget and my morale. Plus, the food was delicious. Not one week went by without at least one of these parties, always with themes like "Come as Someone You Like," "Come as Someone You Hate," "Come As You Are," and other variations on just about any theme. The most elaborate gathering was held each year in honor of Elsa's birthday, for which she always took over the entire ground floor and adjoining gardens of the Ritz Hotel in Paris. In addition to a magnificent dinner, there was invariably spectacular entertainment.

I remember one particular party with the Ballets Russes performing in a garden with fountains and colored lights, while inside, name bands imported from the United States played for dancing in various rooms. As if this weren't enough, Fred and Adele Astaire were performing their famous routines in another room on a specially constructed stage. It was like wandering through the sideshows of a gala circus that one could not possibly afford. It was at this party that there was considerable buzzing as to the identity of a handsome, middle-aged couple who were apparently not regulars of the Elsa set. A friend of theirs later satisfied everyone's curiosity by explaining that the couple was, in fact, Mr. and Mrs. Jay O'Brian, who had a house in Biarritz, and that they certainly had every reason to be there—not only because of their decorative value—but also because they had paid for the entire party.

There was another incident concerning a subsequent birthday party that is worth repeating. A wealthy Philadelphian had given Elsa a $5,000 Cartier brooch as a present, and she promptly asked him if she could return it and have the money instead. He was delighted, as it was a constant source of concern for Elsa's friends that she was not paying proper attention to her personal finances. She didn't this time either, because the money was used to import renowned violinist Fritz Kreisler from Berlin to make one of his infrequent appearances at a private party. And so the brooch was transmuted into music, and the evening became the talk of Paris.

Elsa did have her moments, however brief, of financial introspection, and these could lead to some frenetic promotional activity. For example, one of her ventures involved constructing a rubber beach at Monte Carlo. I should probably explain this further.

The south of France was undergoing a violent seasonal change. Whereas it had once been most fashionable in the winter—and, believe it or not, deserted during the summer—those positions were now in a state of reversal. In fact, Monte Carlo had been designed as a winter resort, built around a compact, tiny, exquisitely laid out square. The casino was on one side, the Hotel de Paris on another, and the Café de Paris on a third. But alas, for summer there was no beach; and the new summer customers were flocking to Eden Roc and Cannes, where they could splash and sunbathe to their hearts' content. Elsa took this all in and marched into the office of the comptroller of Monte Carlo with a definite plan. If they would give her an important executive position in the management—at, I suspect, a considerable salary— she would create a new development that would include the attractions they were lacking for summer visitors. The management accepted her deal, and work on the project began.

There was a long and narrow shorefront property belonging to Monte Carlo, but it was considered useless as a beach because of its rocky terrain. But Elsa convinced them that no, on the contrary, the area was absolutely ideal. Four new deluxe hotels soon sprang into being, as well as a beautiful casino with a nightclub, dining terrace, and large and attractive private gambling room. An enormous swimming pool followed, along with two small restaurants. But after everything was completed, there was still no beach. Elsa assured the powers that be that this would soon be remedied. The next day, a battalion of engineers arrived bearing a colossal sheet of rubber, which they proceeded to install. One end was anchored about fifty yards offshore. It was then stretched inland over the rocks and fastened to the edge of the colony's swimming pool, which overlooked the sea.

It was a great success. Guests flocked to Elsa's "rubber beach," and everything was fine until one night, when an above-average wind blew up. In the early hours of the morning, the most terrific snap I have ever heard brought all heads to all windows. The "beach" shot toward the shore like a gigantic rubber band and was subsequently torn to shreds by the wind and waves. The clientele was not discouraged, however. The hotels remained full, and the galas at the casino became all the more elegant. They still had the pool, and they still had Elsa.

We met again a few years later at a dinner party at Anita Loos's in New York. Even with competition from Aldous Huxley and Ina Claire, Elsa managed to monopolize all discussion before, during, and after dinner. None of us got a word in edgewise. As she was leaving, Elsa flashed a sweet smile around the room and gaily observed, "Thank heaven the art of conversation is not dead!"

In spite of her current success on network television, I doubt that she is any better off financially than when she played *Aida* on the sidewalk in Paris, but it would be interesting to know how many millions have passed through her hands in support of her chosen calling to give people a good time.

~

CHAPTER THIRTEEN

Broadway Director

In 1941, *Blithe Spirit* was my first directorial job on Broadway. Owing to the war, Noel was forced to remain in England, and when I cabled to ask whom he wanted as director, he laconically replied, "Why not you?" And so that was settled. We then had a series of caustic cables about casting. Noel was in agreement regarding Clifton Webb as Charles and Peggy Wood as Ruth but faintly dubious about Leonora Corbett as Elvira. [Leonora Corbett (1908–1960) was an elegant British actress on stage and in films who excelled at sophisticated comedies.] This was rather odd, as I had suggested her because of his enthusiasm for her performance in his 1939 drama *This Happy Breed*. To this day she thinks that Noel selected her for the part, but he didn't. I did, and she was excellent. He was also against Mildred Natwick as Madame Arcati, as he felt that a more robust comedienne was needed, but I again stuck to my guns and she was hired. Many years later, Noel was to change his mind about Millie, for he cast her in the television version of the same play. He adored her performance and her.

Rehearsals were smooth and amiable, but there were one or two moments of absolute panic. After a week, Millie informed me that she hadn't the faintest idea what Madame Arcati was all about. As I had expected her to create the character herself and was already scared to death, this came as a definite shock; however, we resolved our mutual insecurity via a series of private rehearsals, and the results were highly successful. She absorbed my ideas, adapted them for herself, and, of course, arrived at a really brilliant performance.

Blithe Spirit is Noel Coward's most frequently produced comedy in both Great Britain and the United States, a farce fantasy that premiered in London in 1941. When writer Charles Condomine (Cecil Parker) and his second wife Ruth (Peggy Wood) hold a séance at their home with the eccentric Madame Arcati (Margaret Rutherford) as medium, Charles' first wife Elvira (Kay Hammond) materializes, although only Charles can see or hear her. With difficulty, Charles explains the situation to Ruth, but Ruth soon dies in a car crash and also returns as a spirit. With the help of Arcati, Charles eventually gets both wives to return to the hereafter, and he is happy to be rid of them both.

The West End production, produced by Wilson and H. M. Tennent, Ltd., and directed by Coward, ran for 1,997 performances, a new long-run record for a nonmusical in England. The 1941 Broadway version, produced and directed by Wilson, featured Clifton Webb, Mildred Natwick, Peggy Wood, and Leonora Corbett. It won the Drama Critics Circle Award and ran for a profitable 657 performances. A 1945 British movie version, directed by David Lean, stars Rex Harrison and Constance Cummings, with Kay Hammond and Margaret Rutherford reprising their stage roles. In addition to hundreds of stage revivals throughout the English-speaking world, *Blithe Spirit* showed up on American and British television in 1946, 1948, 1956, 1964, and 1966.

Clifton Webb (1893–1966) was an agile, dapper, sophisticated actor-singer-dancer who many mistakenly thought was British because of his precise, affected manner. He started his career at the age of ten, as a singer and, as an adult, was a ballroom dancer in New York. Webb made his Broadway debut in 1913, and later became a Broadway star for his hoofing and singing in such popular musical revues as *The Little Show* (1929), *Three's a Crowd* (1930), *Flying Colors* (1932), and *As Thousands Cheer* (1933), in which he introduced Irving Berlin's song classic "Easter Parade." Webb appeared in a few silent films, but his screen career did not take off until his stunning performance in *Laura* (1944). His other notable screen credits included *Sitting Pretty* (1948), *Cheaper By the Dozen* (1950), *Three Coins in the Fountain* (1954), and *The Remarkable Mr. Pennypacker* (1959).

Mildred Natwick (1908–1994) was a versatile American character actress on the stage, on television, as well as in movies, who often stole the show in eccentric but charming roles. Because of her mature looks and voice, she was often cast as women older than herself. Natwick made her Broadway debut in 1932, and her first movie eight years later. She could easily play dramatic roles, for instance, the biblical Miriam in *The Firstborn* (1958), but she is most fondly remembered for her comic creations on Broadway, including love-starved Widow Quin in *Playboy of the Western World* (1946), hypochondriac Madame St. Pé in *The Waltz of the Toreadors* (1957), bewildered Mrs. Banks in *Barefoot in the Park* (1963), which she reprised on film in 1967, resulting in an Oscar nomination, and, most memorably, the wacky medium Madame Arcati on Broadway in *Blithe Spirit* (1941).

Our trials on the road were rather squalid. Due to the war, railway space was at a premium. On the train, I was only able to obtain one drawing room, which was emphatically occupied by Clifton. He was apparently determined to prove that he was the star, and the ladies were forced to sit, granted in Pullman seats, down the passage. Later, in New Haven, we had a head-on collision. I had assigned the so-called star dressing room to Peggy Wood, with the assumption that "ladies come first." But on the afternoon of the opening, Clifton stormed into the theater to say that he would refuse to appear unless Peggy's trunks were removed and his installed in their place. Although we were intimate friends and had been for years, I found myself saying, "Clifton, I'm sorry about the mix-up, but I had assumed you were a gentleman." He drew himself up on his heels and once again explained that he was the only star of the play and left the theater in an obvious huff. Deflated by his persistence, I had the dressing rooms changed. It became all too clear that a star complex can effortlessly vanquish poor, old-fashioned gallantry.

I was to have further dressing room trouble in New York. Leonora had become emotionally involved with an elderly gentleman, an executive at NBC named John Royal, whom she finally married. He decided that since she was playing a ghost, the atmosphere of her dressing room should be more sympatico, and so he had it painted pale gray and hung with the most hideous glass chandeliers I have ever seen. When Peggy saw the completed décor, she described her costar as a "touring Gaby de Lys." [Wood's pun is a reference to exotic French singer-dancer Gaby Deslys from the turn of the century.] There was still the problem, however, of which dressing room, gray or otherwise, would accommodate which star. This was solved with simple expediency. I had a gold star put on each of the four doors, and if there were any complaints, I never heard them.

On the production side, Stewart Chaney designed the set, and Mainbocher, in his first theatrical assay, did a magnificent job on the clothes. [Stewart Chaney (1906–1969) was a costume, lighting, and set designer who did dozens of Broadway shows between 1934 and 1964. Mainbocher was the professional moniker for Main Rousseau Bocher (1891–1976), an American couture who was much in demand in Europe and the United States from the 1930s through the 1960s.] Peggy Wood, who played fashionable wife Ruth, came on stage looking chic and shiny, and was more glamorous than she had ever been in her long and distinguished career.

There was a slight difficulty, however, with Leonora, the ghost. She only wore one dress—very special, very gray, and very beautiful—but when we opened in New Haven, she decided it was clumsy and impossible to work in. She demanded that it be redone in less-bulky material, although she was perfectly content with the design. In fact, she threatened that if a new dress was not ready for the Boston opening, which was only three days away, she would not appear. This threw the Mainbocher establishment into an understandable panic. It was the weekend, which meant double time, but miraculously the gown was accomplished, and Main personally delivered it to Boston in time for the opening performance. Nonetheless, by now Leonora had decided that the original dress was suddenly workable and that nothing in the world would induce her to part with it. But she had a charmingly naive idea that she thought would compensate the waste to the management: that we give her the second dress to wear to parties in New York as the ghost in *Blithe Spirit*, thus advertising the production.

Her little scheme fell flat, because instead of taking advantage of her talent for promotion, which still burns vividly, I deliberately gave the dress to my wife. [Mainbocher had, for many years, employed Wilson's wife Natasha to wear the designer's clothes and represent the house in public relations activities. The Wilsons' closets were constantly restocked with the latest Mainbocher designs, and it was through these connections that Mainbocher was hired to work on *Blithe Spirit*.] Millie, as Madame Arcati, on the other hand, was no trouble. We found her a dress in a thrift shop on Second Avenue in New York. She put it on, and it was exactly right; we never heard a peep out of her again.

Minor and customary difficulties beset any production during rehearsals and out-of-town tryouts. In this case, they turned out to be well worth the trouble, as the show ran two years on Broadway and two more on the road.

As the New York company was still firmly dug in at the Morosco Theatre, I decided to form a second group to do a road tour until the Broadway company was ready to go out on its own. The preparations for this presented certain problems. Dennis King had been pursuing me for weeks, wanting to play Clifton's part. I firmly pointed out to him his reputation for refusing to take direction. But he swore loyalty, fidelity, and cooperation so emphatically that I relented, and during rehearsals he couldn't have behaved more beautifully. Still, on the first night of our tryout in Wilmington, Delaware, the debacle occurred. Everything we had done in rehearsals was disregarded, and he romped off on a version all his own. How he managed the legerdemain of accepting one performance and then performing another was, I must admit, sheer masterful chicanery. I was so desperately angry that after the first act, I went backstage and posted a closing notice on the bulletin board to be effective at the end of the week. By midnight Mr. King's agent had arrived for a tripartite conversation in my hotel sitting room. The agent guaranteed that Dennis would behave himself, and Dennis, full of apologies, succumbed to his remonstrative blandishments. Hence, the closing notice was rescinded, and the play continued on its travels: Buffalo, Indianapolis, Columbus, and finally the Selwyn Theatre in Chicago, where we were warmly received by a friendly audience and press. Dennis was described as a "new" Mr. King: polished, elegant, subtle, and as giving a performance far beyond any of his previously witnessed in their "divine and windy city."

Dennis King (1897–1971) was a prolific British-born performer who played everything from Shakespearean tragedies to comic operettas during his forty-year stage career. He made his London debut in 1919 and his Broadway bow two years later, settling in the United States and becoming a U.S. citizen. Although King acted in Shaw and Shakespeare works on Broadway, he did not become a star until he originated the role of Canadian fur trapper Jim Kenyon in the operetta favorite *Rose-Marie* (1925). His other musical successes include *The Vagabond King* (1925), which he reprised on film in 1930; *The Three Musketeers* (1928); the 1932 revival of *Show Boat*; and *I Married an Angel* (1938). Among his many Broadway plays are *Romeo and Juliet* (1923), *Peter Ibbotson* (1931), *Three Sisters* (1942), *Medea* (1948), *Billy Budd* (1951), and *A Patriot for Me* (1969). King made a handful of films, *Between Two Worlds* (1944) being the most memorable, and several television dramatic and musical specials, in particular *The Mikado* (1960).

The next day, bursting with pride (not only for myself but for Dennis as well), I went to his dressing room to congratulate him on his wonderful notices. Apparently unimpressed, he glanced at the press clippings carefully piled on his dressing table and nonchalantly remarked, "Well, if that's the way you want me to play it, all right." A few weeks later I surreptitiously returned to Chicago for a "checkup." I needn't have bothered because what I expected had happened. Dennis was back to his Wilmington performance and thus vanished the "new" Mr. King.

I had my problems with movie star Annabella too, not that she wasn't invariably charming and sweet, but because of her acute difficulty in mastering English. [Annabella (1907–1996) was a French screen actress, born Suzanne Georgette Charpentier in Paris, who never lost her thick French accent.] I had engaged her on the basis of her Westport performance in the Hungarian drama *Liliom*, where the accent was almost an asset. But in a modern Coward comedy it interfered with her timing and unmistakably hindered her effectiveness as the ghost Elvira. Early in rehearsals it was obviously necessary to engage someone to polish her diction, and so I hired a fat, amiable woman who only too willingly took on the job of vocal coach. The two labored together during rehearsals, but the effect on Annabella's accent was negligible. During the tour, however, the tutor's value unequivocally proved itself, for with frightening vigor and painstaking adoration she laundered and pressed her pupil's more intimate garments. Unfortunately, in addition to her abilities as a laundress, she had a slight flair for alcohol and, somewhere near Indianapolis, or maybe it was Columbus, went missing for three days. She eventually reappeared, battered and bruised, with the explanation that she had been run over by a taxi. I still have my doubts.

There were no difficulties with the rest of the cast. Estelle Winwood played Madame Arcati with zany precision, and Carol Goodner was appealing and dependable as wife Ruth. In spite of Annabella's accent and Dennis King's personal and somewhat frenetic interpretation of his role, backed by the solid performances of Estelle and Carol, we ran for several months in Chicago; however, my fondest recollection of that engagement will always be my favorite laundress, the vocal coach. The original Broadway company eventually went on their tour. We had to avoid Chicago for obvious reasons, but the safari was an extensive one, embracing, among other cities, San Francisco and Los Angeles. It was in Hollywood that I decided to give a large party for the company and members of the film colony who chose to accept. They all did.

Lady Mendl, born Elsie de Wolfe, was the quintessence of international chic. [Elsie de Wolfe (1859?–1950) was an actress who later became a celebrated interior designer famous in Europe and the United States. She married British diplomat Sir Charles Mendl in 1926.] She had long been a friend of Clifton's, as well as mine, and graciously allowed me to use her beautiful house in Beverly Hills for the gala. Hilda West, her trusted secretary, made the arrangements: invitations, food, and the inevitable liquor. Elsie was then the queen of Hollywood, and a great percentage of the guests had never been allowed to so much as step across that hallowed threshold. I sometimes think it might have been the reason why many of them came at all. Nevertheless, it was overcrowded and painfully respectable.

The list of guests is too long to remember, but I do recall Louis B. Mayer striding up and down, his daughter Edie Goetz and her husband Bill, Hedda Hopper and Luella Parsons, Mary Pickford and her inevitable Buddy Rogers, Ethel Barrymore as gracious as always and smiling from a corner, but predominately Gypsy Rose Lee, who, with no effort, was in both dress and manners the most respectable of them all. [Wilson is not exaggerating when he says they all came. Hilda West's invitation list survives and reads like a Hollywood who's who. Among the 170 guests who accepted the invitation were such diverse celebrities as Fanny Brice, Walt Disney, Fred Astaire, Ginger Rogers, Orson Welles, Arthur Rubenstein, Moss Hart, Samuel Goldwyn, Frank Sinatra, Cole Porter, Monty Woolley, Mrs. William Paley, William Powell, Harold Arlen, Michael Romanoff, Katharine Hepburn, Ingrid Bergman, Irving Berlin, Charles Laughton, and David Selznick. See appendix B for the complete list.] Anyway, both the party for and the tour of *Blithe Spirit* were successes, and at the show's end, no one, particularly myself, could feel anything but gratitude for our good fortune.

Five years later I did another Coward play on Broadway with Clifton called *Present Laughter*. It was partially autobiographical in that it was laid in Noel's London studio and that the characters—a somewhat dubious valet, a mad housekeeper, and Coward's secretary Lorn—were clearly defined. Even London producer Binkie Beaumont and I were impersonated; amicably but, I must say, with a certain amount of Coward acidity. [Wilson was the model for the character Morris Dixon, Garry Essendine's manager.] Due to film commitments, Noel was unable to play the lead in New York, but Clifton was available and enthusiastically accepted. I also engaged Evelyn Varden and an unknown young lady named Jan Sterling, who is no longer unknown. [Jan Sterling (1921–2004) was a glamorous and popular actress in films and on television in the 1950s and 1960s. Evelyn Varden (1893–1958) was an American character actress who found fame late in her career playing mothers and other mature women in plays, on television, and in movies.] Donald Oenslager did the set, and I directed, as well as produced.

Present Laughter is a 1942 comedy by Noel Coward that played on Broadway in 1946. Veteran London actor Garry Essendine (Coward) is of an age when sex is less interesting to him than a good book, but on the eve of his international tour he is besieged by several women, including a would-be actress and her mother, a femme fatale out for an affair, his ex-wife, his secretary, and a male wannabe playwright who worships Garry as much as any female. Although thin on plot, the comedy features some of Coward's most stylish dialogue and farcical characters. Wilson and H. M. Tennent, Ltd. presented the comedy in London in 1943, and again in 1947. The Broadway version, featuring Clifton Webb as Essendine, was directed and produced by Wilson and ran for 158 performances. Decades later, the comedy would enjoy long-running revivals in London and New York. *Present Laughter* was never filmed but showed up on British television in 1964 and 1981.

The production was miraculously free from ordinary worries. We did the usual trek out of town, starting in Wilmington, and eventually opened at the Plymouth Theatre in New York. Owing to Noel and Clifton's names, and perhaps even mine, the first night was a social shambles. Bejeweled ladies rushed up and down the aisles, chattering about their private affairs and paying no attention to the play, which, I suspect, they never wanted to see anyway. It was the place to see and be seen, however, and there they were in their glittering glory. [*Present Laughter* was Webb's last Broadway appearance. The rest of his career was taken up with the movies.]

CHAPTER FOURTEEN

~

Hollywood

In 1940, following *Idiot's Delight,* the Lunts did a production of another Robert Sherwood play called *There Shall Be No Night.* The Playwrights Company, in which Bob was a partner, acted as producer, and the Theatre Guild, with which the Lunts had been associated for so many years, was permitted to participate as coproducer.

As usual, Alfred directed, and Richard Whorf, who was also in the cast, handled the scenic design. The production lived up to the excellence of its total ambiance. Lynn was, of course, the costar, and supporting the Lunts was a great cast, which included Sydney Greenstreet, Thomas Gomez, Phyllis Thaxter, and a young hopeful, Montgomery Clift. I recall Alfred saying, "I'll teach that boy to act if it kills me!"

Monty was inexperienced at the time. He had a lot to learn and knew it, but he had warmth, determination, and sincerity—mostly sincerity, actually—which, under Alfred's guidance, fused into a touching performance. Emotionally high-strung, Monty had a proclivity for getting engaged to a series of young ladies, who were only too willing. He would come to me for advice, which I would promptly give him, although I hardly qualified as a consultant. Perhaps it satisfied him that I was willing to serve as a sounding board. [Clift, who had many affairs with both women and men, was close platonic friends with several female Hollywood stars, none more so than Elizabeth Taylor.]

In fact, my affiliation with the play was only as a beneficent friend. I was one of the backers but otherwise had no official connection with the management. I would eventually produce it in London—again working with

There Shall Be No Night is a potent 1940 drama by Robert E. Sherwood that was timely and quite disturbing when it opened during the early days of World War II. Nobel Prize–winning scientist Dr. Kaarlo Valkonen (Alfred Lunt) and his American-born wife Miranda (Lynn Fontanne) are reluctant to believe that the Russians will invade his beloved Finland, nor can they see much purpose in resistance should the Russians stage an invasion. But when war breaks out and their son Erik (Montgomery Clift) enters the army, Kaarlo joins the medical corps. He concludes that this war will not be the end of civilization, but rather the "long-deferred death rattle of the primordial beast."

While reviews were mixed, the drama won the Pulitzer Prize and ran for a healthy 181 performances. After the Russian defeat of the Finns, Sherwood changed the locale of the play to Greece and made the Germans the villains. The Lunts also starred in the 1943 London production, which was produced by Wilson and H. M. Tennent, Ltd., and directed by Lunt. Perhaps because of the timely nature of the play, *There Shall Be No Night* was never made into a film or television drama.

H. M. Tennent, Ltd.—a few years later in 1943. It was there that we had to make a considerable change in the mise-en-scène. The script centers on a family of Finns, whom Bob Sherwood had glorified in the original production by dramatizing their heroic resistance during the Russian invasion of Finland. Rather inconveniently during our New York engagement, Finland

Montgomery Clift (1920–1966) was a unique stage and screen actor who specialized in playing sensitive, troubled heroes. He was born in Omaha, Nebraska, and began acting professionally as a teenager. By 1935, he was playing youths on Broadway but did not get widespread recognition until his performance as doomed son Erik in *There Shall Be No Night* in 1940. After giving commendable performances in such plays as *The Skin of Our Teeth* (1942), the 1944 revival of *Our Town*, and *The Searching Wind* (1944), Clift went to Hollywood in 1948, and concentrated on movies for the rest of his too-short life. His notable films include *The Heiress* (1949), *A Place in the Sun* (1951), *I Confess* (1953), *From Here to Eternity* (1953), *Raintree County* (1957), *The Misfits* (1961), and *Freud* (1962). After a car accident in 1957 left him slightly disfigured, Clift became more and more a recluse and lived the troubled life of his characters until his death from a heart attack at the age of forty-five. A founding member of the Actors Studio, he was one the finest American actors to use Method acting.

Terence Rattigan (1911–1982) was a respected British playwright whose best works were literate and dramatically effective. He was born in London, the son of a diplomat, and educated at Harrow and Trinity College, Oxford. Rattigan scored his first stage success in 1936, with the comedy-drama *French without Tears*. Numbered among his later dramas and comedies were *Love in Idleness* (1944), which played on Broadway as *O Mistress Mine* (1946); *The Winslow Boy* (1946); *The Browning Version* (1948); *The Deep Blue Sea* (1952); *The Sleeping Prince* (1953); *Separate Tables* (1956); *Ross* (1960); and *In Praise of Love* (1973). Most of Rattigan's stage works have been filmed and/or made into television dramas. He also contributed original screenplays for such movies as *Journey Together* (1945), *The Sound Barrier* (1952), *The V.I.P.s* (1963), and *The Yellow Rolls Royce* (1964). Many of Rattigan's plays fell out of favor in the 1960s but have been enjoying new productions on London and New York stages since the 1990s.

had decided to join up with the Russians as World War II allies. Naturally, this somewhat vitiated the entire point of the play and eventually resulted in the setting being altered to Greece, where the Lunts, as stalwart Greek citizens, were now being bitterly and viciously attacked by the Nazis. It was a great success—as it had been in New York—and we played to a usual and very comfortable Lunt season. [*There Shall Be No Night* ran at the Aldwych for a profitable 220 performances, five weeks longer than the Broadway run.]

The next autumn in London, I again produced the Lunts, in association with H. M. Tennent, Ltd. We did Terence Rattigan's *Love in Idleness*, which

O Mistress Mine is a British comedy by Terence Rattigan that was successful in London and New York under two different titles. Because of his political career, Sir John Fletcher (Alfred Lunt) cannot get a divorce and marry his longtime mistress, Olivia Brown (Lynn Fontanne). When Olivia's son Michael (Brian Nissen) returns from the war, he upsets the couple with his disapproval, but once he himself falls in love, he is more understanding.

Using the title *Love in Idleness*, the comedy was a hit in London in 1944, even though the press had little good to say about the script. But they had nothing but adulation for the Lunts, and audiences agreed. The Broadway production, titled *O Mistress Mine*, ran for a surprising 452 performances. The Theatre Guild and Wilson produced the New York version, and Lunt directed. A film version was never made using either title, but the play was turned into the German television movie *Olivia* in 1965.

was called O Mistress Mine the following season in New York. It was a light comedy that featured Alfred as an important government official who was living with an elegant, attractive woman (Lynn) without the benefit of clergy. While not an original situation, Terence's dialogue was packed with wit and swift, well-turned phrases.

For the New York production we needed a completely new décor, and I persuaded Alfred to use young scenic designer Robert Davison. We had a long session together, during which Alfred told Bob exactly what he wanted, as well as one particular thing he did not want—solid cornices on the walls. He felt that painted ones were easier to travel with and equally effective. At the interview, Bob agreed on all points and then went off and did exactly what he pleased, including solid cornices.

We opened in, of all places, Akron, Ohio. Alfred had a lady friend there who owned a small theater, and she had asked for the attraction. As he is fundamentally a kindhearted man, Alfred had agreed. Both Terry and Binkie Beaumont attended the opening, and when the three of us arrived at the theater, we found Alfred seriously distraught. He was satisfied with the set, but Davison had furnished it with bastard French furniture, completely out of character for an eighteenth-century English home. Alfred simply and steadfastly refused to go on. In a panic, I paced the snow-banked streets of Akron hoping for some way out.

Then a miracle happened. I suddenly came upon a shop filled with beautiful English antiques. Within a few hours, two trucks were sent lumbering through the snow to the theater, and the aisles were soon filled with their contents. The French furniture was struck, and I proceeded to redress the set as I would a room in a private house, trying a desk here, a screen there, a lamp here, a chair there—until the setting was accurate and very handsome. In fact, the Coromandel screen and red lacquer desk would later grace the Lunts' house in New York. What wasn't used was piled back into the trucks, but the shop was $10,000 richer and we even gave them program credit.

Alfred was pleased, and our opening went off splendidly, which was vitally important since the play had been sold out long before our arrival. When we moved to the Empire Theatre in New York, the reception was equally enthusiastic. Alfred was certainly right about the solid cornices, however. During one performance, upon Lynn's entrance, a piece of one cornice fell off the wall and conked her smack on the head. As with her broken wrist in Portland, Maine, she continued unabashed. Mr. Davison, on the other hand, wisely left and went to Mexico. [Robert Davison (b. 1922) designed eight other Broadway shows, including Wilson's production of The Day before Spring in 1946.]

In 1947, while Tallulah was still bouncing around on tour in *Private Lives*, I busied myself with another Rattigan play with a more serious theme. It was called *The Winslow Boy*. It was produced by Atlantis Productions, a special combination that included the Theatre Guild, H. M. Tennent, and myself. We again played the Empire Theatre, and the cast included Alan Webb, Frank Allenby, and a charming moppet, Michael Newell. It was a comfortable and cozy success—nice notices and a good season's run—another sinecure for Mr. Rattigan. [*The Winslow Boy* is a 1946 drama about a youth who is wrongly accused of stealing money at his public school and the barrister who defends him all the way to the nation's highest court. The London and Broadway productions were both directed by Glen Byam Shaw. The drama was filmed with success in 1948 and 1999.]

Terry had become one of the most important contemporary playwrights in England. His range is wide—from farces like *French without Tears* to such psychological dramas as *Separate Tables*—interspersed with a series of highly successful films. He is very good-looking and fully aware of it, but a serious, hard-working writer whose output fully justifies the position he has achieved.

Personally, he is amiable and even frivolous, sometimes to an alarming degree. I remember one particular party that he gave for a minor English peer. The guest list included one or two gentlemen who were unfamiliar with the protocol of such relatively exalted society. One of the young men asked Terry the correct form of address with which to approach the guest of honor. "What shall I call him?" he asked. Terry replied, "Say nothing for about twenty minutes and then just call him 'darling.'" He was certainly fun to be with, and at times it was hard to conceive, in view of his social gaiety, the unmistakable fact that he had contributed some of the most popular plays in the English theater.

In London, on another occasion, Natasha and I had gone to a performance of another of Terry's plays, *The Deep Blue Sea*, starring Peggy Ashcroft and Kenneth More, who made the play glow to such an extent that I bought the American rights at once. Then came the problem of local casting. Alfred de Liagre came up with the idea that if I allowed him to coproduce, he could provide Margaret Sullavan for Peggy's original role. Thus, in 1952, we joined forces and went to work.

The play was one of Terry's more serious forays, as it concerned the attempted suicide of a woman who had left her husband because of her uncontrollable love for a charming but worthless idler. Maggie handled her role with sensitivity and intelligence, and was more than ably supported by Alan Webb, Herbert Berghof, James Hanley, and John Merivale. Frith Banbury, who had directed it in London, was brought over in the same capacity. Maggie and Frith didn't always see eye to eye, however, which caused a certain amount of trepidation during the out-of-town preambles. Then again, as Miss Sullavan was famous for her allergy to directors, this situation was rather anticipated. We opened at the Morosco Theatre in New York to polite, if somewhat reserved, notices; and succeeded in achieving a polite, if somewhat reserved, run. [*The Deep Blue Sea* is a 1952 British melodrama by Terence Rattigan that critics dismissed as a two-handkerchief tearjerker, but it was an effective vehicle for talented performers. The 1952 Broadway production ran for 132 performances.]

Soon after *O Mistress Mine*, I decided to have a shot at Hollywood myself. This was arranged by Audrey Wood, one of the most influential agents in the industry. She sent me out to MGM and put me in the charge of a charming woman named Lillie Messenger. That was her stage name. In private life, she was a princess of the noble German family Thurn und Taxis. Lillie's position at the studio was special. She was technically a story editor but was better known on the MGM lot as one of the few people allowed to enter the office of Mr. Mayer by a private, side entrance. She was also one of an extraordinary group of women who were known in the studio as the "Scheherazades." Their unique function was to appear once a week before the executives and producers in Mr. Mayer's office and, in rotation, tell the stories of the scripts they had read that week. It was a fantastic assignment and, for the most part, enabled the studio brass to completely avoid having to read the scripts themselves. On one occasion, a well-known producer tentatively remarked that a certain script might be good for Garbo. I vividly remember Mr. Mayer's

Louis B. Mayer (1884?–1957) was one of Hollywood's top moguls for forty years and the force behind hundreds of movies made by Metro Pictures and Metro-Goldwyn-Mayer. He was born Lazar Mayer in the Ukraine, and in 1886, his family fled Russia and settled in New Brunswick, Canada. He began his career in Boston, managing a burlesque house, and then showing silent films. By 1918, he was involved in making movies with Samuel Goldwyn and Marcus Loewe. As head of MGM, the most prestigious and productive Hollywood studio, Mayer created and destroyed stars, dictated what moviegoers throughout the nation saw, and shrewdly led Hollywood's Golden Age. Mayer could be fatherly and understanding, as well as vindictive and totalitarian. His power was weakened in the 1950s, and Mayer had been pushed out of the business by the time he died in 1957.

Greta Garbo (1905–1990) was Hollywood's most enigmatic, mystifying, and unique leading lady, the quintessential screen icon. She was born in Stockholm, Sweden, and worked in a department store and as a model before studying at the Royal Dramatic Theatre's acting school. Before she had much of a chance to act on stage, Garbo was appearing in silent films, where it was obvious that the camera loved her striking features. After starring in some Swedish and German films, she was signed by Hollywood and came to the United States in 1925, when she was only twenty years old. After a few films, she was a star, known both for her beauty and mesmerizing acting ability.

Garbo made her first talkie with *Anna Christie* (1930), and her deep, exotic voice made her a star all over again. Although she made only two dozen movies, they include such favorites as *Flesh and the Devil* (1926), *Love* (1927), *Susan Lenox* (1931), *Mata Hari* (1931), *Grand Hotel* (1932), *Queen Christina* (1933), *Anna Karenina* (1935), *Camille* (1936), *Ninotchka* (1939), and *Two-Faced Woman* (1941). Garbo was still at the top of her talent and popularity when she retired from movies in 1941, living in quiet privacy for the next fifty years.

laconic reply: "Who wants Garbo?" Considering that she had been the queen of the MGM lot for a full decade, his reaction came as a considerable shock.

Years later, after she moved to New York, I came to know Garbo personally. By this time she had given up the hermit existence that she had persisted with in Hollywood and was actually appearing in shops in the city and at innumerable private parties. She clung to her dark glasses, but at least the fabulous Miss Garbo was on view.

One night there was a party at Valentina's, the well-known couturiere, given for a group of Pittsburgh millionaires to celebrate Russian Easter. Valentina had specifically asked lady guests to dress in their best and for the gentlemen to wear evening clothes. Nonetheless, Margalo Gillmore, an actress of no mean repute, had mistakenly interpreted the invitation as a cocktail party and consequently arrived relatively informally dressed. Valentina asked her to go home and change into full evening array to match her other bejeweled and elegant guests. Margalo graciously complied, returning shortly afterward appropriately bedecked. After an interminable wait, Garbo finally arrived and was dressed—to Margalo's well-contained fury—in a turtleneck sweater and black slacks. The Pittsburgh friends were both puzzled and impressed but, needless to say, Garbo was not asked to go home to change. [Margalo Gillmore (1897–1986) was a beautiful British-born actress of the

American stage who specialized in tragic roles in plays by Eugene O'Neill, Sidney Howard, and S. N. Behrman.]

Subsequently, at another gathering, I discussed with Miss Garbo the possibility of her playing in *The Cherry Orchard*, or, for that matter, any other play she wanted to do on Broadway. She was very enthusiastic at the beginning of our discussion, and it wasn't until the end of the evening that she came to me and said, "I'm excited about your suggestion and I would be happy to go into rehearsal, but you must realize that on opening night, I will be unable to go on!"

Under the beneficent aegis of Lillie, Mr. Mayer and I became friends. The arrangement we arrived at was that I should spend three months at the studio studying and observing and then decide what I wanted to do. I was given a vast office, which included its own dining room and bathroom, and, naturally, my own secretary. I assumed that the office actually belonged to Sir Alexander Korda, as it was packed with bronze statues of Sabu. [Korda was the Hungarian-born British producer with many movie hits. The young actor Sabu was featured in such Korda films as *Drums* (1938), *The Thief of Bagdad* (1940), and *The Jungle Book* (1942).] It also overlooked a mortuary that adjoins—unhappily perhaps—the MGM lot. Mr. Mayer treated me with courtesy and kindness right down the line. I was not only allowed on every sound stage—and there were twenty to thirty of them working simultaneously—but also into the cutting rooms, viewings of the rushes, and major sessions of the big brass at their executive meetings.

Getting to see Mr. Mayer personally without Lillie's backdoor help was somewhat of a problem. I would be summoned for an appointment and then left to sit in the outer office—presided over by the famous Ida Koverman, who had been secretary to several presidents—surrounded by thirty or forty other hopefuls. After an hour or so, I would finally be received by the top man himself. Once inside, seated in a room that would have done shame to Buckingham Palace, I was persistently entertained with imitations of Ethel Barrymore, Guthrie McClintic, or Kit Cornell and told long stories about Mayer's early career at a theater somewhere north of Boston. Realizing that the thirty or forty others were *still* waiting outside, I would try to escape. But this he would have none of, as there were always further imitations or anecdotes to deliver. After one of these sessions, I said to Lillie, "There is only one thing more difficult than getting into Mr. Mayer's office, and that's getting out of it!"

There was, of course, time for dipping into the social life of Hollywood. There was a huge party at Joan Crawford's where the swimming pool was boarded over and turned into a marquee, and intimate lunches with Judy

Ruth Draper (1884–1956) was one of the most famous of all American monologists, an actress who could captivate audiences alone on an empty stage. She was born in New York City, the daughter of a physician, and was encouraged to go into the theater by a family friend, Polish pianist Ignacy Jan Paderewski. Draper made her Broadway debut as a maid in *A Lady's Name* (1916) but shortly thereafter decided that her gifts for mimicry were best disclosed when alone on a bare stage with little more than a scarf and hat for props. She began to write her own monologues, first offering them professionally in London in 1920, and in New York the following year. Some of her monologues dealt with a single character, others with a succession of people.

Draper frequently departed from her own script, improvising as the moment suggested. Her characters ranged from the most lordly to the most beggarly and, on some occasions, as in her depiction of a French wife saying good-bye to her husband, who is leaving to join the Free French in the war, were done entirely in a foreign language. But her unique gift of expression made each line intelligible. She won applause throughout the world and was still offering her show in New York, in her early seventies, when she died in her sleep after a performance.

Garland and Clifton Webb and his famous mother, Maybelle Webb, as well as one in particular with the late Ruth Draper, where we discussed the possibility of my presenting her for a limited engagement in New York, which I eventually did in 1947.

Ruth was one of the greatest character impersonators of all time. She wrote her own material and delivered it with precision and skill. She was a rather solemn person and a lady in the fullest sense of the word. Oddly enough, her major successes were in Germany, Denmark, Norway, and Sweden—more so than in her native New York. Our presentation at the Empire Theatre had only a mildly cordial reception, although during the three previous months, she had packed the Criterion Theatre in London. [Draper did her one-woman show on Broadway seven times between 1932 and 1956. Wilson produced the 1947 version at the Empire Theatre, which ran for twenty-seven performances.]

Mary Pickford was a frequent hostess at other Hollywood parties. These were held at Pickfair, the luxurious showplace where she had lived for many years as the wife of Douglas Fairbanks Sr. Mary was remarkable in appearance. After having been the leading child actress in the United States when I was too young to even be allowed to see her movies, she has defied time and remains an attractive, desirable woman. She has been equally fortunate

Mary Pickford (1892–1979) was one of Hollywood's first and biggest stars, a petite actress with long curly hair who became known as America's sweetheart. She was born Gladys Louise Smith in Toronto, Canada, into a family of immigrants from England. After the death of her father, the family, which included brother Jack and sister Lottie, earned their living touring the United States in cut-rate theatrical companies. Broadway producer David Belasco spotted Gladys, changed her name to Mary Pickford, and put her on the New York stage in 1907. Pioneer filmmaker D. W. Griffith cast her in her first movie in 1909. A year later, she was in Los Angeles making shorts and features for Biograph and then Carl Laemmle's Independent Moving Pictures Company, Famous Players-Lasky, and Paramount Pictures.

By 1920, Pickford was a star, thanks to such hits as *The Poor Little Rich Girl* (1917), *Rebecca of Sunnybrook Farm* (1917), *Daddy-Long-Legs* (1919), and *Pollyanna* (1920). She was a cofounder of United Artists and the Academy of Motion Picture Arts and Sciences, and remained one of Hollywood's top stars until the advent of sound. Because she was outgrowing her youthful roles, Pickford's sound movies were not successful. She made only a handful of movies after 1930 and retired from acting in 1950, but continued to hold her interests in United Artists. Her later life was plagued with bouts of alcoholism and depression. Pickford died in California in 1979, at the age of eighty-seven.

financially. At the height of her career, there was no income tax, and she also had a sagacious mother with a keen eye for real estate. Her mother spotted those endless vacant lots that made up the Beverly Hills of their day, buying them up one by one in Mary's name, and today Mary is probably the richest landowner in that area. As for her parties, they were massive and caviar-heaped but sedate in the extreme. Guests were encouraged to stroll through the gardens but *not* to leap into the fountains.

There were many stories, of course, of truly wild Hollywood parties that always seemed to climax with the guests pushing one another fully clad into a swimming pool. Alas, I never saw one of these—probably because I had a habit of early-to-bed and was always home before the fun started. I preferred the quiet lunches, like those I attended at Ethel Barrymore's house on the beach. There would only be a few close friends, the likes of Katharine Hepburn, Ina Claire, George Cukor, and Ilka Chase. After a relatively modest lunch, we would sit on lawn chairs on the cliffs overlooking the sea and leisurely discuss everything under the sun.

Ilka Chase (1905–1978) was a character actress and writer who became a celebrity on radio and television, as well as on Broadway and in Hollywood. She was born in New York City and educated at private schools there and in France. Chase made her Broadway debut in 1924 and was soon cast as friends of the heroine or tough, worldly women. Her archetypal role was perhaps backbiting Park Avenue wife Sylvia in *The Women* (1936). She served as the London correspondent for *Vogue* magazine (of which her mother was editor) during the 1920s before returning to Broadway, where she was featured in such plays as *Shall We Join the Ladies?* (1925), *The Happy Husband* (1928), *The Animal Kingdom* (1932), *Forsaking All Others* (1933), *Days without End* (1934), and *In Bed We Cry* (1944).

Chase's movie career consisted of twenty-seven feature films, most memorably *Paris Bound* (1929), *Fast and Loose* (1930), *The Animal Kingdom* (1932), *Now Voyager* (1942), *It Should Happen to You* (1954), *The Big Knife* (1955), and *Ocean's Eleven* (1960). She was popular on the radio and appeared in many television series, specials, and dramas, although she is probably most remembered as the wicked, funny stepmother in the television musical *Cinderella* (1957). Chase also wrote plays, a few of which she appeared in; novels; and two autobiographies.

It may have been because of one of these special afternoons that, some years later, Ilka Chase brought me her latest play and asked me to produce it on Broadway. *In Bed We Cry* was originally her best-selling novel, which had encouraged her to do a dramatic adaptation of it, with the idea of starring in it herself. She proceeded to raise $100,000 without my knowledge, until the day she came to my office, put the check on my desk, and asked me to both produce and direct. "After all, Jack," she said, "what can you lose?"

And so the casting began, and rehearsals followed without difficulty. Ilka had two special choices in the way of designers. Joseph Platt, who turned out a series of ornate and somewhat unbelievable sets, was one. The other was Adrian of Hollywood, whose creations for Ilka were, to say the least, eye-filling. One of the features of the production was Ilka's determination to wear roughly $1 million worth of real jewels. Detectives would arrive nightly with their precious cargo, stand in the wings during the performance, and at the end of the show take the jewels back to the vaults from whence they came.

There has probably never been a more glittering production, but it was torn to shreds by the critics and a "friendly" first-night audience, including many who had passionately clamored for tickets, claiming that they knew

Ilka and her mother—the world-famous editoress of *Vogue*, Edna Woolman Chase—intimately. We continued to fight it out for about a month at the Belasco Theatre in New York, but it was obviously a losing battle and Ilka agreed it would be wiser, if not essential, to close. [*In Bed We Cry* was a melodrama about a famous cosmetics mogul (Chase) who is so upset when her husband leaves her that she takes the refugee Kurt (Frederic Tozere) as her lover—with tragic results. Although Chase's novel was successful, the stage version only ran for forty-seven performances on Broadway.]

At the end of my three months in Hollywood. still surrounded by Sabu in that large office, I waited my turn in Mr. Mayer's anteroom for the finale. He couldn't have been more kind but had a definite theory—which has since been upset by other studios and also MGM—that it was necessary to choose between Broadway and film. He offered me a contract to produce or direct, or both, but with the clear expectation that I was to stay in Hollywood and not return to New York. Perhaps it was madness on my part to turn down a berth in that fabulous labyrinth, but I did and also quite frankly told him that I thought Broadway was more my dish. His reaction was amiable, and more than that, he offered MGM backing for my New York shows and sent

---

Bloomer Girl (1944) is a musical comedy supposedly about less-restricting clothes for women, but it is actually about slavery, civil rights, war, and feminism. During the Civil War, Evelina Applegate (Celeste Holm), the rebellious daughter of an upstate New York hoop skirt manufacturer, not only refuses to marry the man her father has selected for her, but also joins her aunt, Dolly Bloomer (Margaret Douglass), in promoting bloomers. Although she is against slavery, she weds Southern slave owner Jeff Calhoun (David Brooks) and convinces her father to manufacture bloomers.

The funny yet pointed book by Sig Herzig and Fred Saidy is filled with provocative ideas and even includes a musical version of *Uncle Tom's Cabin* put on by the local abolitionists. Harold Arlen (music) and E. Y. Harburg (lyrics) wrote the rich score, which includes the hit song "Right as the Rain" and the moving freedom song "The Eagle and Me," as well as such memorable numbers as "Evelina," "It Was Good Enough for Grandma," and "I Got a Song." Despite the serious issues that *Bloomer Girl* raised, the Broadway show was enjoyable and a major hit for Wilson, running for 654 performances. One of the highlights of the Broadway production was Agnes de Mille's choreography, in particular her "Civil War Ballet." Film or London versions never came to be, but in 1956, there was an abridged adaptation of *Bloomer Girl* on NBC-TV.

me to discuss the details with Nicholas Schenck, head of Loew's, owners of MGM. Soon thereafter, I was producing on Broadway, with Loew's backing.

I shall always be grateful to Mr. Mayer for his warmth and generosity. It is none of my business, but I always felt that when the "powers-that-were" *allowed* him to resign, they made a grave mistake. Surely, the prestige of MGM suffered and has never been quite the same since he was there.

The first show I did under financial sponsorship from Loew's was *Bloomer Girl*. Its birthing pains were somewhat complicated—one might even call it a caesarean. It had been written as a serious, straight play by Lilith and Dan James, and been submitted to Nat Goldstone, a Hollywood agent. He was apparently unable to place it and eventually hit on the idea of transforming it into a musical. Nat enlisted the services of many talented people, including Harold Arlen, who wrote a beautiful score, and Yip Harburg, who adapted the book for musical purposes with his friends Sig Herzig and Fred Saidy. Then the lot of them took off for New York, opened an office; and prepared to produce it by themselves.

Celeste Holm (1919–2012) was a versatile, bright-eyed blonde singer-actress who played everything from the classics to musical comedy on stage, in the movies, and on television. The native New Yorker grew up in various cities in Europe because of her father's job with Lloyd's of London but lived in Chicago for her high school years. After studying theater at the University of Chicago, Holm got experience working in stock and made her professional debut in 1936. Later that year, she understudied Ophelia in Leslie Howard's *Hamlet*. Widespread recognition came when she created the comic role of the irrepressible Ado Annie in *Oklahoma!* (1943), followed by the leading role of abolitionist Evelina in the musical *Bloomer Girl* (1944). She briefly replaced Gertrude Lawrence in *The King and I* and later led a touring company of *Mame*.

Holm's other New York credits include *Anna Christie* (1952), *Invitation to a March* (1960), *Candida* (1970), *Habeas Corpus* (1975), the one-woman program *Paris Was Yesterday* (1979), *I Hate Hamlet* (1991), and *Don Juan in Hell* (2000). She acted in two dozen movies, most memorably *Gentleman's Agreement* (1947), *The Snake Pit* (1948), *Champagne for Caesar* (1950), *All about Eve* (1950), *The Tender Trap* (1955), *High Society* (1956), *Tom Sawyer* (1973), and *Driving Me Crazy* (2012). She was even busier on television, where she appeared in dozens of series, specials, and television dramas between 1950 and 2004. Holm was still performing at the time of her death at the age of ninety-five.

I don't know what went wrong, except perhaps that they came to realize that they were not equipped with the experience to do a big musical production on Broadway. Hence, they gave up their office and returned to Hollywood. After a reasonable period of cogitation, it was suggested that I come out to listen to the finished script and score—thus another journey to Hollywood.

I was immediately sold—particularly with Harold's score—and threw myself into it with a vengeance. We went to MGM and enlisted their financial assistance and additional private funding from some of their wealthy top executives. There was a slight hitch with casting. Celeste Holm—who up until that point had only played, albeit successfully, a low comic part in Oklahoma!—seemed to me to be the ideal lead. My confreres disagreed however, and it was only after Celeste had done several auditions at Harold Arlen's house that they finally assented and she got the part. This was a very good idea, as it turned out. On opening night in New York, she scored a great success and would go on to achieve even more renown in the years that followed.

The original Bloomer Girl cast also included Margaret Douglass; David Brooks; Joan McCracken, who sang "Tomorrow, Tomorrow"; and Dooley Wilson, who sang "The Eagle and Me." There were also Mabel Taliaferro and Matt Briggs, both of whom had fairly straight parts.

Yip Harburg, who had put the show together and was on the liberal side, had a great theory that the play should be a communal organization and everyone involved should have his way. In consequence, after every performance in Philadelphia, the technical staff would sit solemnly together to give their individual opinions on the play's production. These discussions naturally included Nat, Yip, Sig, Fred, the original writers, Agnes de Mille, Lemuel Ayers, Miles White, and even Leon Lombardi, the musical director. I'm not at all sure there weren't others, but I do recall that the consumption of sandwiches was prodigious.

It has always fascinated me trying to determine the machinations of the critical grapevine of coastal cities from Boston to Washington. I mention this because only twenty-four hours after Bloomer Girl opened in Philadelphia, there was a line halfway around the block at the Shubert Theatre in New York, which was to be our eventual home. How the news of our success could have been transmitted so rapidly will never cease to amaze me. It is also true that news of a failure travels with equal speed. Thanks to this mysterious grapevine, we opened to an advance of $200,000 and did even better after that. The early ticket buyers proved to be right, and we ran for almost three years.

My next production for MGM was at their insistence and not of my own choice. It was a war play about the marines called *The Streets Are Guarded*, by Laurence Stallings, who had achieved enormous acclaim for his earlier collaboration with Maxwell Anderson on the renowned World War I drama *What Price Glory*. The studio must have believed that this sole venture would be a repetition of his former success. It was not. Directed by John Haggott, the cast included Paul Crabtree, Joel Marston, Jack Manning, and Miss Jeanne Cagney (in the only female part). The play had drive, distinction, and vitality, and was ensconced in the Henry Miller Theatre, but it did not appeal to local critics and we were forced to close in fairly short order. [*The Streets Are Guarded* is a 1944 war drama that mixes mysticism and reality. Three sailors, a pharmacist, and a nurse are stranded on a remote island in the South Pacific, surrounded by Japanese forces during World War II and in need of food and medicine. A lone marine appears, helps the castaways raid a Japanese supply station, and then disappears into the sea. The question of whether the man was real or some sort of miracle did not interest the press or the public, and the play closed after three weeks.]

The last show under MGM's financial backing was a musical called *The Day before Spring*, written by two young men who have since gone far: Alan Jay Lerner and Frederick "Fritz" Loewe. It was a beautiful production with Irene Manning and the late Bill Johnson. We played Boston to an enthusiastic sellout. There was one painful evening, when Arthur Hornblow—sent east by MGM to inspect their property—arrived at the Shubert Theatre to find that his seats had not been retained. It was not a very nice situation, and quite frankly, he was not very nice about it.

The Day before Spring is a 1945 musical comedy that brought modest attention to Alan Jay Lerner (book and lyrics) and Frederick Loewe (music). When coed Katherine (Irene Manning) was at Harrison University, she and Alex Maitland (Bill Johnson) almost eloped, but his car broke down, they had second thoughts, and she married Peter Townsend (John Archer) instead. Ten years later, the couple returns to Harrison for a class reunion, Katherine and Alex are reunited, and they again plan an elopement, but his car once again breaks down and Katherine returns to her husband.

Critics found the libretto lacking but commended the score by the young songwriting team, in particular the songs "My Love Is a Married Man," "I Love You This Morning," and "God's Green World." Wilson produced and directed the Broadway production, which managed to find an audience for 165 performances.

Lerner and Loewe are considered the American musical theater's finest songwriting team, after Rodgers and Hammerstein. Lyricist and librettist Alan Jay Lerner (1918–1986) was born into a wealthy New York family and educated at selective private schools, including Choate in Connecticut and Harvard, where he collaborated on two Hasty Pudding musicals. At Choate and Harvard, he was a classmate of John F. Kennedy. He worked as a radio scriptwriter before teaming up with German-born composer Frederick Loewe (1901–1988), the son of a popular leading man in operetta.

Loewe studied with such notable figures as Ferruccio Busoni and Eugène d'Albert before coming to the United States in 1924. For a decade, he could not make a living with his music and took numerous odd, unrelated jobs. Some of his songs were interpolated into *Petticoat Fever* and *The Illustrators' Show*, and his full score was heard in the short-lived operetta *Great Lady* (1938).

The new team of Lerner and Loewe scored the unsuccessful Broadway musicals *What's Up* (1943) and *The Day before Spring* (1945), before finding success with the Scottish-set musical *Brigadoon* (1947). The gold rush musical *Paint Your Wagon* (1951) enjoyed a modest run, but their masterpiece *My Fair Lady* (1956) broke all records and remains a triumph of the Broadway stage. The final Lerner and Loewe stage collaboration was *Camelot* (1960), although the team supplied a few new songs for the 1973 Broadway version of their 1958 hit film-musical *Gigi*. Lerner wrote the innovative but failed musical *Love Life* (1948), with music by Kurt Weill, and years later, after Loewe's retirement, he wrote two Broadway musicals with Burton Lane, *On a Clear Day You Can See Forever* (1965) and *Carmelina* (1979). Other Lerner credits without Loewe include *Coco* (1969), *1600 Pennsylvania Avenue* (1976), and *Dance a Little Closer* (1983).

Most of the Lerner and Loewe musicals were made into films, and Lerner also wrote original scripts or songs for such screen musicals as *Royal Wedding* (1951), *An American in Paris* (1951), *The Band Wagon* (1953), and *The Little Prince* (1974), the last with Loewe. While Lerner's librettos offered excellent dialogue, they sometimes betrayed an inability at proper construction and a lack of theatrical tension. On the other hand, as a writer of elegantly literate and witty lyrics, he had no peer among his contemporaries. Loewe was a traditionalist whose music followed long-established patterns, but it was marked by his uncommon gift for fresh melody and ability to capture the essence of a far-off time or place.

We should have stayed in Boston with our capacity houses. The critical reception in New York wasn't desperate, but it did lean toward the apathetic. In the end, we managed to hold on for a considerable number of months. Then the authors came to me with the suggestion that I take it to Chicago. At this point, MGM decided to withdraw, so I sent it out on my own money with a friendly and courteous understanding with the authors that if it didn't come off, they would forego their royalties.

The situation in Chicago was the sort of thing that can only happen in the theater. It got rave notices from the press, starting with the late Ashton Stevens—dean of the local critical fraternity—to Claudia Cassidy, whose influence and popularity were supposed to ensure the success of any show to which she gave her approval. Alan, Fritz and I read the notices the morning after opening night, and there was no question that we were in for a big hit. The only problem, however, was the box office; no one—and I mean *no one*—came to buy a ticket. It might have been Miss Cassidy's statement that, "Mr. Wilson serves caviar and champagne," which I know she meant in good faith and as a compliment. But apparently Chicago likes neither caviar nor champagne. Despite the authors' gesture of no royalties, I had to close the show at the end of two weeks. We burned the scenery in Chicago to save the expense of shipping it back to New York. MGM had been right. [Unfortunately, *The Day before Spring* was Wilson's only collaboration with Lerner and Loewe. Had they stuck together, Wilson would have enjoyed considerable success with such upcoming Lerner and Loewe hits as *Brigadoon*, *My Fair Lady*, and *Camelot*.]

CHAPTER FIFTEEN

~

One-Night Stand

In 1945, I journeyed back to England for the opening of Noel's revue *Sigh No More*. The trip itself was quite a problem, as World War II had just ended and passports were technically forbidden. I had to go to Washington for a session with the famous Ruth Shipley, head of passports for the State Department. She was a little recalcitrant at first, but my arguments for going sounded reasonable and she ended up giving me the necessary papers.

A few weeks later, I left for LaGuardia Airport, waved off by my mother in a flood of tears and, ironically enough, Natasha. I say "ironically" because her first husband, Lucien Lelong, was also a passenger, and she had the privilege of bidding bon voyage to two husbands at once. Incidentally, he and I became great friends during the trip.

At the time, transatlantic planes were only designed to land on water. Thus, our stop at Gander, Newfoundland, was on some sort of lake, where we were towed to shore for dinner, and our stop in Ireland was on the Shannon River. The chief steward courteously informed me there that if struck by even one small piece of driftwood, the plane could easily sink. After a delicious breakfast in the local inn and an endless bus ride through the beautiful Irish countryside, we were conveyed to London in another plane that was considered suitable to hold the air without the safeguard of water landings. I finally arrived in time for the end of rehearsals and had to journey on to Manchester for the preliminaries and opening night.

The show was presented by me, with Binkie Beaumont as coproducer, and directed by Noel, who wrote it, in conjunction with Joyce Grenfell and Richard

Sigh No More is a 1945 British musical revue by Noel Coward and others that enjoyed a run of 213 performances in the West End. Coward wrote the songs and sketches, with contributions to the latter by Joyce Grenfell, Richard Addinsell, and Norman Hackworth. The sterling cast featured Grenfell, Cyril Ritchard, Madge Elliott, Tom Linden, and Graham Payn, who sang the show's hit ballad "Matelot." Other notable numbers from the score include "Nina," "Old Soldiers Never Die," and the title song. An unusual feature of the revue was a full orchestra directed by Mantovani.

Addinsell. It starred Cyril Ritchard and his late wife Madge Elliott and featured, among others, Graham Payn, who was destined to follow Noel in *Tonight at 8:30*. The production had charm, humor, and nostalgia, but it was not a critical success. Soon after its transition to London, *Sigh No More* quietly folded.

A few years later, my first producing partnership with the Shuberts occurred. Noel had been urging me to do a play by a new writer, Michael Clayton Hutton, called *Power without Glory*. It was an intellectual melodrama that

The **Shuberts** were the most illustrious producing team and theater owners in the American theater during the twentieth century. Lee (1873?–1953), Sam S. (1876?–1905), and J. J. (1878?–1963) Shubert were born in Shervient, Lithuania; their years of birth have never been verified and are estimates. The brothers were brought to the United States in 1882, and the family settled in Syracuse, New York. Lee and Sam soon had odd jobs at local theaters, and Sam quickly became box office treasurer at one.

When Sam purchased the touring rights to the Charles Hoyt play *A Texas Steer* in 1894, the brothers' careers were launched. By 1900, the Shuberts had tackled New York with the hit melodrama *Arizona* (1900), and they eventually became the largest theater owners in New York and elsewhere, as well as the most active producers in the United States. Between 1901 and 1954, the "Messrs Shubert," as their billing read, produced 520 plays on Broadway. Their emphasis was largely on musicals. Among their principal New York playhouses were the Shubert, Winter Garden, and Princess theaters. Although the brothers' tactics were often deemed crass and ruthless, they often gave substantially reduced rents to struggling, worthwhile attractions and kept many theaters that might otherwise have been lost to movies or burlesque in the legitimate fold. The vast collection of records, manuscripts, and other materials left behind by the brothers has been reorganized into the Shubert Archive, housed in the Lyceum Theatre in New York.

had impressed me enormously when I first saw it in London. But I was faintly doubtful about its American potentialities and so set sail for New York without committing myself. While mid-ocean on the *Queen Elizabeth*, I was called from London by Lee Shubert, who said that he was very enthusiastic about the play, and if I was still interested, he would be willing to put up 50 percent of the venture. That was good enough for me, and soon thereafter we went ahead with the arrangements. The author and leading members of the cast were imported, and after the usual preliminary tryout, we made our bow at the Booth Theatre. Although it was meticulously written and beautifully acted, the play was not to the American taste, as I had originally feared. We closed after just a few weeks. [*Power without Glory* was a 1947 British play about a London aristocrat who seduces his brother's fiancée and then murders a neighbor who threatens to expose the affair. Critics praised the fine cast but disparaged the melodrama, which closed after thirty-one performances.]

My last association with the Shuberts was more disastrous still. In fact, *The Starcross Story* was one of my two most magnificent flops.

The first had occurred in 1942, with *The Wife Takes a Child*, written by Phoebe and Henry Ephron, who later became prominent Hollywood writers. In the cast were Henry Hull, Evelyn Varden, and Nedda Harrigan. [*The Wife Takes a Child* is a 1942 American play about a wartime Manhattan family trying to live in a small apartment with too many family members, including a pregnant daughter-in-law who gives birth to yet another resident. The strained melodrama closed before opening in New York. Rewritten by the Ephrons as a farce and retitled *Three's a Family*, the comedy was produced on Broadway by John Golden in 1943 and ran a surprising 497 performances. The play was filmed by Hollywood as *Three Is a Family* in 1944.]

Nedda came to me one day, rather moist-eyed, with the information that she was about to be served with a subpoena. She said it would be necessary for her to leave town for a week to avoid having to accept it, missing subsequent rehearsals and perhaps even the opening. I needed her present, of course, but naturally agreed to let her go. Luck was against her, however, as it was one chance in a million that I should run into Alan Campbell, who enthusiastically described to me the wonderful week he had just spent in Miami. Dorothy Parker, his intermittent wife, had gone down to stay with him, and Nedda had gone down to stay with Josh Logan and they had a whale of a time. I like to think I behaved well because, of course, I could have had Nedda up on charges at Equity but instead settled for one quiet quip: "How were the subpoenas in Florida?" I never mentioned the matter again. [Dorothy Parker (1893–1967) was one of America's most quoted wits and a member of the celebrated Algonquin Round Table in New York. She

Joshua Logan (1908–1988) was a prominent stage and film director, and sometime playwright, who had several musical, dramatic, and comedy successes during his thirty-year career. Born in Texarkana, Texas, he studied at Princeton and with Konstantin Stanislavsky in Moscow. Logan's first solo directorial assignment on Broadway was *To See Ourselves* (1935), but it was his staging of the dark comedy *On Borrowed Time* (1938) that called attention to his talent and inaugurated a string of successes and interesting productions: *I Married an Angel* (1938), *Knickerbocker Holiday* (1938), *Stars in Your Eyes* (1939), *Morning's at Seven* (1939), *Two for the Show* (1940), *Higher and Higher* (1940), *By Jupiter* (1942), *This Is the Army* (1942), *Annie Get Your Gun* (1946), *Happy Birthday* (1946), *John Loves Mary* (1947), *Mister Roberts* (1948), *South Pacific* (1949), *The Wisteria Trees* (1950), *Wish You Were Here* (1952), *Picnic* (1953), *Fanny* (1954), *Kind Sir* (1953), *Middle of the Night* (1956), *Blue Denim* (1958), and *The World of Susie Wong* (1958). He cowrote and/or coproduced several of these.

Logan directed the screen versions of *Mister Roberts* (1955), *Picnic* (1955), *South Pacific* (1958), and *Fanny* (1961), as well as such films as *Bus Stop* (1956), *Sayonara* (1957), *Tall Story* (1960), *Camelot* (1967), and *Paint Your Wagon* (1969). At his best, his direction was distinguished by deep insight into character and remarkable fluidity, the latter especially evident in his staging of often-cumbersome musicals.

was an accomplished poet who also reviewed plays for different journals and collaborated on movie scripts. Her husband, Alan Campbell (1904–1963), was a successful screenwriter.]

As for the show, it didn't seem good enough for New York, and after careful deliberations, we closed it in Boston. Some time later, John Golden—a dean of New York's producers—bought the rights, had it rewritten into hokum farce, and managed a success where I had lost out. Nedda came out all right though, marrying Josh Logan.

Josh's theatrical record needs no recording, as he is one of the most successful producer-directors on Broadway and subsequently in film as well. His vitality, which occasionally reaches frenetic peaks, is almost unbelievable. When he is on the beam, there is no one who can surpass him at his job. I have never actually worked with him, but we have known each other personally for many years. He and Nedda lead a lavish life: lunches in their country home for forty or fifty people at one time and parties in the River House, one of the most elegant apartment buildings in New York, for as many as two hundred or more guests. Considering that Josh started out as a bit player in a Cape Cod summer theater, he has certainly done all right for himself.

But back to my really triumphant fiasco some twelve years later: *The Starcross Story* by Diana Morgan. We had done it at Westport with considerable success, and several months later, Mr. Lee Shubert suggested that we do it on Broadway. I had always liked the play, and as Shubert, his brother J. J., and a mysterious partner named Mr. Krellberg were willing to put up the money, I was happy to take the assignment.

Lee Shubert was obviously one of the great figures of the American theater. He was shrewd, canny, and a man who drove a hard bargain. In a vast office furnished with bogus Italian antiques, he sedulously occupied a small cubicle that could hardly seat three people. He liked me, I think, and I liked him. As tough as he was, he was also fair. Once he had drilled you into the arrangement he fancied and said, "That's a deal," you knew that it was. I never doubted his word, and we always operated on a handshake; I actually never had a contract with him in my life. He was a tireless worker, and his hours would have exhausted any stevedore. After a long day at his office, he would dine with his wife (usually at Le Pavillon) but afterward return to his cubicle to await the telegraphic returns of the grosses from each theater that the Shuberts owned from coast to coast. Only after the last report was in would he get into his car, which stood patiently in Shubert Alley—a private street in the theater district that they also own—and presumably go home to rest up for the next day. His dominance in the theater was unmistakable, and doing business with him was always a stimulating pleasure, even though he invariably had to have his own way.

The Starcross Story is a 1954 drama by Diana Morgan that closed on opening night on Broadway despite a superb cast. Hollywood wants to make an adventure film about heroic explorer Christian Starcross, who died, along with his crew, on a polar expedition. Even though Starcross was actually a self-centered cad, his widow Christine (Eva Le Gallienne) approves of the project, against the complaints of Starcross's mistress, Ann Meredith (Mary Astor), who wants to reveal the real Starcross. Christine prevails, and the hero's image remains untarnished. Also in the cast were Anthony Ross, Christopher Plummer, and Una O'Connor.

Wilson had directed the drama the summer before at the Westport Country Playhouse, with Le Gallienne giving a vibrant performance as Christine. Wilson brought her and Christopher Plummer to Broadway, where he, S. S. Krellberg, and the Shuberts produced *The Starcross Story*. Although the press did not think it the worst offering of the season, it closed on opening night all the same.

I was especially enthusiastic about *Starcross*, as it was to star Eva Le Gallienne, who had also done the Westport production. Her costar was Mary Astor, and there were also Anthony Ross, Christopher Plummer, Margaret Bannerman—of the London *Fallen Angels* fame—and Una O'Connor, who had been with us in *Cavalcade*. I was not only one of the producers, but also director, and my sympathetic liaison with Miss Le Gallienne came as a happy surprise. Our methods in the theater are diametrically different. She is an intellectual, an artsy personality, and I—let's face it—am more inclined toward Broadway and commercial theater. Thus, I did not expect that after doing Ibsen, Hauptmann, O'Neill, Chekhov, and Edna St. Vincent Millay, plus her two experimental repertory theaters, that we would be entirely compatible. Strangely enough, however, we saw eye to eye from the start of rehearsals. She was completely devoid of any affectation, was solidly shrewd, and gave a compelling, honest performance.

A few days before the opening, Lee Shubert died. I was one of the honorary pallbearers, along with roughly thirty others of our profession. But despite his sad and unexpected death, we decided to press on and opened *The Starcross Story* to polite, if somewhat equivocal, notices. It had been an open secret on Broadway for many years that Lee and his brother J. J. had not always seen eye to eye. They had always maintained separate offices in separate buildings, and although they jointly managed their vast empire, they were apparently not on the most amicable terms. In fact, it was rumored at the time that J. J. did not even attend his brother's funeral. I only mention this because it may be the story behind the fate of *Starcross*.

The night after we opened, I went to the theater, as is my custom on every second night. Amazingly, I found the cast pacing in the alley outside a dark house. Without warning and to the surprise and fury of us all, the play had been closed after just one performance. It was humiliating for them—a distinguished group of actors—and, for that matter, pretty humiliating for me as well. Since I was not on intimate terms with J. J. Shubert, I was never able to find out any explanation and have never been certain of the reasons behind such a sudden decision to shut down. As for the other investor, Mr. Krellberg, I have never heard of him since and trust that he returned to wherever he came from.

It was the only one-night stand I ever had.

[Wilson's track record as a producer includes several short runs, but he did quite well throughout the course of his career. Of the thirty-seven Broadway productions he produced or coproduced, fifteen were hits (meaning they made a profit). His record in London was even better. Of the seventeen West End shows he presented, thirteen were hits. Ironically, Wilson directed and others produced the two longest-running Broadway successes of his career: the musicals *Kiss Me, Kate* and *Gentlemen Prefer Blondes*.]

~

CHAPTER SIXTEEN

Cole and *Kiss Me, Kate*

Kiss Me, Kate has a particularly peculiar history. It was born in a lawyer's waiting room one afternoon, when Arnold Subber (as he was known then) happened to sit down next to Lemuel Ayers. They didn't know one another but fell into a desultory conversation. Subber had just come from a summer theater on Long Island, where they had done a musical version of *The Taming of the Shrew*, and was enthusiastic about its commercial possibilities. That same afternoon, he succeeded in convincing Lem that they should join forces and produce it on Broadway.

The problems associated with that wild idea were almost insurmountable. They had no book and no composer. But Bella Spewack was approached to do the adaptation and accepted. Before the script was completed, however, certain marital difficulties developed in the Spewack home. I know nothing of the cause, but as a sort of plum to settle one spousal disagreement, Sam Spewack was strategically created coauthor, and forthwith they collaborated in companionable felicity.

The next problem was finding a composer. They had the impertinent good taste to attempt Cole Porter, and that's where I came into the picture. Cole phoned one day to ask if I was still interested in doing a musical together. We had discussed it many times before, and he thought that perhaps *Kate* might be the one. But although he was fond of Lem and Arnold, he distrusted their lack of managerial experience and was calling to ask me to coproduce. I declined on the grounds that it would be unfair to the boys, as, in the parlance of Broadway, the show would become *mine* and they—who, after all, had created it—would

Saint Subber (1918–1994) was a successful theater producer whose hits ranged from dark dramas to tuneful musicals to Neil Simon comedies. He was born Arnold Subber, the son of ticket brokers, and grew up in Manhattan learning about different aspects of theater. After studying at New York University, Subber broke into the business as an assistant stage manager for the Broadway hit *Hellzapoppin'* (1938). The next year, he was assistant to producer John Murray Anderson, who was presenting *Billy Rose's Aquacade* at the New York World's Fair. It was while working backstage on the 1940 revival of *The Taming of the Shrew*, starring the Lunts, that Subber got the idea for a musical about a married couple squabbling during a musical version of Shakespeare's comedy. While he worked as a production assistant and other behind-the-scenes jobs, Subber made plans for producing his *Shrew* musical. Those preparations came to fruition in 1948, when he produced his first Broadway show, *Kiss Me, Kate*.

Subber's subsequent musicals included *Out of This World* (1950), *The Grass Harp* (1952), *House of Flowers* (1954), *Gigi* (1973), and *1600 Pennsylvania Avenue* (1976), none of which came close to matching the success of *Kiss Me, Kate*. Among the distinguished dramas he produced are *The Dark at the Top of the Stairs* (1957), *The Tenth Man* (1959), the 1967 revival of *The Little Foxes*, and *K2* (1983). Most memorable of the many comedies Subber presented are such early works by Simon as *Barefoot in the Park* (1963), *The Odd Couple* (1965), *Plaza Suite* (1968), *Last of the Red Hot Lovers* (1969), *The Gingerbread Lady* (1970), and *The Prisoner of Second Avenue* (1971).

Bella and Samuel Spewack were a husband-and-wife writing team most remembered for their sterling book for the musical *Kiss Me, Kate*. Samuel Spewack (1899–1971) was born in the Ukraine, raised in the United States, and served for several years as a journalist after attending Columbia University. Bella Spewack (1899–1990) was born Bella Cohen in Bucharest and raised in New York, and she was also a journalist for several New York papers and a theatrical press agent, before joining with her husband to write approximately a dozen plays or musicals that reached Broadway.

The most successful of the Spewack creations were the comedies *Poppa* (1928), *Clear All Wires* (1932), *Boy Meets Girl* (1935), and *My Three Angels* (1953). The team also wrote books for musicals, most memorably *Leave It to Me!* (1938) and *Kiss Me, Kate* (1948). On his own, Samuel wrote *Two Blind Mice* (1949) and also directed many of their plays. The Spewacks were also active in Hollywood, writing scripts for such films as *Should Ladies Behave* (1933), *The Cat and the Fiddle* (1934), *My Favorite Wife* (1940), *Week-End at the Waldorf* (1945), and *Move Over, Darling* (1963). The team was known for their satirical tone, wisecracking characters, and lively dialogue.

fade into the shadows. Instead, I made a counterproposal to take over as director. This idea was not entirely unsatisfactory to Cole, nor to Bella, who insisted that clauses be inserted in their contracts allowing me complete control of the production. This meant that I was not only to stage the show and supervise the casting, but also make all immediate and important decisions, even to the

Cole Porter (1891–1964) was one of America's most distinctive and beloved songwriters, the author of dozens of song standards written for Broadway and Hollywood. Born into a family of wealth in Peru, Indiana, he was educated at Yale and Harvard. Although he interpolated a few songs into earlier musicals, Broadway did not hear his first complete score until the short-lived *See America First* (1915). While some songs he wrote for *Hitchy-Koo* (1919) and *Greenwich Village Follies of 1924* were noticed, it was his score for *Paris* (1928) and its hit song "Let's Do It" that finally launched his career. It was followed by *Fifty Million Frenchmen* (1929), *Wake Up and Dream!* (1929), *The New Yorkers* (1930), *Gay Divorce* (1932), *Anything Goes* (1934), *Jubilee* (1935), *Red, Hot, and Blue!* (1936), *You Never Know* (1938), *Leave It to Me!* (1938), and *Du Barry Was a Lady* (1939). Porter's wartime musicals were mostly star-driven vehicles for Ethel Merman or Danny Kaye, but some superb songs could still be found in *Panama Hattie* (1940), *Let's Face It!* (1941), *Something for the Boys* (1943), *Mexican Hayride* (1944), and *Seven Lively Arts* (1944).

One of his rare flops was *Around the World in Eighty Days* (1946), followed by his biggest hit, *Kiss Me, Kate* (1948). Porter's later musicals were *Out of This World* (1950), *Can-Can* (1953), and *Silk Stockings* (1955). He had an equally successful film career. In addition to the screen versions of some of his stage musicals, he wrote original songs for the movie musicals *Born to Dance* (1936), *Rosalie* (1937), *Broadway Melody of 1940: You'll Never Get Rich* (1941), *The Pirate* (1948), *High Society* (1956), and *Les Girls* (1957). Porter's songs trafficked in a knowing, witty sophistication, and his generally silken melodies were combined with lyrics that ranged from suave and blasé to sexually obsessive. Like Noel Coward, his famous high-flying lifestyle seems to be reflected in his songs.

extent of selecting the eventual New York theater. In fact, I never invoked any of those bonus privileges but allowed the management to handle the production and confined myself to my directorial duties.

We had our casting problems, of course. Alfred Drake was obviously ideal for the male lead but recalcitrant about accepting it. In spite of his magnificent singing voice, he had temporarily developed an allergy to musicals and was only interested in important drama. At one point in our negotiations he suggested that if I could offer him an established classic, he would do it for one-third of the fantastic salary that he was asking for Kiss Me, Kate. I think he finally accepted the part solely because of the Shakespearean sequences, which he played beautifully and I'm sure were close to his heart.

The role of "Kate" presented another problem. Cole had seen a young singer on television named Patricia Morison whom he thought might be suitable. She was in Hollywood at the time, and so we telegraphed her to come to the East Coast for an audition. She was not financially able to come to New York, however, and as the producers were, quite naturally, unwilling

---

Alfred Drake (1914–1992) was a favorite leading man in 1940s and 1950s Broadway musicals and a respected classical actor as well. He was born Alfredo Capurro in New York City and studied at Brooklyn College before getting work in the chorus of Gilbert and Sullivan stock companies. Drake made his Broadway debut in the chorus of The Mikado in 1935. After playing increasingly important roles in Babes in Arms (1937), The Two Bouquets (1938), One for the Money (1939), The Straw Hat Revue (1939), and Two for the Show (1940), he won widespread recognition when he created the role of Curly in Oklahoma! (1943). He was applauded for his performances in Sing Out, Sweet Land (1944), The Beggar's Holiday (1946), The Cradle Will Rock (1947), and Joy to the World (1948), before starring as the shrew-taming Fred Graham in Kiss Me, Kate (1948).

After a brief appearance as the egotistical David Petri in The Gambler (1952), Drake scored again as the wily Hajj in Kismet (1953) and played Othello and Benedick for the American Shakespeare Festival. His most famous classical role was King Claudius opposite Richard Burton in Hamlet (1964). Drake garnered excellent notices in three failures, Kean (1961), Lorenzo (1963), and the stage version of Gigi (1973). He helped adapt several Italian plays, including The Gambler, and directed a number of shows. Curiously, the handsome actor made only three movies but appeared on several television specials and musical adaptations. Drake was the quintessential leading player, combining a superb baritone voice with exceptional acting and comic skills.

to hire her without a tryout—and also refused to pay her fare—the situation became a deadlock. It was she who solved it, however. A U.S. Air Force plane was flying an assembly of entertainers to New York for a splurge at Madison Square Garden, and she managed to include herself among the group. The cost of the trip, therefore, was picked up by the government. Pat sang the benefit that Saturday night but by ten o'clock the next morning was auditioning for the composer, the management, and me. The session was relatively brief, as she had to fly back to Hollywood that afternoon. Her unmitigated determination may have been exhausting, but it unquestionably paid off. She was hired and three weeks later returned to New York to begin rehearsals.

We started working at the Ziegfeld Roof and ended up at the Century Theatre, where the show was eventually to be housed. The usual rehearsal problems were practically nonexistent. Lem had done a beautiful collection of costumes and a group of sets that were as elegant as they were subtle. Hanya Holm's dances matched his every mood with delicacy and finesse, and established her as one of Broadway's finest choreographers. [Hanya Holm (1893–1992) also staged the dancing in other hits, for example, *Out of This World* (1950), *My Fair Lady* (1956), and *Camelot* (1960).] I certainly had no trouble cast-wise either. Pat Morison took direction with understanding and cooperation, and emerged with a glowing performance. Alfred

Patricia Morison (b. 1915) is a dark-haired beauty with blue eyes and a warbling soprano voice who spent several years in Hollywood without getting much recognition, but she triumphed on Broadway in one of the musical theater's best roles: fiery actress Lilli Vanessi playing Katharine in *Kiss Me, Kate.* She was born in New York City, the daughter of an actor and a theatrical agent, studied theater at the Arts Students League and the Neighborhood Playhouse, and was trained in dance by Martha Graham. Yet, despite this background, Morison worked as a fashion designer before going on the stage. She made her Broadway debut in 1938, before being signed to a Hollywood studio, where she made numerous films throughout the next ten years, but with little success. After touring in USO shows during World War II, Morison returned to Broadway as Kate and was roundly applauded. Much of her subsequent career was in touring musicals, as well as nightclub and television appearances, although she was on Broadway one last time in 1954, as one of the replacements for Anna in *The King and I.*

Kiss Me, Kate (1948) is an American musical comedy classic with Cole Porter's most famous stage score and one of the best musical books in the history of Broadway. The stars of the new musical version of *The Taming of the Shrew*, currently trying out in Baltimore, are egomaniac Fred Graham (Alfred Drake) and the temperamental Lilli Vanessi (Patricia Morison), who were once married but are now divorced and still bickering with one another. Lilli receives a bouquet from Fred, leading her to believe he still loves her, but when she learns the flowers are meant for the flirty Lois Lane (Lisa Kirk), she determines to get revenge by walking out on the show. Fred's problems are compounded when another member of the company, Bill Calhoun (Harold Lang), signs Fred's name to a gambling debt. Opening night is peppered by warfare between Fred and Lilli, and the demands of two comic gangsters for payment of the IOU. Fred convinces the hoods that they must force Lilli to perform to get their money, which they do, until their boss is wiped out and the IOU becomes invalid. Just as Shakespeare's Kate and Petruchio come to terms on stage, Fred and Lilli make up backstage.

Sam and Bella Spewack wrote the sparkling book, and the scintillating Porter score included such gems as "Wunderbar," "So in Love," "Always True to You in My Fashion," "Brush Up Your Shakespeare," "Too Darn Hot," and "Why Can't You Behave?" Porter's songs seem to come out of and be part of the libretto, both in the *Shrew* scenes and the backstage story. The Saint Subber–Lemuel Ayers production, directed by Wilson, was an immediate hit and went on to enjoy a run of 1,077 performances. Moreover, in the first year that the Tony Awards were given, it won the award for Best Musical. *Kiss Me, Kate* has since been revived in other venues, most recently a 1999 production that was popular on Broadway and in the West End. The 1953 movie version of *Kiss Me, Kate*, starring Howard Keel, Kathryn Grayson, and Ann Miller, took many liberties with the original script but was still enjoyable and successful. There have been television adaptations in 1958, 1964, 1967, 1968, 1975, and 2003.

Drake, although never refusing direction, had definite ideas of his own. As a matter of fact, in the middle of rehearsals I asked him to help me with the Shakespearean episodes, which he did expertly, possibly because he was the leading figure in each one. There was also Lisa Kirk, somewhat unknown and inexperienced at that point, who boomed out "Always True to You in My Fashion" and sold it to the customers like hotcakes. Harold Lang, who was certainly not inexperienced, danced with his usual alacrity and, in spite of his acting, which was on the weak side, was enormously valuable to the show. Adding it all together—plus Cole's magnificent score—*Kate* became one of the resounding musical hits of the decade. It happily proved that Lem and Arnold, despite their managerial immaturity, knew their business after all, and that I had been wise to leave them to their own devices.

[It is curious that the producers of *Kiss Me, Kate* agreed to Wilson's counterproposal to direct the musical. He had previously staged only two musicals: the 1943 revival of *A Connecticut Yankee* and the unprofitable *The Day before Spring*. Yet, the young producers chose wisely, because among the raves for *Kiss Me, Kate* were praises for Wilson's direction. William Hawkins, in the *World-Telegram*, put it most succinctly: "John C. Wilson keeps a complicated show sliding hitchlessly along and has toned the performances with a smooth ease that makes the rambunctious plot all the more effective." The runaway success of *Kiss Me, Kate* quickly put Wilson in the top ranks of Broadway directors, and he was offered many musicals during the next four or five years.]

It was during the tryout in Philadelphia that Arnold decided to change his name. It was a complicated process in some respects, because he was already billed on the out-of-town program as Arnold Subber. But he felt that a more suitable name was necessary in view of his new position in the theater. It turned out that during an early apprenticeship with John Murray Anderson—who was notorious for his ironic and often vitriolic nicknames—Arnold had been called "Saint" because of Murray's conviction that he was born of the devil. There is even a rumor that Murray forced him to walk around with a bell fastened around his neck. This nomenclature was apparently not all that upsetting, for in Philadelphia his billing suddenly changed to Arnold *Saint* Subber. Then Cole stepped in and subtly suggested that "Arnold" was a rather common name and recommended that he drop it. And so at last the confusion was resolved—and he's been known as Saint Subber ever since. Actually, Cole's concern regarding Saint's name was rather unlike him, and I'm not sure to this day that he really cared one way or the other.

I first met Cole Porter in the 1920s, when he was socially prominent but theatrically unknown. He was living with his exquisite wife Linda, who had one of the most beautiful houses in Paris. She was—as Anita Loos would have phrased it—"loaded, darling." At that point, Cole had no intention of becoming a commercial composer. Only on a private whim would he slip off to the piano after lunch to turn out some of the best songs he had ever written. His disinterest in monetary compensation was such that after dashing off a relatively important song, he would simply give it to a singer in one of the Montmartre boîtes that he frequently patronized or, more often than not, Elsa Maxwell, who would invariably claim that she had written it herself. In those days, he even had an aversion to the lyrics being written down. I can still see Linda sitting behind a handsome Coromandel screen in their music room, scribbling away as fast as she could while Cole amused himself with his latest chef d'oeuvre. In later years, he was to change his views about money and became one of the highest-paid composers in the business.

Cole—as almost everyone already knows—is a very rich man. He not only inherited large sums from his family, who owned endless acreage in Indiana, but also received a considerable fortune upon Linda's death, which saddened us all. Then, of course, there are his royalties from Broadway, Hollywood, phonograph records, and what are known as "subsidiary rights," which combine to bring him a significant income, making touching principal totally unnecessary. And, alas, to add to his financial comfort, one of the largest natural gas deposits in the United States was discovered on the Indiana property. [Wilson and Porter had known one another for more than twenty years, especially during Wilson's visits to Venice and Paris, and with their wives they had often vacationed throughout the world together. Linda Porter and Natasha Wilson were close friends, and Linda, who died in 1954, even left Natasha some of her one-of-a-kind Cartier jewels. A portrait of Natasha painted by Pavel Tchelitchew hung in the Porters's Manhattan apartment.]

At the moment Cole maintains three establishments. For years, he has kept a charming Hollywood pied-à-terre to use when he's there. But there is a story concerning the other two properties. Linda bought a huge old-fashioned house in Williamstown, Massachusetts, where she installed her famous collection of French furniture. She later had another home built on the grounds for Cole's personal use—on the modern side, with its own swimming pool—where he could play the piano all night long without disturbing her. As she was never very well, this was a wise and convenient arrangement. But after she died, Cole made some extensive alterations to his real-estate life. In Williamstown, he tore down the original house and had his own relocated in its place. In New York, he rented, on a long-term lease, the Presidential Suite at the Waldorf Towers, which he had redecorated at a fabulous price. Linda's fine furniture and objets d'art were moved there, and the ensemble totals what is certainly the most extraordinary apartment in Manhattan. The pity is that with so many lovely houses, he is naturally unable to spend much time at any one of them. But more unfortunate still is his personal tragedy, which success and wealth could not allay.

It was in 1937 that Cole suffered a terrible accident from which he never fully recovered. While staying at a house party on Long Island, he was persuaded to join the other guests for a morning ride through the woods of the Piping Rock Club. His mount turned out to be the friskiest horse in the stable and, during the course of the outing, got out of hand, fell, and rolled on top of Cole. This turned out to be more than just a matter of broken bones and included a severance of the nerves in both legs. It led to innumerable operations and forced him to be bedridden for many, many months. His gallantry and fortitude during this period were amazing. A piano was constructed to fit over his bed, and even while in acute pain, he turned out some of his best scores, including *You Never Know* and *Leave It to Me*. He not only never mentioned his illness, but also refused to allow any visitor to mention it. Many years later, during the rehearsals for *Kate*, Cole would arrive each day with the inevitable pink carnation but required the help of a walking stick and a personal attendant to guide him up and down the aisles. He was always chipper and amiable, but the lingering effects of the accident were still palpably evident. [Porter continued to suffer from pain, and following a series of operations, his right leg was amputated in 1958, after which time he became a recluse, mainly living in his Waldorf Towers apartment until his death in 1964.]

It was inevitable during our long run of *Kiss Me, Kate* on Broadway that there should be a road company to fulfill the out-of-town demand. It was here that Edwin Lester, the West Coast entrepreneur, stepped in with the suggestion that the new company be formed in California. His plan was to book it in the Los Angeles Philharmonic for five or six weeks and then send it on to the Curran Theatre in San Francisco for a similar engagement. The deal was accepted, and off we went—Lem, Saint, Hanya, myself, and even Cole—to work an entirely new cast into the already-familiar pattern. We were fortunate to be able to obtain Anne Jeffreys, who turned in a beautiful performance as Kate, and Keith Andes, who was excellent in the role originally created by Alfred Drake. Marc Platt played the dancing juvenile, and there was also a little soubrette named Julie Wilson, who would go on to have a successful career. [Julie Wilson (b. 1924) has appeared in numerous musicals in New York, on tour, and throughout the country but is most known for her cabaret and nightclub appearances.] Rehearsals followed virtually the same format as we had used in New York, and our labors proved well worthwhile. The opening in Los Angeles was triumphant; to me, it seemed even better than in New York. There was a warmth and response from the audience that must have inspired the cast to special heights. We left the theater tired but happy, Cole to his luxurious Brentwood home and the rest of us to our various hotels.

After more than two years of this double-company run, we began to make certain changes. Jack Hylton, an important London producer, had bought *Kiss Me, Kate* for the Coliseum there, and I was again asked to direct it. There were some difficulties reaching an agreement, however. I had neglected to insert in my original contract that my fee for any London engagement would automatically be equivalent to my New York percentage. Lem Ayers took advantage of this oversight and insisted that as it was my third job on *Kate*, I should settle for half of my previous royalty. I must say that Jack Hylton was for me all the way, but Lem was firm and I was firmer, and in consequence the London version was directed by Sam Spewack, who had the courtesy and good manners to have my original production acknowledged in the playbill.

This new situation, of course, involved an exchange of stars. Pat Morison elected to throw in her lot with the London company, and Anne Jeffreys replaced her in New York. Julie Wilson also voted for London, which turned out wisely for her, as she became a favorite there. She was followed in New York by Betty George, a buxom, ebullient performer who made up in vitality what she lacked in experience. Alfred Drake had long since bowed out. Keith Andes had been reclaimed by the movies—mostly owing to his success in *Kate*—and Robert Wright, who had done the backers auditions years before, came into his own and finally clinched the part of Petruchio. Bill Johnson, a newcomer to the show, was engaged for the London production and built up an impressive following for himself there, too. As I was in England at the time, I went to the final performance at the Coliseum. The audience hysteria over Patricia, Julie, and Bill was so great that the management added an extra performance to give their fans a chance to see them one last time. [*Kiss Me, Kate* opened at the London Coliseum in 1951 and ran for 501 performances.]

And with this climax, the saga of a very fine musical was ended.

CHAPTER SEVENTEEN

~

Anita, Carol, and
Gentlemen Prefer Blondes

During the preliminary proceedings of *Gentlemen Prefer Blondes*, the Lunts decided to do a production of *I Know My Love*, which was adapted by S. N. Behrman from Marcel Achard's *Aupres De Ma Blonde*. The sets, lighting, and costumes were done by Stewart Chaney, and Alfred—to nobody's surprise—directed. It was a rather interesting play; I suppose one might have even called it "experimental." For one thing, it was played backward. At the opening, Alfred and Lynn played a devoted couple celebrating their fiftieth wedding anniversary, and the story retrogressed through majestic sequences until the final scene, which showed their adolescent courtship. It was a tour de force of acting and makeup. The cast would rush to their dressing rooms between scenes to reorganize their grease paint in an assiduous effort to grow younger and younger as the evening progressed.

The play had been a huge success in Paris but apparently caused considerable confusion among American audiences when it opened in San Francisco. The problem was serious enough that Sam Behrman phoned me and threatened to leave unless I came immediately. So, of course, I went. We had a series of endless conferences late into the night. Alfred, Lynn, Sam, and I finally decided that perhaps the show would be more comprehensible if we played it forward instead of backward. This substantially altered the makeup schedule, but as always, the Lunts took it in stride and in no time at all were enthusiastically growing older instead of younger. Unfortunately, our major operation was far from successful, and by the time we opened in New York at the Shubert Theatre, we had reverted to playing it backward again. There

I Know My Love is a 1949 comedy by S. N. Behrman based on Marcel Achard's French play *Aupres de Ma Blonde*. Thomas (Alfred Lunt) and Emily Chanler (Lynn Fontanne) are celebrating their fiftieth wedding anniversary with family and friends, but there is tension in the air because their granddaughter (Betty Caulfield) wishes to marry, against her parents' wishes. The scene shifts back half a century to when Tom and Emily were wooing and defying their elders in marrying. Scenes from the past reveal that the couple has weathered many crises in their marriage, and they reach their golden anniversary as proud survivors. Behrman adapted the French comedy as a vehicle for the Lunts, who were celebrating their twenty-five years together on the stage with this production. Some critics carped about the script, but audiences kept the play on the boards as long as the Lunts stayed with it, for 246 performances. The Theatre Guild and Wilson coproduced *I Know My Love*, and it was directed by Lunt.

Anita Loos (1893–1981) was a screenwriter, playwright, and novelist who is most known for *Gentlemen Prefer Blondes*, one of the greatest comic novels in American literature. She was born in Sisson, California, the daughter of two newspaper writers, and grew up in San Francisco. By the time she was four years old, Loos was acting on stage, but as she grew up she was more attracted to writing, penning her first screenplays as a teenager. In 1912, she was hired as a scriptwriter for the Biograph Film Company, and during the next three years, she wrote more than 100 scenarios for the company. In 1915, Loos began working with D. W. Griffith and wrote feature films for such stars as Douglas Fairbanks and Lillian Gish. By the 1920s, she was one of the highest-paid writers in Hollywood and nationally known for her articles in *Vanity Fair* and other magazines.

Gentlemen Prefer Blondes began as a series of stories in *Harper's Bazaar*. When they were published in book form in 1925, the collection became a surprise best-seller and has remained in print ever since. Loos wrote several subsequent books, including the sequel *But Gentlemen Marry Brunettes* (1928), many nonfiction works, and three autobiographies. She continued writing screenplays into the 1940s. Although Loos spent much of her career in Hollywood, she was represented on Broadway with a handful of plays, most notably *The Whole Town's Talking* (1923), *Happy Birthday* (1946), and her dramatization of Colette's novel *Gigi* (1951). She contributed to both the play version and the musical version of her *Gentlemen Prefer Blondes* in 1926 and 1949.

was a fine cast, including Geoffrey Kerr, whom the Lunts had imported from London, as well as Betty Caulfield, Esther Mitchell, and Katharine Bard. The play was only moderately received by the critics. Yet, due to the Lunts' popularity, we managed to run the full season.

I became involved with *Gentlemen Prefer Blondes* through Anita Loos, who had written the original book. I had never met, let alone worked for, producer Herman Levin, although I did know his business partner, scenic designer–producer Oliver Smith. But because of Anita's suggestion—plus my recent success with *Kiss Me, Kate*—I was engaged as director.

Anita was an extraordinary person and a rare friend. The word *petite* must have been invented for her, as she looks like a tiny sixteen-year-old child, which, according to records, she couldn't possibly be. She started her career in Hollywood, writing silent pictures for such luminaries as Lillian Gish, Mary Pickford, and many others of that historic era. Somewhere along the line, she elected to marry a distinguished man named John Emerson, who is now deceased. It was with John that I first met Anita at Cole Porter's house

---

Gentlemen Prefer Blondes is a 1926 comedy by Anita Loos and John Emerson based on the best-selling comic novel by Loos. Lorelei Lee (June Walker), a gold-digging blonde from Little Rock, Arkansas, has her expenses paid by a rich button manufacturer, Gus Eisman (Arthur S. Ross). He even sends Lorelei and her friend Dorothy (Edna Hibbard) to Europe, where Lorelei wangles a tiara from an English lord and dates dashing young Henry Spofford (Frank Morgan). When she learns that Spofford may be richer than Eisman, she plans to dump Eisman. By that time, however, Dorothy has claimed Spofford.

The Edgar Selwyn production capitalized on the book and the current Roaring Twenties setting, and the comedy ran for 199 performances. The story became a popular musical of the same title in 1949, with a book by Loos and Joseph Fields, lyrics by Leo Robin, and music by Jule Styne. The score included three song favorites: "A Little Girl from Little Rock," "Bye Bye Baby," and "Diamonds Are a Girl's Best Friend." The Herman Levin and Oliver Smith production, directed by Wilson, ran for 740 performances and made Carol Channing, who played Lorelei, a Broadway star. Yvonne Adair was Dorothy, Jack McCauley was Gus, and Eric Brotherson was Spofford. The musical has been successfully revived both in its original version and a revised version with Channing called *Lorelei* (1974). On screen, *Gentlemen Prefer Blondes* was a silent film in 1928, with Ruth Taylor as Lorelei, and the musical was filmed in 1953, with Marilyn Monroe as the heroine.

in Paris. It was just after the publication of the book of Blondes, and she was one of the most talked about authors of the moment.

To this day, Anita is an indefatigable worker, rising at five or six in the morning and writing until lunch time. She goes on turning out plays and articles at a profligate rate—witness Happy Birthday and Gigi, two of her latest Broadway successes—and is usually working on at least three plays at a time. She doesn't drink or smoke and lives simply in a large apartment in New York opposite Carnegie Hall, where she is sedulously attended to by a devoted housekeeper named Gladys. Gladys is more than a servant, however; she is a companion and friend, and Anita never travels without her. We always get postcards—from a boat, from Paris, Montecatini, Rome, or some other exotic locale—explaining how Gladys' social successes have been far more impressive than Anita's, although that is difficult to believe.

[For Wilson's version of the casting of Carol Channing as Lorelei, see the prologue. According to Channing's autobiography, it was coproducer Smith who approached her during intermission at a summer theater on Long Island and offered her the role. After Channing had been cast, Wilson and Natasha

---

Carol Channing (b. 1921) remains one of Broadway's favorite comediennes, a tall, blonde performer whose voice runs the gamut from babyish squeals to baritone. She was born in Seattle, raised in San Francisco, and educated at Bennington College, before going to New York. While she understudied and played small roles, Channing developed her stage persona in nightclubs, singing songs with a broad naiveté as she flashed her giant smile and opened her round eyes from beneath her bleached-blonde wig. She first gained attention when she appeared in the Broadway musical revue Lend an Ear (1948), where her superb comedic talents flourished, most notably as a wildly energetic chorus girl in a spoof of 1920s musicals. She consolidated her reputation when she essayed the role of Lorelei Lee in the musical Gentlemen Prefer Blondes (1949).

In 1954, Channing succeeded Rosalind Russell in Wonderful Town and then appeared in the title role of The Vamp (1955), as well as in Show Girl (1961), an intimate revue designed around her talents. Her greatest success was as the pushy Dolly Levi in Hello, Dolly! (1964), a role she would return to throughout her career, with extensive tours and Broadway returns in 1978 and 1995. She also returned to the character of Lorelei Lee for Lorelei (1974), a revised version of Gentlemen Prefer Blondes. Channing made only a handful of movies but was a familiar face on television, appearing on series and specials.

invited her to Pebbles for a party, in which the Lunts were also present. Channing soon found herself in a quiet room with the Lunts, who quizzed her about her ideas for the character of Lorelei. After the conversation, the Lunts went back to the party and informed Smith that they were going to invest in *Gentlemen Prefer Blondes*. During the rehearsals, Channing admits, "Jack and I never got close, but we drained each other's talents dry." Just as Wilson writes that Channing was a delight to direct, she states, "Jack Wilson really did have great taste. He staged 'A Little Girl from Little Rock,' 'Bye Bye Baby,' and 'Diamonds' and all my songs. . . . Agnes de Mille, our choreographer, refused to touch anything to do with me. She said to Jack Wilson, 'Anyone who tinkers with Carol's concept of Lorelei's walk, talk, dance, song, or pantomime is a fool.'" Channing also describes Wilson's theatrical sense: "Jack Wilson insisted they buy a black velvet curtain to go behind me during 'Diamonds.' They originally had a busy ocean liner scene. Well, that black curtain made every thought, every flicker of an eyelash stand out like a neon sign. . . . I wish I had told John C. Wilson how I appreciated him and how I felt he helped the audience appreciate the show."]

At Carol's gentle insistence, we engaged Yvonne Adair for *Blondes*. She had been with her as a cast member in *Lend An Ear*, and she later graduated to become the "orchid queen" of North Jersey due to her marriage to Harold Patterson, the "orchid king." We also had Alice Pearce, as brilliant a comedienne as she was sweet, and Jack McCauley, as charming as he was debonair. Agnes de Mille's dances and Jule Styne's music were superb, and Oliver Smith did wonderful sets. Miles White was engaged to do the clothes. There is no question but that his contribution was of enormous value to the show. He was ably assisted by a young gentleman named Frank Thompson, who claimed to be a Cherokee Indian and later became a successful designer in his own right. [Thompson went on to design costumes for twenty-six Broadway shows, including *The Little Hut* (1953), for Wilson.]

Rehearsals progressed with a reasonable amount of regular irregularity. Herman Levin was one of the nicest men whom I have ever worked for and had a habit that other producers would be wise to copy. He would arrive at the theater after an obviously comfortable lunch and, puffing on a huge cigar, ask, "Is everything all right?" or "Is there anything you want?" or "Can I do anything for you?" Having been properly reassured on all points, he would slap me on the back and say, "Well, all right then, I'll see you tomorrow!" and vanish from the theater. He was a director's dream.

We had some trouble after the first run-through. Naturally, we were all in a state of the jitters. I was standing in a corner with Agnes de Mille, waiting for the inevitable conference, when she spotted producer Billy Rose approaching

Herman Levin (1907–1990) was an esteemed Broadway producer who presented a diverse range of plays and musicals. He was born in Philadelphia and educated at the University of Pennsylvania, the University of Missouri, and St. John's University Law School for a legal career. Instead of practicing law, Levin joined Mayor Fiorello La Guardia's administration in the mid-1930s and advanced to become director of the Bureau of Licenses in the Welfare Department. He left city politics in 1946, when he coproduced the Broadway musical revue *Call Me Mister* and the Sartre drama *No Exit*. In 1949, he produced the popular musical version of *Gentlemen Prefer Blondes*, but his greatest success came when he presented *My Fair Lady* (1956). The drama *The Great White Hope* (1968) was his only subsequent hit. Among Levin's other Broadway productions were *Richard III* (1949), *Bless You All* (1950), *The Girl Who Came to Supper* (1963), *Lovely Ladies, Kind Gentlemen* (1970), and *Tricks* (1973).

us and murmured, "If he makes one single suggestion, I'll scream the place down and leave." [Billy Rose (1899–1966) was a colorful showman and theater owner who wrote songs and presented everything from classy Broadway musicals, to "Aquacades," to girlie shows.] Sure enough, he had quite a list of suggestions. Needled by Agnes' preliminaries, I turned to the great Mr. Rose and asked, "Are you speaking as the owner of this theater or as the producer of the Diamond Horseshoe?" He drew himself up to what I presume was his full height and replied, "I am speaking as a man who's made a million dollars in the theater." It was only later that I discovered, to my great embarrassment, that Herman had personally invited him to make comments on the performance, and I think, taken all in all, that I really behaved very badly. Oddly enough, after this set-to, Mr. Rose and I healed the breach. He used to invite me for coffee—to which he was passionately addicted—in that famous and capacious office where I had first met Ziegfeld.

In any case, *Gentlemen Prefer Blondes* was a hit and made Carol a star. Herman gave a magnificent party at the St. Regis Roof, with bands galore and the entire theatrical profession present. Noel was there too, and I was deeply touched when he turned to me and said, "That show is a hit, and there are two fundamental reasons. First, Carol Channing, and second, you." However fundamental the reasons may have been, Noel was right, and we ran for two years. [Anita Loos, in one of her autobiographies, explains that Wilson was chosen to direct *Gentlemen Prefer Blondes* because "he had directed *Present Laughter* and was geared to put the most exquisite taste into a show that was basically rowdy."]

Soon after *Blondes*, Herman and Oliver again engaged me to stage a revue called *Bless You All*. The songs were by Harold Rome and the skits by Arnold Auerbach. Oliver, of course, did the sets and Miles White the costumes—and extremely varied they were. I can recall one specific sequence in which the girls descended an elaborate staircase with champagne glasses miraculously adhered to their bosoms and bunches of grapes you know where. The choreographer was Helen Tamiris, whose favorite dancer, Valerie Bettis, took up most of her attention. We had a good, solid cast, including Jules Munshin, who had scored an enormous hit in Herman's first revue, *Call Me Mister*, the inimitable Mary McCarty, and the unpredictable Pearl Bailey, who would implore me for direction and then totally disregard it. Although her material was relatively set, one could never be quite sure what lyrics Pearl was going to sing or how she was going to sing them. Accurate or inaccurate, however, she's a fine artist. I sometimes got the impression during performances that the audiences preferred her improved lyrics to those written by the authors.

Herman booked the show at the Mark Hellinger Theatre, which I felt was a great mistake. The theater is so vast that I think I'm right in saying that the only show that ever filled it solidly, completely, and night after night was Herman's subsequent production, *My Fair Lady*. In any case, *Bless You All* was greeted with amiable notices, and we limped along to three-quarter houses, which would have been capacity in any ordinary New York theater. But perhaps because of the overhead, or the lack of public interest, or whatever other factors the management could blame, it was not a huge success, and after a reasonable number of months, we stumbled out.

[By 1950, Wilson was no longer involved with Noel Coward's finances or management, but he still took an active part in the Englishman's career.

Bless You All was a 1950 topical musical revue by Arnold Auerbach (sketches) and Harold Rome (music and lyrics) that boasted a superior cast. The material may have been suspect, but the performers were first rate. Jules Munshin, Mary McCarty, and Pearl Bailey provided the comedy in songs and sketches; the ballads were handled by Byron Palmer; and the featured dancers included Donald Saddler and Valerie Bettis. Among the topics spoofed were Peter Pan, Tennessee Williams, and politics, the last being the source of a production number that showed how campaigns in the future will be held on television. The critics were not impressed with either the skits or the score but applauded the fine cast, and the revue ran for eight weeks. Herman Levin and Oliver Smith coproduced the revue, which was directed by Wilson.

That year, Richard Rodgers used his friendship with Wilson to try and make a deal for Coward to play the King of Siam in *The King and I*, with his childhood pal Gertrude Lawrence. Wilson worked up a lucrative deal for Coward, but the master hated long runs and Rodgers and Hammerstein's musicals ran forever, so he turned down the role. Five years later, history repeated itself, when Alan Jay Lerner asked Wilson to try and get Coward to play Henry Higgins in their planned musical of *Pygmalion*. Wilson again interceded, but Coward turned down the role. How the history of *The King and I* and *My Fair Lady*, not to mention Coward's career, would have been altered if he had agreed to either part.]

~

CHAPTER EIGHTEEN

Television

When I was asked the next year to stage a new musical called *Make a Wish*, I was naturally intrigued by the general setup. The producers were Harry Rigby, Jule Styne, and Alex Cohen. The star was Nanette Fabray. It was written by Preston Sturges, based on Molnar's *The Good Fairy*, with music and lyrics by Hugh Martin, dances by Gower Champion, and settings and clothes by Raoul Pene Du Bois. It also featured Harold Lang, Melville Cooper, and Helen Gallagher. One would have reasonably assumed that with such a lineup, a hit would be almost inevitable; however, many difficulties arose to disturb the calm of our voyage. During the tryout in Philadelphia, Mr. Sturges returned to Hollywood in a huff concerning alterations in his script, and we were forced to recruit other authors, whose names unfortunately escape me, to patch it up. [Abe Burrows and Anita Loos worked on the script, but only Sturges was credited in the program.] Their repairs were not very successful. When we opened at the Winter Garden in New York, the notices were tepid and the public reaction equally apathetic. In spite of Nanette and her impressive cohorts, we lasted only two or three months, as I recall.

I managed to achieve, through my association with H. M. Tennent, Ltd., the American rights to two enormous European successes: *Nina* and *The Little Hut*. Every producer in New York was attempting to snare these two properties, but, unfortunately, I won the game—unfortunately, because in spite of their European acclaim, they turned out to be disastrous failures in the United States.

Make a Wish is a 1951 Broadway musical comedy based on Ferenc Molnar's 1931 Hungarian play *The Good Fairy* and the 1935 film version written by Preston Sturges. When French orphan Janette (Nanette Fabray) grows too big for the orphanage, she goes to Paris, where she encounters a host of colorful characters, including raffish millionaire Marius Frigo (Melville Cooper), who tries to seduce her but ends up helping Janette and struggling artist Paul Dumont (Stephen Douglass) get together.

Also featured in the cast were Harold Lang and Helen Gallagher. *Make a Wish* drew from both the original play and the movie to write the musical's book, but critics found it lacking, just as the songs by Hugh Martin failed to impress. Wilson directed the fine cast, which were were highly praised, as was the choreography by newcomer Gower Champion, and *Make a Wish* managed to run for three months.

The first was André Roussin's Parisian hit *Nina*, adapted by Samuel Taylor. Alan Webb, David Niven, and—to my initial delight—Gloria Swanson were all engaged for this amour à trois. Gregory Ratoff, an old friend of Miss Swanson's, took over the direction; Charles Elson designed the set; and the usual preliminaries began. In Boston, we became aware of the first rumbles of disaster. After several skirmishes at lunches with Gloria—during which she prescribed endless diets for better health and improved regularity—she summoned Gregory and me to her suite one morning. We arrived to find her sitting on a sofa, dressed like a Chinese empress, and without undue hesitation,

Nina is a 1949 French comedy by André Roussin that was a success in Paris but failed in New York in 1951. Parisian hypochondriac Adolphe (Alan Webb) is fed up with his wife Nina (Gloria Swanson) and her longtime affair with Gerard (David Niven), so he goes to Gerard's apartment to shoot him. Instead he comes down with a nasty cold, Gerard pampers him in his illness, and the two men become close friends, even considering poisoning Nina so that they could be rid of her. To the contrary, Gerard is involved in a traffic accident, and Nina and Adolphe are reunited to nurse him back to health.

Samuel Taylor adapted the French comedy, but except for compliments for Webb, the reviewers had little good to say about it. Even with Hollywood stars Swanson and Niven in the cast, *Nina* closed after five weeks. Wilson produced the comedy with H. M. Tennent, Ltd., and it was directed by Gregory Ratoff.

Gloria Swanson (1899–1983) was one of Hollywood's biggest stars during the silent era, and she continued to act in talkies, on Broadway, and on television into the 1980s. She was born in Chicago, but because her father was in the military, Swanson mostly grew up in Puerto Rico. She quit school at the age of fifteen and worked as an extra in movies until she started getting featured parts and then leading roles. Under the direction of Cecil B. DeMille, she became a major star and the very image of a glamorous screen icon. Among her many popular silent films are *Male and Female* (1919), *The Affairs of Anatole* (1931), *The Love of Sunya* (1927), *Sadie Thompson* (1928), and *Queen Kelly* (1929).

Swanson's popularity waned with the advent of sound movies, but she still made a few talkies, none more famous than *Sunset Boulevard* (1950), in which she plays a faded silent-screen star much like herself. She acted in five Broadway plays, *A Goose for the Gander* (1945), *Bathsheba* (1947), *Twentieth Century* (1950), *Nina* (1951), and *Butterflies Are Free* (1969), and made many television appearances. Swanson was an exotic beauty known for her lavish clothes and many love affairs, but she was also an eccentric, volatile personality who retained a grande dame attitude throughout her life.

---

we were emphatically informed that she would not continue under Gregory's direction any longer and wanted me to take over. Gregory, being Russian, promptly burst into a flood of tears and reminded her of their intimate friendship and his financial kindness during the lean periods of her histrionic past. Gloria, however, was a wisp of steel, as I soon began to discover for myself. She firmly stuck to her point, and that afternoon I took over the rehearsals.

Unfortunately, there seemed to be little improvement under my guidance, and Gloria must have felt the same way. Two weeks later, when I arrived at a rehearsal in Philadelphia, there sat Constance Collier, who had been imported to Boston and retained by our star to see what she could do to save the performance. Constance was at first conscientious about her assignment, but her efforts turned out on the negligible side. In fact, her major contribution was provided by her predilection to smoking cigarettes through a veil. One afternoon, she galvanized the cast by bursting into flames in the middle of a run-through. Luckily, her faithful assistant, Phyllis Wilbourn, was on hand to extinguish the blaze and the rehearsal resumed—without the further benefit of Constance, who left the theater slightly charred and majestically returned to New York.

About a week later, Gloria blew her top and made one of the greatest theatrical "goofs" of all time. Without consulting me, she announced to the New York press, the Associated Press, and United Press International that she hated her part and was only doing the play under managerial duress. At once, I received innumerable letters from my backers urging me to close the show immediately and not attempt to bring it to New York following the bad publicity that Miss Swanson had gratuitously given it. I disregarded their advice, however, because we had already sold forty or fifty benefit nights at the Royale Theatre, and it seemed that with this backing it might pull through.

Opening night was pretty close to torture. It was apparent that *Nina* was being poorly received, although Alan gave a magnificent performance as the husband, and David, as the lover, was absolutely charming. But Miss Swanson was brittle and sharp, which somehow compensated for her total lack of technique. To add to her other first-night problems was the unfortunate fact that Gloria had insisted on designing her own costumes, and during the performance one of these creations started to behave in a frankly eccentric fashion. Shortly after her first entrance, a wire stay sprang from the bodice of her gown and hit her smack in the face. With amazing aplomb she immediately stuffed it back into its intended haven and continued the performance. But alas, her handiwork outwitted her again. Five minutes later, the wire whipped up from below and again hit her in the face, only this time a little more sharply. Of course, by now the audience was in complete hysterics, and the scene was ruined.

It couldn't have mattered less, however, as the play never got off the ground. We left the theater with the fateful knowledge of what the next day's notices would be and were all too right. I could have written them myself. During the ensuing weeks, supported entirely by reluctant benefits, Alan and David managed to endear themselves to the audiences. But I don't think they endeared themselves to Miss Swanson, because on the last night—although I dutifully went to see her—Alan and David walked out of the theater without even a "good-bye"!

The second of these European disappointments came in 1953. It was called *The Little Hut* and had run in London for about three years. There was a distinguished group of people responsible for its production there: the author, again André Roussin; the adapter, Nancy Mitford; and Oliver Messel, who did the superb décor; however, the only one we brought to New York was the original director, Peter Brook. Peter was considered by many to be a very talented young man, which his record in Stratford-on-Avon and the English theater in general undoubtedly proved. But I'm afraid that on this particular safari he spent more time in the National Gallery in Washington

The Little Hut is a 1947 French comedy by André Roussin that played in London with success but failed on Broadway. When Philip (Robert Morley), his wife Susan (Joan Tetzel), and her lover Henry (David Tomlinson) are shipwrecked on an island, they are very sophisticated about it all and decide to share the woman equally. When a brawny stranger enters the picture, the wife is smitten with him, thinking he is a native prince of the island, but he turns out to be the cook from their sunken ship. It looks as if he will also share the wife, but the quartet is rescued and returns to civilization.

British novelist Nancy Mitford adapted the satirical commentary on human relationships, and it was a hit in Paris, where it ran for more than 1,500 performances, and in London, where it ran for three years. But *The Little Hut* lasted less than a month on Broadway. Peter Brook directed both the West End and New York productions. Robert Morley was the star of the 1950 London production and largely responsible for its success. The 1953 Broadway version, produced by Wilson and H. M. Tennent, Ltd., featured Roland Culver, Anne Vernon, and Colin Gordon as the trio, and they could not generate the kind of reviews needed to sell the oddball comedy. Despite its short American run, *The Little Hut* was made into a movie by Hollywood in 1957, with Ava Gardner, Stewart Granger, and David Niven as the trio.

Peter Brook (b. 1925) is an internationally acclaimed theater director who found fame for his innovative interpretations of the classics and continued to experiment with world theater. London born and educated at Oxford, he established himself as a major British director with his productions for the Royal Shakespeare Company, in particular his dynamic *Marat/Sade* (1964) and minimalist *A Midsummer Night's Dream* (1970). Both productions were successes on Broadway, as was *The Visit* (1950), in which the Lunts gave their final performances. Other New York productions directed by Brook include *The Little Hut* (1953), *House of Flowers* (1954), *The Fighting Cock* (1959), *Irma La Douce* (1960), *The Physicists* (1964), *The Conference of the Birds* (1980), *La Tragedie de Carmen* (1984), *The Mahabharata* (1987), *The Man Who* (1995), and revivals of *The Cherry Orchard* in 1988 and *Hamlet* in 2001.

In 1970, Brook cofounded the Centre Internationale de Créations Théâtrales, a Paris-based company comprised of actors from throughout the world, and he has been active with the company ever since. He has directed the film versions of some of his stage productions, as well as such movies as *The Beggar's Opera* (1953), *Lord of the Flies* (1963), and *Meetings with Remarkable Men* (1979). Brook is author of seven books about theater and the recipient of numerous international awards and honors.

enjoying their admirable collection than concentrating on the frenetic futility of our efforts with *The Little Hut*. I expect he was bored to death with it by then anyway.

It seems that most French comedies are invariably based on the fundamental formula of amour à trois, and this play was no exception. Three people are marooned on a desert island: a husband, a wife, and another gentleman, who turns out to be the madame's lover of long standing. The eventual solution was reasonable and natural enough. They would share her favors on alternate occasions, with the odd man out sulking. This sounds very wicked, of course, but as directed it was actually as harmless as *Alice in Wonderland*. Robert Morley had played the husband in London, and during its long run there, the play virtually became known for his performance. But he refused to come to the United States for tax reasons, and I frankly think we suffered by his absence. We had an excellent trio in New York, with Roland Culver, Anne Vernon, and Colin Gordon, but the local audiences were not sufficiently attracted, and what had been a three-year run in London went out of office in just three weeks on Broadway.

That same year, I elected to have a shot at television. The idea was put to me by Lester Shurr, another of New York's important agents. I accepted the terms he arranged and found myself with the Kudner Agency, a vast organization with many departments handling, supervising, and promoting every aspect of the amusement business. My particular assignment was called *The Buick Circus Hour*, and it must have cost the sponsors a pretty penny. We not only had a ballet and a singing chorus, but also an entire menagerie of live animals, frequently including lions, tigers, and elephants. Our resident stars were Dolores Gray, John Raitt, and Joe E. Brown. Various shows also featured special guests the likes of Milton Berle, Bert Lahr, and Ed Wynn. Stars or guest stars notwithstanding, those huge, smelly elephants stole the show. I've directed some difficult theatrical personalities in my time, but they were the toughest. We even paid some of the show girls extra money to ride on their trunks—a feat that always fascinated me but one that I never had nerve enough to try myself.

The job was deceptive. I had a producing-directing contract and was to be paid for each show. But they aired only once a month, and each show required an entire month of preparation. The first three weeks were spent selecting songs, discussing material with authors, planning ballets with the choreographer, and trying to formulate an overall plan. I was given every courtesy and support by the head of Kudner's television department, Myron Kirk, who always seemed to have headaches and inevitable ulcers. He assigned me their top cameraman and technical advisor, Mann Holliner—an old-timer in show business who knew every trick of the trade and, more valuable than that, every song ever written. We worked together in great harmony and became close friends.

I invented a regular sequence for the show that featured old songs done in period, for instance, "By the Sea," "Row, Row, Row," "In the Good Old Summertime," and other numbers of that ilk. Some of them were sung by the stars with or without the chorus, some danced by the ballet. It was far and away the outstanding feature of the program. The sponsors thought so highly of it, in fact, that I was flown to Detroit in one of their private planes to attend a dinner presided over by the top-flight executives of the company. Their special praise was not for the script, not for the tigers, and not even for the stars. It was for the nostalgic musical sequences. They liked them even better than the elephants.

After the three weeks of preparation, we would go into rehearsal, where I would change my role from producer to director. As theaters were not available, these were held in the Henry Hudson Hotel on West 57th Street, in private dining rooms and the ballroom. It was not exactly the ideal atmosphere for work, and to hear Dolores singing one of her numbers surrounded by chicken-patty remnants from some ladies-club lunch was, frankly, not in the best theatrical tradition. But we weren't the only ones. Milton Berle was fighting his way through the melting ice cream down the hall, and Martha Raye was belting out her act in another room among the remains of slightly tired potato salad. For the early days of television, it was the usual routine, and so I didn't feel I had any right to protest. Way, way down in the basement of the hotel was a large gymnasium, where we rehearsed the ballets and bigger choral numbers. Even with a show of this size, one is only allowed a single "camera day." After the numbers were presumably ready, we would move onto the stage of the Center Theatre for our one and only run-through in front of the cameras. I would go to the theater the night before with our scenic designer, Stewart Chaney, and Frank Thompson (who supervised the costumes) to be present at the hanging and arranging of the sets. Then we would tuck into cots in various dressing rooms so we could be on time for the rehearsal, which started rolling at seven the next morning.

I got into a spot of trouble with a cameraman during one of these run-throughs. While Dolores was doing one of her numbers, I walked onto the stage and motioned for him to close in on her. He promptly climbed off his camera, went to the side of the stage, and lit a cigarette, whereupon all hell broke loose. Being an amateur in the television business, I was not aware that it was necessary to go all the way to the control room at the rear of the theater to ask the head cameraman to ask the stage cameraman to do what

I had innocently wanted him to do in the first place. We later became fine pals, and on the night of our last broadcast, he even gave me a wristwatch.

I had worked with Dolores Gray before but under very different conditions. The Theatre Guild owned the musical rights to *Pygmalion*, and they asked me to direct Dolores as "Eliza Doolittle" at our playhouse at Westport. There was no question but that she could sing the role, but there was a certain amount of doubt as to whether she could act it. Nonetheless, she worked hard and turned in a fine performance. At the end of the Westport run, Alan Lerner and Fritz Loewe—who had been asked by the guild to do the musical adaptation for Broadway—arrived to appraise the production. They were enthusiastic not only about Dolores, but also about my direction, Tom Helmore and Bramwell Fletcher's performances, and, in fact, the entire Westport production. We all went home on a series of pink clouds, but one month later Alan and Fritz went to the guild to say that they had been unable to find any story line or continuity in George Bernard Shaw's play and felt it best to

Dolores Gray (1924–2002) was a vibrant stage, film, and television performer whose brassy persona and Broadway belt allowed her to shine in every medium. Born in Chicago, she was given singing and dancing lessons by her mother, who was then singing in San Francisco nightclubs and performing on the radio. Gray was only a teenager when she started singing in clubs, where she was later discovered by Rudy Vallee, who made her a regular on his radio show. Her Broadway debut was in the revue *Seven Lively Arts* (1944), followed by character parts in the short-lived book musical *Are You With It?* (1945) and *Sweet Bye and Bye* (1946), which never made it to New York.

Gray became a London star when she played Annie Oakley in *Annie Get Your Gun* (1946) for three years. Returning to Broadway, she enthralled audiences in the revue *Two on the Aisle* (1951) and the western musical *Destry Rides Again* (1959). Gray was even well-reviewed in the flops *Carnival in Flanders* (1953) and *Sherry!* (1967). She once again became a favorite in London when she played Mama Rose in *Gypsy* in 1973, and was finally in a Broadway hit again when she was a replacement for Dorothy Brock in *42nd Street* in 1986. She made her last hurrah on the London stage in *Follies* in 1987. Gray made only three movie musicals, but each role was choice: television star Madeline Bradbille in *It's Always Fair Weather* (1955), sultry Lalume in *Kismet* (1955), and Park Avenue gossip Sylvia in *The Opposite Sex* (1956). Gray frequently returned to supper clubs and appeared on many musical programs on television.

relinquish their connection with the idea. Armina Marshall persuaded them to give it another try, but after several more weeks they reappeared to reiterate that, try as they had, they could not manage to work a musical out of it. The Theatre Guild was truly discouraged and consequently allowed their option on the property to expire. Only a few weeks later, Alan and Fritz bought the rights themselves, proceeded rather quickly with the story and music, which heretofore they had been unable to do, and eventually emerged with a little number called My Fair Lady. [Herman Levin ended up being the producer and Moss Hart the director of My Fair Lady when it opened in 1956.]

One of the main problems with television, as I was to learn, was the necessity of finishing the program exactly on the final moment of the air time that has been assigned to you—not one second sooner or later. This required a certain amount of sweating in the control room as to whether we were ahead of or behind schedule. It was during these perilous periods that Victor Young, who conducted our orchestra, habitually saved our lives. He wore a headphone that was directly connected to the control booth, and we would call him—sometimes in a panic—to add or subtract a chorus or two, depending on whether we found ourselves ahead or behind. He never failed, and, amazingly enough, the show usually came off on time.

Those of us involved in the show managed the allocated ten months to considerable success and then returned to our former activities, but I still often wonder what became of those damn elephants. [The Buick Circus Hour ran from October 1952 to June 1953, on NBC-TV, as a variety show that replaced Milton Berle's The Texaco Star Theatre every fourth week.]

Victor Young was an extraordinary man. During the ten months of the television series, he was also involved in the composition of several motion-picture scores but somehow managed for each of our shows to fly out from Hollywood on the Friday before, rehearse the stars and the chorus, correlate the music, go through "camera day" and the show, and then fly back to his West Coast obligations that same night. I was to work with him again in 1955, on a Broadway show that he composed and I directed, called Seventh Heaven. It was produced by Gant Gaither and a mysterious but vital gentleman from Hollywood named William Bacher. Although Stella Unger was only credited with working on the book with Victor Wolfson and doing the lyrics, she also seemed to be an important part of the management team. She was present at all of the production meetings and made many of the key decisions. I suspect she was also responsible for a great deal of the money.

The show starred Gloria DeHaven, who was fragile and charming, if somewhat inaudible; Ricardo Montalban, who was also charming and very good looking, if somewhat lacking in stage experience at the time; and Kurt

Victor Young (1900–1956) was a prolific composer, conductor, arranger, band leader, and songwriter who worked on more than 350 movies and also had an extensive career in radio, television, theater, and records. He was born in the slums of Chicago, the son of Polish parents who loved music and saw that the boy received violin lessons. When he was ten, Young's mother died, and he and his sister were sent to live with their grandparents in Warsaw, Poland, where he studied at the Warsaw Imperial Conservatory.

After graduation, Young made his concert violinist debut with the Warsaw Philharmonic Orchestra. The young musician quickly gained a lauded reputation in Europe, and in 1917, he was performing in St. Petersburg for the czar when the Russian Revolution broke out. Young was arrested by the Bolsheviks and sentenced to die, but a revolutionary who admired Young's musical skills helped him escape. Back in Poland, he was arrested by the Germans and sentenced to die but was saved by his musical gifts. He survived the rest of the war and didn't return to the United States until 1920, when he picked up his violinist career and performed for top orchestras in Chicago.

Young realized that there was more money to be made in silent movies when he was hired by the movie house chain Balaban and Katz to write, arrange, and conduct music for their many cinemas. By the end of the 1920s, he had begun his recording career, arranging and conducting music for Brunswick Records. Young's movie scores include *Golden Boy* (1939), *Reap the Wild Wind* (1942), *Palm Beach Story* (1942), *For Whom the Bell Tolls* (1943), *Samson and Delilah* (1949), *The Greatest Show on Earth* (1952), *The Quiet Man* (1952), *Johnny Guitar* (1954), and *Around the World in Eighty Days* (1956). He also wrote music for the Broadway musicals *Murder at the Vanities* (1933), *Blackbirds of 1933*, *Arms and the Girl* (1950), and *Seventh Heaven* (1955), and was active in television specials.

Kasznar, an old pro who, in consequence, lacked nothing. There was also an ebullient, eccentric young Robert Clary and an exciting new personality, Chita Rivera, and they both contributed enormously. [Chita Rivera (b. 1933) found widespread recognition two years later in *West Side Story* and went on to become one of the American musical theater's favorite dancing-singing stars.] The production was exquisite, as we had been fortunate to obtain the services of great international artist Vertes, who did both sets and costumes. Victor's score was a pillar of strength. He again proved—in another medium—that in addition to being a brilliant musician, he was a wonderful person with whom to work. In spite of the expert hands that

Seventh Heaven is a 1955 musical play based on a popular 1922 melodrama by Austin Strong that had been successful as a silent film in 1927 and a talkie in 1937. The musical featured Ricardo Montalban as street sweeper Chico and Gloria DeHaven as his wife Diane, who is faithful to him when he goes off to war and returns home blind. Victor Wolfson and Stella Unger wrote the book, and the songs were by Victor Young (music) and Unger (lyrics). Peter Gennaro choreographed, and Wilson directed a cast that also featured Kurt Kasznar, Chita Rivera, Robert Clary, and Beatrice Arthur. The critics felt that the teary story was showing its age, and the lackluster libretto and score did little to freshen it up, although there were compliments for the fine cast. *Seventh Heaven* managed to run for forty-four performances.

cradled the production, *Seventh Heaven* was only a moderate success, and when it came to New York, it only managed a run of about five weeks before we closed down.

[In the early 1950s, Lawrence Langner described Wilson as "tall and handsome, whose premature gray hair contradicted his boyish appearance." But by the time of *Seventh Heaven*, Wilson's looks, not to mention his streak of major hits, like *Bloomer Girl*, *Kiss Me, Kate*, and *Gentlemen Prefer Blondes*, had begun to decline. By the mid-1950s, this reversal of fortune began to impact his income, and a number of friends, colleagues, and family members often noticed signs of alcohol abuse. In 1957, Noel Coward sent a detailed and affectionate letter explaining that Wilson would no longer be involved in producing his plays in the United States, and that same year, Wilson ended his relationship with the Langners at Westport and sold his Connecticut house. Still active and hopeful—but not always upbeat or well—he permanently moved with Natasha to their Park Avenue apartment.]

CHAPTER NINETEEN

~

Winding Down

Michael Abbott, a young producer, asked me to stage a light comedy that he had bought entitled *Late Love*, written by a lady from Pittsburgh named Rosemary Casey. Michael and I got Arlene Francis to accept the starring role, which turned out to be a jolly good idea. She was enchanting and then and there became one of my great loves in the theater. In spite of the fact that she regularly appears on *What's My Line* and many other television productions, she remains unaffected, unimpressed by her success, and always warmly affectionate. [Arlene Francis (1908–2001) was a popular television personality who also enjoyed a successful theater career. She first gained recognition on Broadway in 1942, for her Russian sniper Natalia in the comedy *The Doughgirls*, followed by noteworthy performances in *The Overtons* (1945), *Once More with Feeling* (1958), and the 1966 revival of *Dinner at Eight*. But Francis's fame rested on her many television appearances in series, game shows, talk programs, and original dramas.] After several required tea sessions commandeered by Lucile Watson, we managed to cajole our elegant hostess into the fold as well. As always, Miss Watson was excellent in her role but persistently disagreeable from the start of rehearsals to the last performance. It may have had something to do with her advanced age, which she seldom failed to mention. Personally, I do not consider immaculate manners over a silver tea tray sufficient compensation for bad manners in the theater. [Lucile Watson (1879–1962) was a busy actress on the stage and in films who often played overbearing matrons and other formidable types. She was in numerous plays on Broadway between 1902 and 1953, and acted in thirty-five movies between 1934 and 1951.]

Late Love is a 1953 comedy by Rosemary Casey that charmed Broadway audiences for three months. The stuffy writer and widower Graham Colby (Neil Hamilton) does not allow strong drink, smoking, the radio, or the television in his elegant house and insists that his daughter Janet (Elizabeth Montgomery) and visitors be punctual and act in a civilized manner at all times. Colby explains that his regulations are for the benefit of his conservative and demanding mother (Lucile Watson), who lives with him. When Colby's publisher sends artist Constance Warburton (Arlene Francis) to paint his portrait, she finds that this pretense is a sham and that it is Colby who is so suffocating. Constance helps Janet elope with Colby's secretary Matthew (Cliff Robertson) and treats the mother to a fun-filled trip to New York City. Wilson directed the comedy, which fell short of being a hit. A movie version of *Late Love* was never produced, but a television adaptation was broadcast on NBC-TV in 1956.

We also had among us Neil Hamilton, a model of polite behavior, and Frank Albertson, who was perhaps more animated but equally well behaved. There were also some newcomers, including Cliff Robertson, who went on to many leading roles, and Elizabeth Montgomery, daughter of actor Robert Montgomery, who has since managed to mingle Broadway, television, film, and marital excursions with remarkable finesse. [Cliff Robertson (1923–2011) is mostly remembered for his film career and praised performances in *Picnic* (1955), *The Best Man* (1964), and *Charly* (1968). Elizabeth Montgomery (1933–1995) was most famous for her television series *Bewitched* in the 1960s.] With sets by Stewart Chaney and clothes by Frank Thompson, we had a handsome production. The acting was beyond reproach, but *Late Love* was a little too gentle and, at moments, a little too contrived, which the critics spotted and the audiences must have sensed. The result was not a failure but, like the play itself, a rather gentle success.

It was the Theatre Guild, egged on by Terry Helburn, that talked me into joining them as coproducer on a play called *The Burning Glass*. It was by Charles Morgan, who had a somewhat overrated position in the London theater. [Charles Morgan (1894–1958) was a British novelist who also worked in the theater and in television.] The guild had an eye on his plays, and he obviously had an eye on the guild. It was even in our contract that following the "expected success" of *Glass*, we were required to do another of Mr. Morgan's creations called *The River Line*, a play that I distrusted from the moment I read it. In any case, we went ahead with *The Burning Glass* and gave

The Burning Glass is a 1954 British drama by Charles Morgan that was profitable in London but closed inside of three weeks on Broadway. English scientist Christopher Terriford (Michael Goodliffe) discovers a method of solar energy that is as powerful as the hydrogen bomb, but he won't give it to the British government. An enemy government kidnaps Terriford, and his wife (Dorothy Green) and associate Tony Lack (Michael Gough) try to re-create the method in his absence. Terriford is released when he refuses to talk, and Tony, fearing he will be kidnapped next, commits suicide.

The thriller was produced by Wilson and then the Theatre Guild later that same year in New York, with a laudable cast that included Cedric Hardwicke, Isobel Elsom, Walter Matthau, Scott Forbes, and Maria Riva. There were some appreciative nods to the players, but the play was dismissed as claptrap. *The Burning Glass* was never filmed, but it showed up on British television in 1956 and 1960.

Cedric Hardwicke (1893–1964) was a distinguished classical actor with a long list of stage credits and character parts in films. He was born in Lye, England, and trained at the Royal Academy of Dramatic Art. By 1912, he was on the professional stage in London and went on to play much of the classical repertory throughout the next twenty years. His first American appearance was in 1936, in the short-lived *The Promise*, but he won Broadway audiences over the next year with his diabolical criminologist in *The Amazing Dr. Clitterhouse*. Other highlights in Hardwicke's stage career include the icy Reverend Skerritt in *Shadow and Substance* (1938), Creon to Katharine Cornell in *Antigone* (1946), Caesar to Lili Palmer's young queen in *Caesar and Cleopatra*, and Japanese businessman Asano in *A Majority of One* (1959).

Hardwicke's movie career started to blossom in the 1930s, and he went on to make more than 100 films. Among them are *Becky Sharp* (1935), *King Solomon's Mines* (1937), *The Hunchback of Notre Dame* (1939), *The Keys of the Kingdom* (1944), *The Winslow Boy* (1948), *Richard III* (1955), *The Ten Commandments* (1956), and *The Pumpkin Eater* (1964). Hardwicke had stern, Roman features and a clear, authoritative voice that made him ideal for classical roles, but in Hollywood he usually played heavies and sinister aristocrats. He was also a respected stage director. Hardwicke was knighted in 1934, at the time the youngest British actor to receive that honor.

it a first-rate production. Sir Cedric Hardwicke was the star and eventually became the director. Oliver Smith did the sets; Noel Taylor the costumes; and—to add to its other embellishments—Walter Matthau, Isobel Elsom, and Maria Riva were in the cast. I had first introduced Maria to the stage in *Foolish Notion* when she was a shy, frightened, eager young actress, but by the time of this production, primarily through radio and television work, she had become an established personality of her own, so much so that she was given costar billing with Sir Cedric. [Maria Riva (b. 1924), the daughter of Marlene Dietrich, is most remembered for her many dramatic roles on television in the 1950s.]

Maria's mother, better known as Marlene Dietrich, naturally appeared when we did our tryout in Washington, DC. Marlene adores her daughter and watches over her like a mother hen, although "hen" is scarcely the word to describe her. During several days of rehearsals, she hung around outside the theater looking absolutely lovely. I finally realized that as she was obviously altering Maria's performance each night in their suite at the Mayflower, it would be wiser to invite her to rehearsals and allow her to make suggestions in front of everyone. Sir Cedric agreed with me, and so from that time onward, Marlene became an unofficial member of the production staff, albeit one who was discreetly garbed in sable. [Marlene Dietrich (1901–1992) was one of Hollywood's most glamorous and exotic stars, remembered in her early days for such romantic movies as *The Blue Angel* (1930), *Morocco* (1930), *Blonde Venus* (1932), *Shanghai Express* (1932), and *The Garden of Allah* (1936). She later gave outstanding performances in character parts in such films as *Witness for the Prosecution* (1956), *Touch of Evil* (1958), and *Judgment at Nuremberg* (1961).]

Marlene's concern for her daughter has a strong domestic strain, and Maria was sometimes inclined to repel it. Maria married an apparently impecunious young man, set herself up in a cold-water flat on Third Avenue in New York, and refused to accept financial assistance from her relatively wealthy parents; however, none of this appeared to alter Marlene's determination to display her maternal devotion. One morning in New York, I remember her descending the steps of the St. Regis Hotel, where she was then living, hung with pearls and swathed in mink and on her way, as she explained to me, to scrub the floors of Maria's flat. Shortly thereafter, when Maria had a child, Marlene happily graduated to babysitting and became one of the world's best-looking grandmothers.

The Burning Glass was well received in Washington. Maria was pretty and competent, even though her performance may have lacked some of the ominous undertones that Mr. Morgan had originally intended. Cedric was excellent: suave and elegant. I found him a most amiable companion, which came as a considerable surprise. Not having known him before and only having seen him from across the floodlights, I had expected a level of self-satisfied pomposity. But this was definitely not the case. He had a dry wit and an unfailing sense of humor, and was not averse to having a few cozy drinks.

When we finally got the play to New York, the results were as some of us had begun to anticipate. The notices were respectful but dull, and after a few weeks, we came to an inevitable, if distinguished, close. No one ever said a word against it, but no one came to see it either. Well anyway, we never had to do *The River Line*! [Broadway never saw *The River Line*, which had been a success in London in 1952, but it was made into a German film in 1964.]

Noel had always made it a rule never to write a play for specific people. On some occasions, however, he was just as likely to break his own rules as he was to follow them. This was the case with *Point Valaine* and *Design for Living*, and most particularly in the case of *Quadrille*. The play was carefully designed to fit the personalities of Lynn and Alfred. Noel conceived for her an elegant English marchioness, and for Alfred, a stalwart American railroad magnate. The basic plot is that the marquis falls in love with the tycoon's wife, and during the patching up of this arrangement (which involves a trip to the south of France), the tycoon falls in love with the marchioness and eventually marries her.

We first did *Quadrille* in 1952, in London, where it ran for a season and then assayed New York two years later. Alfred and Lynn were eager to have

---

Quadrille is a 1952 romantic comedy by Noel Coward that ran in London and in New York on the strength of the Lunts' acting prowess and popularity. The American manufacturer Axel Diensen (Alfred Lunt) goes to Europe in 1873 to chase down his wife (Marian Spencer) who has eloped with the Marquis of Heronden (Griffith Jones). He meets up with Herondon's wife Serena (Lynn Fontanne) and the two find they like each other much more than their spouses. Critics felt the limp play was only a vehicle for the Lunts and as such gave the couple a chance to shine gloriously for eight months. Lunt directed and Cecil Beaton designed the exquisite period sets and costumes. Wilson and H. M. Tennent, Ltd. produced *Quadrille* on Broadway in 1954 with Brian Aherne and Edna Best joining the Lunts. Again the press adulated the players (Lunt won the Tony Award) but thought the comedy feeble. All the same, it ran nearly five months. Although *Quadrille* was never made into a film, it showed up on German television in 1961 and 1966.

a strong supporting cast. They were so eager, in fact, that they were willing to accept far less than their normal salaries so that we could engage Brian Aherne for the marquis, Edna Best to play Alfred's flighty wife, and Brenda Forbes, Dorothy Sands, and Jerome Kilty in other important roles. Cecil Beaton had designed a magnificent production in London, but as he was unable to come to New York, his original designs were supervised here, including sets by Charles Elson and costumes by Stanley Simmons. The production was big, involving a railway station, a Mayfair drawing room, and a Cote d'Azur villa. The cast, out of necessity, was large as well, but the play managed to survive its financial overhead and we ran for another full season with great success.

The day following the closing, the Lunts departed, flustered but elegant on the *Twentieth Century* bound for Genesee Depot, Wisconsin, Lynn to her solitaire and Alfred to his cows. [Unfortunately, *Quadrille* marked the end of Wilson's professional and personal relationship with the Lunts. During the New York run of the play, the Lunts fired their business manager, Larry Farrell, because of his excessive drinking. They hired Donald Seawell to handle their finances and severed business ties with Wilson, also because of his growing drinking problem.]

Beginning in 1957, I became involved with a relatively new setup for me: Off Broadway productions. This has unmistakably become an important aspect of New York's theatrical milieu. There is the Theatre de Lys, the Phoenix, the Cherry Lane, and, among many other downtown theaters, the Circle-in-the-Square, where experimental plays, as well as Broadway leftovers, flourish. For example, there is *The Threepenny Opera*, which, when it was first presented on Broadway in 1933, managed only three weeks at the Empire Theatre, but in 1954, Off Broadway, it achieved three years at the de Lys. The Theatre Guild first produced Eugene O'Neill's *The Iceman Cometh* with modest success in 1946, but it too has since had an apparently endless run at the Circle-in-the-Square. And then there was *Uncle Vanya* at the Fourth Street Theatre and *Mary Stuart* at the Phoenix.

This must indicate a resurgent audience willing to go through geographical difficulties and often acute discomfort because of their obvious interest in and love of the theater. Off Broadway has done no harm to Broadway, where hits still flourish, but, on the contrary, it has proved to be a shot in the arm for the entire theatrical scene. Off Broadway has also become an invaluable springboard for actors, writers, and directors. Witness Geraldine Page, Jason Robards, and Jose Quintero, to mention a few. In addition, there have been countless established Broadway figures who have elected to work there for minimum salaries, including Franchot Tone, Eva Le Gallienne, Siobhàn

McKenna, and Alan Schneider. And then Tennessee Williams, for reasons of his own, temporarily joined the ranks. He was determined that his two new one-act plays—known collectively as *The Garden District*—be done Off Broadway and through his director, Herbert Machiz, I was given the present of producing them.

Since the other theaters were unavailable, we were lucky to stumble into a new playhouse, the York Theatre, which is uptown on First Avenue. The theater had been acquired by a young man from Hollywood named Warner

Tennessee Williams (1911–1983) was one of the American theater's finest playwrights, with a poetic style of writing that has rarely been equaled. He was born Thomas Lanier Williams in Columbus, Mississippi. His father was a violent, aggressive traveling salesman; his mother the high-minded, puritanical daughter of a clergyman; and his elder sister a young woman beset by mental problems that eventually led to her being institutionalized. Thus, his family provided him with the seeds for characters who would people so many of his plays.

Williams attended several universities before graduating from the State University of Iowa. During this time, some of his early works were produced at regional and collegiate playhouses while he held numerous odd jobs. Williams's first play to receive a major production was *Battle of Angels* (1940), which folded on the road. Success came with his *The Glass Menagerie* (1945), followed by such popular dramas as *A Streetcar Named Desire* (1947), *Summer and Smoke* (1948), *The Rose Tattoo* (1951), *Cat on a Hot Tin Roof* (1955), *Garden District* (1958), *Sweet Bird of Youth* (1959), *Period of Adjustment* (1960), and *The Night of the Iguana* (1961). During these years he had a number of failures, including *You Touched Me!* (1945), *Camino Real* (1953), and *Orpheus Descending* (1957), but in later years they were reexamined and some found favor.

Although Williams continued to write and be produced, the plays that followed *The Night of the Iguana* were neither critical nor commercial successes. His preoccupation with social degeneracy and homosexuality, which had heretofore been contained by his sense of theater and poetic dialogue, overcame these saving restraints and lost him a public for the newer works. Many of his plays were filmed by Hollywood but usually in abridged or sanitized forms. More faithful adaptations were later found on television. Among his original screenplays are *Baby Doll* (1956), *The Fugitive Kind* (1959), and *Boom!* (1968). Williams's strengths in playwriting were his vivid characterizations and glistening dialogue. His subject matter was sometimes crude or brutal, but his writing remained elegant and poetic.

Garden District is a 1958 program of two plays by Tennessee Williams that played Off Broadway. The shorter play, *Something Unspoken,* concerns an aging Southern lady, Cornelia (Eleanor Phelps), and her longtime companion Grace (Hortense Alden), who live together and help delude one another about the reality of their relationship. *Suddenly, Last Summer* centers on the wealthy Mrs. Venable (Alden), who tries to convince a doctor (Robert Lansing) that her niece Catharine (Anne Meacham) is hopelessly insane and should have a lobotomy. When the doctor gives Catharine a truth serum, the horrible truth that Mrs. Venable wants hidden is revealed. Her son Sebastian was a homosexual who used his beautiful cousin Catharine to lure handsome men into his bedroom. While following the usual routine on an exotic island, the native boys turn on him and then kill and cannibalize him.

Wilson produced the double bill, which was directed by Herbert Machiz and ran for nearly six months. While *Something Unspoken* is infrequently produced today, *Suddenly, Last Summer* has received many revivals. The 1959 film version of *Suddenly, Last Summer* starred Katharine Hepburn as Mrs. Venable, Elizabeth Taylor as Catharine, and Montgomery Clift as the doctor. Both Hepburn and Taylor received Academy Award nominations for Best Actress for their roles.

LeRoy, the son of well-known film director Mervyn LeRoy. More important financially, Warner was the grandson of Harry Warner of Warner Brothers. Warner the younger bought a former movie house and spent a considerable amount of his family's money installing a stage, building dressing rooms, repainting, and making it into a charming theater. Although he would rather be a director—and for all of his twenty-two years had some definite ideas on the subject—he succumbed to my suggestion that opening his theater with a new Tennessee Williams bill might not be a bad start. My counsel turned out to be well-advised, as *Garden District* became a sellout success.

Tennessee is probably the most important playwright in the United States today and certainly the most controversial. As a person, he is gentle and soft-spoken, but in the theater, he is determined to get his own way—a right that, in my opinion, he unquestionably deserves. It has been a pleasure and a privilege to work with him. But then I have always been fortunate in that respect. Noel Coward was not a bad introduction to this perilous occupation. And to graduate to a producer of the Lunts was another step of no mean importance. My association with Binkie Beaumont and subsequently the Theatre Guild were also tempting dishes on the theatrical buffet. And then, of course, as added spice there was always Tallulah Bankhead. The directorial phase, with all its frenetic variances, was generally lucrative and usually satisfactory. My career, in various capacities, has consisted of approximately one hundred shows, including those at Westport. In addition, for more than thirty years I was in close contact with nearly every actor and actress of note in the American and English theaters, witnessing an endless parade of them rise and fall, come and go, or come and stay. Even with their occasional tiresomeness and vagaries, they will always hold a warm spot in my heart. It was all so fascinating. What a life!

Epilogue

John C. Wilson ended his memoir on a highly optimistic note, even though in 1958 he was at the low point of his career. In the previous ten years he had only one successful Broadway production, *Quadrille*, which enjoyed a modest run mostly because of the presence of the Lunts. On the other hand, his Off Broadway venture, Tennessee Williams's *Garden District*, was a surprise hit. It was his last producing effort.

Two months after his sixty-second birthday, Wilson died from a heart attack in his Manhattan apartment on October 29, 1961. It was a sad occasion for his past and current friends, who mourned his last difficult years, as well as his passing. Noel Coward served as an honorary pallbearer for Wilson's funeral on October 31, at St. Bartholomew's Church in Manhattan. The other honorary pallbearers were Wilson's longtime office manager Edwin Knill, actors Alfred Lunt and Clifton Webb, Cole Porter, and four of the American theater's most distinguished producers: Alfred de Liagre Jr., Gilbert Miller, Lawrence Langner, and Herman Levin. Wilson was buried in the Ewing Presbyterian churchyard in Ewing, New Jersey, just outside his birthplace, Trenton.

His widow Natasha continued to live in the Park Avenue apartment, although she seldom went to the theater—something she never enjoyed much anyway. She remained a close friend to Coward and went to Jamaica, often for weeks at a time, to stay with him and see old friends. In New York, she was often seen out on the town with Anita Loos and was in constant touch with Wilson's extended family in New Jersey and Pennsylvania. Sadly, she developed glaucoma in the late 1970s and lost much of her vision, and then became less active. Natasha died in 1981, at the age of seventy-six, and is buried next to Wilson in the Ewing churchyard.

Most of Wilson's personal and professional friends outlived him. Cole Porter died three years later, but most survived much longer, for instance, Alfred Lunt (1977), Lynn Fontanne (1983), Anita Loos (1981), S. N. Behrman (1973), Katharine Cornell (1974), Thornton Wilder (1975), Herman Levin (1990), John Gielgud (2000), Ina Claire (1985), Tallulah Bankhead (1968), Gilbert Miller (1969), and Beatrice Lillie (1989). As for Coward, the man who had made such a major impact on Wilson's personal and professional life, he outlived Wilson by eighteen years, dying in Jamaica in 1979.

—Thomas S. Hischak and Jack Macauley

~

John C. Wilson's
Production Credits

Theater

Broadway

Private Lives [Times Square Theatre; 27 January 1931] A comedy by Noel
Coward (256 performances)
Produced by Charles B. Cochran, John C. Wilson. Directed by Noel Coward.
Cast: Gertrude Lawrence, Noel Coward, Laurence Olivier, Jill Esmond.

Point Valaine [Ethel Barrymore Theatre; 16 January 1935] A comedy by
Noel Coward (55 performances)
Produced by John C. Wilson. Directed by Noel Coward. Cast: Lynn Fon-
tanne, Alfred Lunt, Louis Hayward, Osgood Perkins, Philip Tonge.

The Taming of the Shrew [Guild Theatre; 30 September 1935] A revival of
a comedy by William Shakespeare (129 performances)
Produced by John C. Wilson, Theatre Guild. Directed by Henry Wagstaff
Gribble. Cast: Lynn Fontanne, Alfred Lunt, Richard Whorf, Alan Hewitt,
Dorothy Mathews, Sydney Greenstreet.

Tonight at 8:30 [National Theatre; 24 November 1936] A comedy with
songs by Noel Coward, in two separate programs consisting of nine play-
lets (118 performances)
Produced by John C. Wilson. Directed by Noel Coward. Cast: Noel Coward,
Gertrude Lawrence, Alan Webb, Joyce Carey, Moya Nugent, Kenneth
Carten.

Excursion [Vanderbilt Theatre; 9 April 1937] A comedy by Victor Wolfson
(116 performances)
Produced by John C. Wilson. Directed by C. Worthington Miner. Cast:
Whitford Kane, Shirley Booth, J. Hammond Dailey, Frances Fuller, Anthony Ross, Richard Kendrick, Flora Campbell.

George and Margaret [Morosco Theatre; 22 September 1937] A comedy by
Gerald Savory (86 performances)
Produced and directed by John C. Wilson. Cast: Irene Browne, Alan Webb,
Morland Graham, Arthur Macrae, Richard Wagner, Moya Nugent.

Dear Octopus [Broadhurst Theatre; 11 January 1939] A comedy by Dodie
Smith (53 performances)
Produced by John C. Wilson. Directed by Glen Byam Shaw. Cast: Lillian
Gish, Reginald Mason, Lucile Watson, Jack Hawkins, Rose Hobart, Phyl-
lis Povah.

Set to Music [Music Box Theatre; 18 January 1939] A musical revue by Noel
Coward (sketches, music, lyrics) (129 performances)
Produced by John C. Wilson. Directed by Noel Coward. Cast: Beatrice Lil-
lie, Richard Haydn, Robert Shackelton, Maidie Andrews, Gladys Henson,
Hugh French.

Blithe Spirit [Morosco Theatre; 5 November 1941] A comedy by Noel Cow-
ard (657 performances)
Produced and directed by John C. Wilson. Cast: Clifton Webb, Mildred
Natwick, Peggy Wood, Leonora Corbett.

The Pirate [Martin Beck Theatre; 25 November 1942] A comedy by S. N.
Behrman (177 performances)
Produced by the Playwrights' Company and the Theatre Guild. Directed by
Alfred Lunt, John C. Wilson. Cast: Lynn Fontanne, Alfred Lunt, Alan
Reed, Clarence Derwent, Juanita Hall.

Blithe Spirit [Morosco Theatre; 6 September 1943] A revival of a comedy by
Noel Coward (32 performances)
Produced and directed by John C. Wilson. Cast: Clifton Webb, Mildred
Natwick, Peggy Wood, Haila Stoddard.

A Connecticut Yankee [Martin Beck Theatre; 17 November 1943] A revival
of a musical comedy by Herbert Fields (book), Richard Rodgers (music),
Lorenz Hart (lyrics) (135 performances)

Produced by Richard Rodgers. Directed by John C. Wilson. Choreographed by William Holbrook, Al White Jr. Cast: Dick Foran, Vivienne Segal, Julie Warren, Vera-Ellen, Robert Chisholm, John Cherry.

Lovers and Friends [Plymouth Theatre; 29 November 1943] A drama by Dodie Smith (168 performances)
Produced by John C. Wilson, Katharine Cornell. Directed by Guthrie McClintic. Cast: Katharine Cornell, Raymond Massey, Anne Burr, Henry Daniell, Carol Goodner.

Bloomer Girl [Shubert Theatre; 5 October 1944] A musical comedy by Sig Herzig, Fred Saidy (book), Harold Arlen (music), E. Y. Harburg (lyrics) (654 performances)
Produced by John C. Wilson. Directed by E. Y. Harburg. Choreographed by Agnes de Mille. Cast: Celeste Holm, David Brooks, Dooley Wilson, Joan McCracken, Matt Brigs, Mabel Taliaferro.

In Bed We Cry [Belasco Theatre; 14 November 1944] A drama by Ilka Chase based on her novel (47 performances)
Produced and directed by John C. Wilson. Cast: Ilka Chase, Frederic Tozere, Paul McGrath, Ruth Matteson, Francis DeSales, Eleanor Audley.

The Streets Are Guarded [Henry Miller's Theatre; 20 November 1944] A drama by Laurence Stallings (24 performances)
Produced by John C. Wilson. Directed by John Haggott. Cast: Morton L. Stevens, Jeanne Cagney, Phil Brown, George Matthews, Len Doyle.

Foolish Notion [Martin Beck Theatre; 13 March 1945] A comedy by Philip Barry (104 performances)
Produced by the Theatre Guild. Directed by John C. Wilson. Cast: Tallulah Bankhead, Donald Cook, Henry Hull, Mildred Dunnock.

The Day before Spring [National Theatre; 22 November 1945] A musical comedy by Alan Jay Lerner (book, lyrics), Frederick Loewe (music) (167 performances)
Produced and directed by John C. Wilson. Choreographed by Anthony Tudor. Cast: Irene Manning, Bill Johnson, John Archer, Tom Helmore, Patricia Marshall.

O Mistress Mine [Empire Theatre; 23 January 1946] A comedy by Terence Rattigan and retitled production of *Love in Idleness* (452 performances)
Produced by John C. Wilson, Theatre Guild. Directed by Alfred Lunt. Cast: Lynn Fontanne, Alfred Lunt, Dick Van Patten, Ann Lee, Margery Maude.

Present Laughter [Plymouth Theatre; 29 October 1946] A comedy by Noel Coward (158 performances)
Produced and directed by John C. Wilson. Cast: Clifton Webb, Matra Linden, Cris Alexander, Doris Dalton, Jan Sterling.

Bloomer Girl [City Center; 6 January 1947] A revival of a musical by E. Y. Harburg and others (48 performances)
Produced by John C. Wilson. Directed by E. Y. Harburg. Choreographed by Agnes de Mille. Cast: Nanette Fabray, Dick Smart, Hubert Dilworth, Mabel Taliaferro.

Ruth Draper [Empire Theatre; 12 January 1947] A solo performance by Ruth Draper (42 performances)
Produced by John C. Wilson. Directed and performed by Ruth Draper.

The Importance of Being Earnest [Royale Theatre; 3 March 1947] A revival of a comedy by Oscar Wilde (81 performances)
Produced by John C. Wilson, Theatre Guild, H. M. Tennent, Ltd. Directed by John Gielgud. Cast: John Gielgud, Pamela Brown, Margaret Rutherford, Robert Flemyng, Jane Baxter.

The Eagle Has Two Heads [Plymouth Theatre; 19 March 1947] A drama by Jean Cocteau, Donald Duncan (29 performances)
Produced and directed by John C. Wilson. Cast: Tallulah Bankhead, Helmut Dantine, Clarence Derwent, Kendall Clark.

Love for Love [Royale Theatre; 26 May 1947] A revival of a comedy by William Congreve (48 performances)
Produced by John C. Wilson, Theatre Guild, H. M. Tennent, Ltd. Directed by John Gielgud. Cast: John Gielgud, Pamela Brown, Cyril Ritchard, Robert Flemyng, Marian Spencer.

The Winslow Boy [Empire Theatre; 29 October 1947] A drama by Terence Rattigan (214 performances)
Produced by John C. Wilson, Theatre Guild, H. M. Tennent, Ltd. Directed by Glen Byam Shaw. Cast: Frank Allenby, Alan Webb, Madge Compton, Michael Newell.

Ruth Draper [Empire Theatre; 28 December 1947] A solo performance by Ruth Draper (27 performances)
Produced by John C. Wilson. Directed and performed by Ruth Draper.

Power without Glory [Booth Theatre; 13 January 1948] A drama by Michael Clayton Hutton (31 performances)

Produced by John C. Wilson, Messrs. Shubert. Directed by Chloe Gibson. Cast: Peter Murray, Joan Newell, Trevor Ward, Hillary Liddell.

Private Lives [Plymouth Theatre; 4 October 1948] A revival of a comedy by Noel Coward (248 performances)
Produced by John C. Wilson. Directed by Martin Manulis. Cast: Tallulah Bankhead, Donald Cook, Barbara Baxley, William Langford.

Kiss Me, Kate [New Century Theatre; 30 December 1948] A musical comedy by Bella and Sam Spewack (book), Cole Porter (music, lyrics) (1,070 performances)
Produced by Saint Subber, Lemuel Ayers. Directed by John C. Wilson. Choreographed by Hanya Holm. Cast: Alfred Drake, Patricia Morison, Lisa Kirk, Harold Lang.

I Know My Love [Shubert Theatre; 2 November 1949] A comedy by S. N. Behrman (246 performances)
Produced by John C. Wilson, Theatre Guild. Directed by Alfred Lunt. Cast: Lynne Fontanne, Alfred Lunt, Betty Caulfield, Thomas Palmer, Noel Leslie, Hugh Franklin.

Gentlemen Prefer Blondes [Ziegfeld Theatre; 8 December 1949] A musical comedy by Joseph Fields, Anita Loos (book) based on the novel by Loos, Jule Styne (music), Leo Robin (lyrics) (740 performances)
Produced by Herman Levin, Oliver Smith. Directed by John C. Wilson. Cast: Carol Channing, Yvonne Adair, Jack McCauley, Eric Brotherson, Rex Evans, Reta Shaw.

The Lady's Not for Burning [Royale Theatre; 8 November 1950] A comedy-drama by Christopher Fry (151 performances)
Produced by John C. Wilson, Theatre Guild. Directed by John Gielgud. Cast: Richard Burton, John Gielgud, Pamela Brown, Peter Bull, Penelope Munday.

Bless You All [Mark Hellinger Theatre; 14 December 1950] A musical revue by Arnold Auerbach (sketches), Harold Rome (music, lyrics) (84 performances)
Produced by Herman Levin, Oliver Smith. Directed by John C. Wilson. Choreographed by Helen Tamiris. Ballets choreographed by Byron Palmer. Cast: Jules Munshin, Pearl Bailey, Mary McCarty, Gene Barry, Robert Chisholm, Swen Swenson.

Make a Wish [Winter Garden Theatre; 18 April 1951] A musical comedy by Abe Burrows, Preston Sturges (book), Hugh Martin (music, lyrics) (102 performances)
Produced by Harry Rigby, Jule Styne, Alexander H. Cohen. Directed by John C. Wilson. Choreographed by Gower Champion. Cast: Nanette Fabray, Melville Cooper, Stephen Douglass, Helen Gallagher, Harold Lang.

Nina [Royale Theatre; 5 December 1951] A comedy by André Roussin, Samuel Taylor (45 performances)
Produced by John C. Wilson, H. M. Tennent, Ltd. Directed by Gregory Ratoff. Cast: Gloria Swanson, Alan Webb, David Niven.

Kiss Me, Kate [Broadway Theatre; 8 January 1952] A revival of a musical by Cole Porter and others (8 performances)
Produced by Saint Subber, Lemuel Ayers. Directed by John C. Wilson. Choreographed by Hanya Holm. Cast: Robert Wright, Holly Harris, Marilyn Day, Frank Derbas.

The Deep Blue Sea [Morosco Theatre; 5 November 1952] A drama by Terence Rattigan (132 performances)
Produced by John C. Wilson, Alfred de Liagre Jr. Directed by John C. Wilson. Cast: Margaret Sullavan, Alan Webb, James Hanley, Herbert Berghof, Philip Merivale.

The Little Hut [Coronet Theatre; 7 October 1953] A comedy by André Roussin, Nancy Mitford (29 performances)
Produced by John C. Wilson, H. M. Tennent, Ltd. Directed by Peter Brook. Cast: Roland Culver, Anne Vernon, Colin Gordon.

Late Love [National Theatre; 13 October 1953] A comedy by Rosemary Casey (95 performances)
Produced by Michael Abbott. Directed by John C. Wilson. Cast: Arlene Francis, Neil Hamilton, Cliff Robertson, Elizabeth Montgomery, Lucile Watson.

The Starcross Story [Royale Theatre; 13 January 1954] A drama by Diana Morgan (1 performance)
Produced by John C. Wilson, Messrs. Shubert, Sherman S. Krellberg. Directed by John C. Wilson. Cast: Eva Le Gallienne, Mary Astor, Anthony Ross, Lynn Bailey, Christopher Plummer, Una O'Connor.

The Burning Glass [Longacre Theatre; 4 March 1954] A drama by Charles Morgan (28 performances)

Produced by John C. Wilson, Theatre Guild. Directed by Luther Kennett. Cast: Cedric Hardwicke, Scott Forbes, Walter Matthau, Maria Riva, Isobel Elsom.

Quadrille [Coronet Theatre; 3 November 1954] A comedy by Noel Coward (150 performances)
Produced by John C. Wilson, H. M. Tennent, Ltd. Directed by Alfred Lunt. Cast: Alfred Lunt, Lynn Fontanne, Brian Aherne, Edna Best, Jerome Kilty, Brenda Forbes, Dorothy Sands.

Seventh Heaven [ANTA Playhouse; 26 May 1955] A musical by Victor Wolfson (book), Victor Young (music), Stella Unger (book, lyrics) (44 performances)
Produced by Gant Gaither, William Bacher. Directed by John C. Wilson. Choreographed by Peter Gennaro, Jerome Robbins (uncredited). Cast: Ricardo Montalban, Gloria DeHaven, Kurt Kasznar, Chita Rivera, Robert Clary, Beatrice Arthur.

Eugenia [Ambassador Theatre; 30 January 1957] A drama by Randolph Cater based on Henry James's *The Europeans* (12 performances)
Produced by John C. Wilson. Directed by Herbert Machiz. Cast: Tallulah Bankhead, Scott Merrill, Tom Ellis, Anne Meachum, Irma Hurley.

London

The Shining Hour [St. James Theatre; 4 September 1934] A play by Keith Winter (213 performances)
Produced by John C. Wilson. Directed by Raymond Massey. Cast: Gladys Cooper, Raymond Massey, Adrianne Allen, Marjorie Fielding.

Theatre Royal [Lyric Theatre; 23 October 1934] A comedy by Edna Ferber, George S. Kaufman. A retitled production of *The Royal Family* (174 performances)
Produced by John C. Wilson. Directed by Noel Coward. Cast: Marie Tempest, Laurence Olivier, Madge Titheradge, George Zucco, W. Graham-Browne.

Tonight at 8:30 [Phoenix Theatre; 9 January 1936] A comedy with songs by Noel Coward in three separate programs consisting of 10 playlets (157 performances)
Produced by John C. Wilson. Directed by Noel Coward. Cast: Noel Coward, Gertrude Lawrence, Joyce Carey, Alan Webb.

Mademoiselle [Wyndham's Theatre; 15 September 1936] A comedy by Jacques Deval (103 performances)
Produced by John C. Wilson. Directed by Noel Coward. Cast: Madge Titheradge, Isabel Jeans, Cecil Parker, Greer Garson.

You Can't Take It with You [St. James Theatre; 22 December 1937] A comedy by George S. Kaufman and Edna Ferber (c. 60 performances)
Produced by John C. Wilson. Directed by William McFadden. Cast: A. P. Kaye, Hilda Trevelyon, Daphne Raglan, Edward Underdown.

Operette [His Majesty's Theatre; 16 March 1939] An operetta by Noel Coward (book, music, lyrics) (133 performances)
Produced by John C. Wilson. Directed by Noel Coward. Cast: Fritzi Massary, Griffith Jones, Peggy Wood, Irene Vanbrugh.

Blithe Spirit [Piccadilly Theatre; 2 July 1941] A comedy by Noel Coward (1,997 performances)
Produced by H. M. Tennent, Ltd., John C. Wilson. Directed by Noel Coward. Cast: Cecil Parker, Margaret Rutherford, Fay Compton, Kay Hammond.

Present Laughter [Haymarket Theatre; 29 April 1943] A comedy by Noel Coward, in repertory with *This Happy Breed* (38 performances)
Produced by H. M. Tennent, Ltd., John C. Wilson. Directed by Noel Coward. Cast: Noel Coward, Joyce Carey, James Donald, Beryl Measor, Judy Campbell.

This Happy Breed [Haymarket Theatre; 30 April 1943] A play by Noel Coward, in repertory with *Present Laughter* (38 performances)
Produced by H. M. Tennent, Ltd., John C. Wilson. Directed by Noel Coward. Cast: Noel Coward, Dennis Price, Joyce Carey, Judy Campbell, Meg Titheradge.

There Shall Be No Night [Aldwych Theatre; 15 December 1943] A drama by Robert Sherwood (220 performances)
Produced by John C. Wilson, H. M. Tennent, Ltd. Directed by Alfred Lunt. Cast: Alfred Lunt, Lynn Fontanne, Terry Morgan, Muriel Pavlow, Norman Williams, Charles Russell.

Private Lives [Apollo Theatre; 8 November 1944] A revival of a comedy by Noel Coward (716 performances)
Produced by H. M. Tennent, Ltd., John C. Wilson. Directed by Noel Coward. Cast: John Clements, Kay Hammond, Peggy Simpson, Raymond Huntley.

Love in Idleness [Lyric Theatre; 20 December 1944] A comedy by Terence Rattigan (213 performances)

Produced by John C. Wilson, H. M. Tennent, Ltd. Directed by Alfred Lunt. Cast: Alfred Lunt, Lynn Fontanne, Brian Nissen, Kathleen Kent, Mona Harrison.

Sigh No More [Piccadilly Theatre; 22 August 1945] A musical revue by Noel Coward, Joyce Grenfell, Richard Addinsell (sketches, music, lyrics) (213 performances)

Produced by H. M. Tennent, Ltd., John C. Wilson. Directed by Noel Coward. Cast: Cyril Ritchard, Madge Elliott, Joyce Grenfell, Graham Payn, Tom Linden.

Present Laughter [Haymarket Theatre; 16 April 1947] A revival of a comedy by Noel Coward (528 performances)

Produced by H. M. Tennent, Ltd., John C. Wilson. Directed by Noel Coward. Cast: Noel Coward, Joyce Carey, Robert Eddison, Moira Lister, Joan Swinstead.

Peace in Our Time [Lyric Theatre; 22 July 1947] A play by Noel Coward (167 performances)

Produced by H. M. Tennent, Ltd., John C. Wilson. Directed by Noel Coward, Alan Webb. Cast: Bernard Lee, Maureen Pryor, Daphne Maddox, Kenneth More, Beatrice Varley, Michael Guard, Dandy Nichols, Dora Bryan.

Relative Values [Savoy Theatre; 28 November 1951] A comedy by Noel Coward (477 performances)

Produced by H. M. Tennent, Ltd., John C. Wilson. Directed by Noel Coward. Cast: Gladys Cooper, Judy Campbell, Angela Baddeley, Simon Lack, Ralph Michael, Hugh McDermott.

Quadrille [Phoenix Theatre; 12 September 1952] A comedy by Noel Coward (329 performances)

Produced by John C. Wilson, H. M. Tennent, Ltd. Directed by Alfred Lunt. Cast: Alfred Lunt, Lynn Fontanne, Marian Spencer, Griffith Jones, Joyce Carey.

Off Broadway

Garden District [York Playhouse; 7 January 1958] Two one-act dramas (*Suddenly, Last Summer* and *Something Unspoken*) by Tennessee Williams (c. 165 performances)

Produced by John C. Wilson, Warner LeRoy. Directed by Herbert Machiz. Cast: Hortense Alden, Anne Meacham, Robert Lansing, Eleanor Phelps.

Touring Productions

Blithe Spirit [1941] A comedy by Noel Coward
Produced and directed by John C. Wilson. Cast: Dennis King, Annabella, Estelle Winwood, Carol Goodner.

Present Laughter [1942–1943] A comedy by Noel Coward (U.K. tour)
Produced by H. M. Tennent, Ltd., John C. Wilson. Directed by Noel Coward. Cast: Noel Coward, Joyce Carey, James Donald, Judy Campbell, Beryl Measor.

Kiss Me, Kate [1949] A musical comedy by Bella and Sam Spewack (book), Cole Porter (music, lyrics)
Produced by Edwin Lester. Directed by John C. Wilson. Choreographed by Hanya Holm. Cast: Anne Jeffreys, Keith Andes, Marc Platt, Julie Wilson.

Westport Country Playhouse

Wilson was hired by Lawrence Langner and Armina Marshall as general manager of Westport Country Playhouse for twelve summer seasons. In 1941, he brought new life to the summer theater company by recruiting Hollywood stars to perform in a converted barn in Fairfield County, Connecticut. The theater was closed during World War II, from 1942 to 1945, but resumed operation in the summer of 1946. Wilson continued as manager and sometime director until the spring of 1957. The following are the summer productions he coproduced there with Langner and Marshall, as well as the productions he directed.

1941

Her Cardboard Lover by Jacques Deval, P. G. Wodehouse. Cast: Tallulah Bankhead.
La Belle Hélène by Jacques Offenbach, Stewart Chaney. Cast: Anne Brown, Hamtree Harrington.
Meet the Wife by Lynn Starling. Cast: Mary Boland.
Little Dark Horse by André Birabeau, Theresa Helburn. Cast: Walter Slezak, Evelyn Varden.
Curtain Going Up! by Ivor Novello. Cast: Constance Collier, Violet Heming, Gloria Stuart.
Love in Our Time by Leslie Reade. Cast: Ilka Chase, Dennis King.
Liliom by Ferenc Molnar. Directed by Lee Strasberg. Cast: Tyrone Power, Annabella.

Mis' Nelly of N'Orleans by Laurence Eyre. Directed by John C. Wilson. Cast: Grace George.

1946

They Knew What They Wanted by Sidney Howard. Cast: June Havoc, Kenny Delmar.

Young Woodley by John Van Druten. Cast: Roddy McDowall.

Design for Living by Noel Coward. Cast: Jean-Pierre Aumont, David Wayne, Marta Linden, Francesca Braggiotti.

Night Must Fall by Emlyn Williams. Cast: Dame May Whitty.

The Devil Takes a Whittler by Weldon Stone. Cast: Patricia Neal, Carol Stone, John Conte, Tom Scott, Paul Crabtree.

Our Town by Thornton Wilder. Cast: Thornton Wilder, Katharine Bard.

Angel Street by Patrick Hamilton. Directed by John C. Wilson. Cast: Frances Lederer, Bramwell Fletcher, Helen Shields, Pamela Gordon, Hazel Jones.

Dream of Fair Women by Reginald Lawrence. Cast: Donald Cook, Ann Burr, Clarence Derwent, Nina Vale, Frank Milan.

What Every Woman Knows by James M. Barrie. Directed by Phyllis Laughton. Cast: Olivia de Havilland, Erik Rhodes, Wesley Addy, Elaine Stritch, J. P. Wilson.

It's a Man's World by Hagar Wilde. Directed by Martin Manulis. Cast: Peggy Conklin, Carmen Mathews, Donald Cook.

1947

The Girl of the Golden West by David Belasco. Directed by Armina Marshall. Cast: June Havoc, Robert Stack, Murvyn Vye, Russell Collins, Philip Langner.

French without Tears by Terence Rattigan. Directed by John C. Wilson. Cast: William Eythe, Erik Rhodes, Virginia Gilmore, Katharine Bard, Paul Crabtree.

Private Lives by Noel Coward. Directed by Martin Manulis. Cast: Tallulah Bankhead, Donald Cook, Buff Cobb, Phil Arthur, Therese Quadri.

The Male Animal by Elliott Nugent, James Thurber. Cast: Buddy Ebsen, Katharine Bard, Lawrence Fletcher, Paul Crabtree, Doris Rich, William Degnan.

The Man Who Came to Dinner by George S. Kaufman, Moss Hart. Cast: Henry Morgan, Marta Linden, Rex O'Malley, Virginia Gilmore, Paul Crabtree, Janet Fox.

Ladies in Retirement by Edward Percy, Reginald Denham. Cast: Estelle Winwood, Fritzi Scheff, Zoyla Talma, Elliott Reid.

Papa Is All by Patterson Green. Cast: Jessie Royce Landis, Guy Spaull, Helen Carew, Emmett Rogers.

The Skull Beneath by Richard Carlson. Directed by Martin Manulis. Cast: Fay Bainter, Hugh Marlowe, Alan Hewitt, Elliot Reid, Flora Campbell, Russell Collins.

The Pursuit of Happiness by Lawrence Langner, Armina Marshall. Directed by Armina Marshall. Cast: Alfred Drake, Mary Hatcher, Russell Collins, Seth Arnold, Dennis King Jr.

My Fair Lady by Otis Bigelow. Directed by John C. Wilson. Cast: Alexander Kirkland, Marta Linden, Jane Seymour, Russell Collins, Kendall Clark.

This Time Tomorrow by Jan de Hartog. Directed by Paul Crabtree. Cast: Sam Jaffe, Ruth Ford, John Archer, Tyler Carpenter.

1948

Lysistrata '48 by Aristophanes, Gilbert Seldes. Cast: June Havoc, Bibi Osterwald, Joan McCracken.

Sundown Beach by Bessie Breuer. Directed by Elia Kazan. Cast: Kim Hunter, Julie Harris, Martin Balsam, Steven Hill, Nehemiah Persoff, Joan Copeland, Robert F. Simon.

The Beaux' Stratagem by George Farquhar. Cast: Brian Aherne, Carmen Mathews, E. G. Marshall, John Merivale, Maureen Stapleton, Richard Temple, Guy Spaull.

John Loves Mary by Norman Krasna. Directed by Martin Manulis. Cast: Guy Madison, Katharine Bard, Paul Crabtree, E. G. Marshall, Matt Briggs, Elliot Reid.

Anna Christie by Eugene O'Neill. Cast: June Havoc, George Matthews, E. G. Marshall, Florence Dunlop.

Perfect Pitch by Sam and Bella Spewack. Directed by Martin Manulis. Cast: Roland Young, Buddy Ebsen, Joyce Arling, Philip Coolidge.

Seven Keys to Baldpate by George M. Cohan. Directed by Paul Crabtree. Cast: William Gaxton, Marianne Stewart, Lawrence Fletcher, Martha Hodge, Edward Platt, E. G. Marshall, Kathleen Comegys.

The Skin of Our Teeth by Thornton Wilder. Directed by John C. Wilson. Cast: Thornton Wilder, Armina Marshall, Betty Field, Fania Marinoff, Richard Hepburn, Guy Spaull, Lois Braun.

The Voice of the Turtle by John Van Druten. Directed by Edwin Gordon. Cast: Joan Caulfield, Edwin Gordon, Jean Casto.

The Silver Whistle by Robert E. McEnroe. Directed by Paul Crabtree. Cast: José Ferrer, E. G. Marshall, John Conte, Phyllis Hill, Kathleen Comegys, Edward Platt.

1949

The Time of Your Life by William Saroyan. Directed by Paul Crabtree. Cast: Eddie Dowling, E. G. Marshall, Lawrence Fletcher, Meg Mundy, Joe Sullivan, Helen Chalzel, John Randolph, Bob Emmett.

Pretty Penny by Jerome Chodorov, Harold Rome. Directed by George S. Kaufman. Choreographed by Michael Kidd. Cast: Peter Gennaro, David Burns, Carl Reiner, Marilyn Day, Barbara Martin, Lenore Lonergan.

Yes, My Darling Daughter by Mark Reed. Directed by Herbert Brodkin. Cast: Ann Harding, Muriel Hutchison, E. G. Marshall, Lawrence Fletcher, Phyllis Kirk.

Accent on Youth by Samuel Raphaelson. Directed by Martin Manulis. Cast: Paul Lukas, Katharine Bard, Elaine Stritch, E. G. Marshall, John Hudson.

A Story for Sunday Evening by Paul Crabtree, Walter Hendl. Directed by Paul Crabtree. Cast: Leora Dana, Cloris Leachman, Paul Crabtree, Lawrence Fletcher.

The Corn Is Green by Emlyn Williams. Directed by Edward McHugh. Cast: Eva Le Gallienne, Richard Waring.

A Month in the Country by Ivan Turgenev, Emlyn Williams. Directed by Garson Kanin. Cast: Ruth Gordon, E. G. Marshall, Howard St. John, Scott McKay, Edmond Ryan.

Out of Dust by Lynn Riggs. Directed by Mary Hunter. Cast: Helen Craig, William Redfield, Berry Kroeger, Joan Loring.

Western Wind by Charlotte Frances. Directed by Martin Manulis. Cast: Cornel Wilde, Patricia Knight, John Baragrey.

The Philadelphia Story by Philip Barry. Directed by Herbert Brodkin. Cast: Sarah Churchill, Jeffrey Lynn, E. G. Marshall, Richard Derr, William Kemp, Peggy French.

Texas Li'l Darlin' by John Wheedon, Sam Moore, Robert Emmett Dolan, Johnny Mercer. Directed by Paul Crabtree. Choreographed by Emy St. Just. Cast: Elaine Stritch, Kenny Delmar, Danny Scholl, Harry Bannister.

Good Housekeeping by William McCleery. Directed by Don Richardson. Cast: Helen Hayes, Kent Smith, Mary MacArthur, Matt Briggs, Jack Manning.

Come Back, Little Sheba by William Inge. Directed by Daniel Mann. Cast: Shirley Booth, Sidney Blackmer, Cloris Leachman, Lonny Chapman, John Randolph.

1950

The Second Man by S. N. Behrman. Directed by Martin Manulis. Cast: Franchot Tone, Cloris Leachman, Walter Brooke, Margaret Lindsay.

Angel in the Pawnshop by A. B. Shiffrin. Directed by Martin Manulis. Cast: Eddie Dowling, Joan McCracken, Hugh Reilly, Marie Murray Hamilton.

The Devil's Disciple by George Bernard Shaw. Cast: Maurice Evans.

The Life of the Party by Lawrence Langner. Cast: John Emery.

The Winslow Boy by Terence Rattigan. Cast: Basil Rathbone, Meg Mundy.

Within a Glass Bell by William Marchant. Cast: Mildred Dunnock, Don Hamner.

The Long Days by Davis Now. Cast: Florence Reed, John Baragrey.

Traveller's Joy by Arthur Macrae. Cast: Gertrude Lawrence, Dennis King.

Miss Mabel by R. C. Sherriff. Cast: Lillian Gish.

Over Twenty-One by Ruth Gordon. Cast: Eve Arden.

My Fiddle Has Three Strings by Arnold Schulman. Cast: Maureen Stapleton, MacDonald Carey, Betsy Blair, J. Edward Bromberg, Fritzi Scheff, Steven Hill.

Blind Alley by James Warwick. Cast: Zachary Scott.

The Amazing Adele by Pierre Barillet, Jean-Pierre Gredy, Garson Kanin. Cast: Ruth Gordon.

Head of the Family by George Norford. Cast: Frederick O'Neal.

1951

The Animal Kingdom by Philip Barry. Directed by John Stix. Cast: Nina Foch, Karl Malden, Scott McKay, Kim Hunter, Louis Lytton.

Candida by George Bernard Shaw. Directed by Norris Haughton. Cast: Olivia de Havilland, Edgar Kent, Kendall Clark, Katherine Squire, Frank Leslie.

For Love or Money by F. Hugh Herbert. Directed by John Loder. Cast: John Loder, Betsy von Furstenberg, Marta Linden, William Kester, Edith Gresham.

Love Revisited by Robert Anderson. Cast: Richard Kendrick, Helen Claire.

The Philanderer by George Bernard Shaw. Directed by Romney Brent. Cast: Claudia Morgan, Tom Helmore, Vanessa Brown.

The Holly and the Ivy by Wynyard Browne. Directed by R. T. Ingham. Cast: Leo G. Carroll, Anne Burr.

The Little Screwball by Walt Anderson. Cast: Walter Abel, Edward Gargan.

Island Fling by Noel Coward. Directed by John C. Wilson. Cast: Claudette Colbert, Edith Meiser, Leon Janney, Reginald Mason.

Glad Tidings by Edward Mabley. Directed by Melvyn Douglas. Cast: Melvyn Douglas, Joan Bennett, Signe Hasso.

Alice in Wonderland by Lewis Carroll, John Charles Sacco, Frances Pole. Directed by Harold Hogan Fuquay. Cast: Florence Forsberg, William Crach, Roy Raymond, John Henson, Bruce Adams, Anita Bolster.

A Foreign Language by S. N. Behrman. Directed by Charles Bowden. Cast: Edna Best, John Hoyt, Brenda Forbes, Howard St. John, James Lipton.

A Case of Scotch by Aimee Stewart, Philip Lewis. Directed by Jerry Epstein. Cast: Margaret Phillips, John Forsythe.

Kin Hubbard by Lawrence Riley. Directed by John C. Wilson. Cast: Tom Ewell, Josephine Hull, June Lockhart, John Alexander.

1952

Pygmalion by George Bernard Shaw. Cast: Tom Helmore, Dolores Gray, Bramwell Fletcher.

Lady in the Dark by Moss Hart, Kurt Weill, Ira Gershwin. Directed and choreographed by Elizabeth Gilbert. Cast: Kitty Carlisle, Jackson Young, Lee Bergere, Russel Gold, Addison Powell.

Idiot's Delight by Robert E. Sherwood. Cast: Scott McKay, Luba Malina.

Three to One by Nancy Hamilton, Morgan Lewis. Cast: Kaye Ballard, Alice Pearce.

Heartbreak House by George Bernard Shaw. Directed by Basil Langton. Cast: Philip Bourneuf, Beatrice Straight.

Ballat Variante. Cast: Mia Slavenska, Frederic Franklin, Alexandra Danilova.

The Hasty Heart by John Patrick. Directed by John Patrick. Cast: John Forsythe, John Dall, Mary Fickett.

Right You Are by Luigi Pirandello. Cast: Alfred Drake, Mildred Dunnock.

Jezebel's Husband by Robert Nathan. Directed by Sherman Marks. Cast: Claude Rains, Claudia Morgan, Carmen Mathews, Robert Emhardt.

Seagulls Over Sorrento by Hugh Hastings. Cast: Rod Steiger.

Dangerous Corner by J. B. Priestly. Cast: John Forsythe, Faye Emerson.

Tin Wedding by Hagar Wilde, Judson O'Donnell. Directed by John C. Wilson. Cast: MacDonald Carey, Maureen Stapleton.

An Evening with Beatrice Lillie. Cast: Beatrice Lillie.

1953

Second Fiddle by Mary Drayton. Directed by Elmer Rice. Cast: Betty Field, Herbert Rudley, Paula Lawrence, Dorothy Donahue, Amy Douglass.

One Thing after Another by Elizabeth Berryhill, Gordon Connell. Directed by Elizabeth Berryhill.

Sailor's Delight by Peter Blackmore, Lawrence Langner. Directed by Harry Ellerby. Cast: Eva Gabor, Tom Helmore, Natalie Schaefer, Katherine Meskill, Philippa Bevans.

What about Maisie? by Ruth and Francis Bellamy. Directed by John C. Wilson. Cast: Claudia Morgan, Beatrice Pearson.

The Play's the Thing by Ferenc Molnar, P. G. Wodehouse. Directed by Ezra Stone. Cast: Ezio Pinza, Frances Compton, Philip Loeb, Alexander Clark.

Once Married, Twice Shy by Lawrence Langner. Directed by Charles Bowden. Cast: Elaine Stritch, Scott McKay, Clarence Derwent, Elizabeth Eustis.

Three Men on a Horse by John Cecil Holm, George Abbott. Directed by John Cecil Holm. Cast: Wally Cox, Walter Matthau, Teddy Hart, Peter Turgeon, Fred Gwynne, Ann Whiteside.

The Road to Rome by Robert E. Sherwood. Directed by Charles Bowden. Cast: Arlene Francis, John Baragrey, Ann Shoemaker, Tige Andrews, Michael Tolan.

The Starcross Story by Diana Morgan. Directed by Luther Kennett. Cast: Eva Le Gallienne, Faye Emerson, Glenn Anders.

Day of Grace by Alexander Fedoroff. Directed by Norris Houghton. Cast: MacDonald Carey, Ben Gazzara, John Alexander, Katherine Squire.

Comin' Tho' the Rye by Warren P. Munsell Jr., Stephen DeBaun, Robert Burns. Directed by Ezra Stone. Cast: David Brooks, Anna Lee, Luella Gear.

The Trip to Bountiful by Horton Foote. Directed by Vincent Donehue. Cast: Lillian Gish, Eva Marie Saint, John Beal, Jo Van Fleet.

A New School for Scandal by Richard B. Sheridan, Albert Marre. Directed by Albert Marre. Cast: June Havoc, Hurd Hatfield.

1954

The Lady Chooses by William McCleery. Directed by Luther Kennett. Cast: Walter Abel, Faye Emerson, Hugh Reilly, Jean Stapleton, Arny Freeman, Lily Lodge.

The Apollo of Bellac by Jean Giraudoux, Maurice Valency. Directed by Joseph Anthony. Cast: Zachary Scott, Ruth Ford, Paula Lawrence, Gaby Rodgers.

The Shewing-Up of Blanco Posnet by George Bernard Shaw. Directed by Joseph Anthony. Cast: Zachary Scott, Ruth Ford, Paula Lawrence, Gaby Rodgers.

Happy Birthday by Anita Loos. Directed by Daniel Levin. Cast: Imogene Coca, William Prince, Daniel Reed, Jack Diamond, Fay Sappington.

Court Olympus by Richard Reardon. Directed by John C. Wilson. Cast: Lee Grant, Rita Gam, Nicholas Joy, Josephine Brown, Tom Tryon.

Candle-Light by P. G. Wodehouse. Directed by Charles Bowden. Cast: Eva Gabor, Richard Kiley, Paula Lawrence, John Baragrey, Gordon Nelson.

Reunion 54 by Justin Sturm. Directed by Lee Bowman. Cast: Lee Bowman, Tom Helmore, Haila Stoddard, George Mathews, Carl White.

Libel by Edward Wooll. Directed by Lexford Richards. Cast: Peter Cookson, June Duprez, Fred Tozere, John Emery, Tammy Grimes.

The Little Hut by André Roussin, Nancy Mitford. Cast: Barbara Bel Geddes, Hiram Sherman, John Granger, Kenneth Mays, Howard Morton.

Darling, Darling by Pierre Barillet, Jean-Pierre Gredy, Anita Loos. Directed by John C. Wilson. Cast: Gypsy Rose Lee, Richard Derr, Florence Sunstrom, Tom Tryon, James Nolan.

My Aunt Daisy by Albert Halper, Joseph Schrank. Directed by Robert Ellenstein. Cast: Jo Van Fleet, Leslie Nielsen, Rusty Lane, Arthur Storch.

Home Is the Hero by Walter Macken. Directed by Worthington Miner. Cast: Peggy Ann Garner, Glenda Farrell, J. Pat O'Malley, Art Smith, Francis Fuller, Christopher Plummer.

Trouble in Tahiti by Leonard Bernstein. Directed by David Brooks, Fred Sadoff. Cast: Alice Ghostley, Richard Eastham, Constance Brigham, Martin Balsam, Gene Saks.

The Thirteen Clocks by James Thurber, Fred Sadoff, Marck Bucci. Directed by David Brooks and Fred Sadoff. Cast: Alice Ghostley, Richard Eastham, Constance Brigham, Martin Balsam, Gene Saks.

1955

Brief Moment by S. N. Behrman. Directed by Peter Turgeon. Cast: Betty Furness, Murray Matheson, Mark Roberts, Jan DeRuth.

Mother Was a Bachelor by Irving W. Phillips. Directed by Frank Carrington, Agnes Morgan. Cast: Billie Burke, Tommy Halloran, Suzanne Jackson, George McIver.

Detective Story by Sidney Kingsley. Directed by Windsor Lewis. Cast: John Forsythe, Kathy Nolan, Henry Silva, Maria Riva, Jack Klugman.

Star Light, Star Bright by S. K. Lauren, Gladys Lehman. Directed by John C. Wilson. Cast: Terry Moore, Frank Albertson, Jean Carson, Effie Afton.

Wedding Breakfast by Theodore Reeves. Directed by Frank Cosaro. Cast: Shelley Winters, Anthony Franciosa, Martin Balsam, Virginia Vincent.

Blue Denim by James Leo Herlihy. Directed by Arthur Penn. Cast: Burt Brinckerhoff, Katherine Squire, Brandon Peters, Patricia Bosworth, Mark Rydell.

Heaven Can Wait by Harry Segall. Directed by Windsor Lewis. Cast: Richard Kiley, Mercer McLeod, Howard Morton, Jack Klugman.

The Rainmaker by N. Richard Nash. Directed by Jeffrey Hayden. Cast: Eva Marie Saint, Sidney Armus, Will Geer, Mark Richman, Arthur Storch.

Gigi by Colette, Anita Loos. Cast: Cathy O'Donnell, Estelle Winwood, Josephine Brown, Marion Morris, Bethell Long.

Hide and Seek by Aurand Harris. Directed by Windsor Lewis. Cast: Jessie Royce Landis, Mark Roberts, Kathy Nolan, Tim Carlin.

The Empress by Elaine Carrington. Directed by William Bulter. Cast: Geraldine Page, Paul Stevens, Michael Galloway, Joseph Campanella, Judith Ives Lowery, Raymond St. Jacques.

Oh, Men! Oh, Women! by Edward Chodorov. Directed by Franchot Tone. Cast: Franchot Tone, Betsy von Furstenberg, Lorette Leversee, Dana Elcar, Patrick O'Neal.

The Great Waltz by Moss Hart, Johann Strauss, Desmond Carter. Cast: Mia Slavenska.

Scandal at Montfort by Hugh Mills. Directed by Windsor Lewis. Cast: Arlene Francis.

A Palm Tree in a Rose Garden by Meade Roberts. Directed by Jose Quintero. Cast: Alice Ghostley, Barbara Baxley, Betty Lou Holland, Herbert Evers, George Voskovec.

1956

The Chalk Garden by Enid Bagnold. Directed by Charles Bowden. Cast: Lillian Gish, Dorothy Gish, Neil Fitzpatrick, Frances Ingalls.

Ballet Theatre. Directed by Joseph Levine. Cast: Nora Kaye, John Kriza, Lupe Serrano, Scott Douglas.

Posket's Family Skeleton by Arthur Wing Pinero. Directed by Peter Turgeon. Cast: Bramwell Fletcher, Betty Sinclair, Ralph Sumpter, Frances Tannehill.

27 Wagons Full of Cotton by Tennessee Williams. Directed by Peter Cass. Cast: Maureen Stapleton, John Cassavetes, Jules Munshin, Ed Heffernan.

A Marriage Proposal by Anton Chekhov. Directed by Peter Cass. Cast: Maureen Stapleton, John Cassavetes, Jules Munshin, Ed Heffernan.

Welcome Darlings. Musical direction by Peter Howard, Ted Graham. Cast: Tallulah Bankhead, James Kirkwood, Sheila Smith, Don Crichton.

The Gimmick by Joseph Julian. Directed by David Pressman. Cast: Larry Blyden, Patricia Smith, Tammy Grimes, Gene Saks, Heywood Hale Broun.

The Doctor in Spite of Himself by Molière. Directed by James Lipton. Cast: Jules Munshin, Betsy Palmer, Lawrence Fletcher, Hal Holbrook, Gemze DeLappe, James Ambandos, Marilyn Clark.

Beasop's Fables. Directed by John Philip. Cast: Beatrice Lillie, Fred Keating, John Philip, Shannon Dean.

Anastasia by Marcelle Maurette, Guy Bolton. Directed by Boris Tumarin. Cast: Dolores del Rio, Lili Darvas, Stephen Elliott, Boris Tumarin.

Knickerbocker Holiday by Maxwell Anderson, Kurt Weill. Directed by Frank Perry. Cast: Will Geer, Susan Cabot, Biff McGuire, Clarence Hoffman.

Anniversary Waltz by Jerome Chodorov, Joseph Fields. Directed by Dan Levin. Cast: Imogen Coca, Jules Munshin, Amy Douglass, Marilyn Clark, Paul Lipson, Rosetta Le Noire, Peter Turgeon.

The Rohm Affair by Larry Ward, Gordon Russell. Directed by John Marley. Cast: Robert Pastene, Martin Brooks, Rudy Bond, Jack Weston, Lois Nettleton, Thomas Carlin.

Television

The Buick Circus Hour [NBC-TV; 7 October 1952–16 June 1953] A variety program that ran every four weeks for one season. Written by Anita Loos, Jerry Seelen.

Produced by John C. Wilson. Directed by Frank Burns, John C. Wilson. Cast: Joe E. Brown, Dolores Gray, John Raitt.

APPENDIX B

~

Guest List for
Blithe Spirit Party (1944)

The following is a transcription of the invitation list for a party at the Los Angeles home of socialite Lady Mendl (née Elsie de Wolfe) on March 12, 1944, to meet the cast of the *Blithe Spirit* tour. The original list is housed in the John C. Wilson Theatre Collection on Noel Coward, General Collection, Beinecke Rare Book and Manuscript Library of Yale University.

indicates a guest was crossed off the list; it is assumed that they responded to say they could not come.

Mr. Jack Wilson's cocktail party for the *Blithe Spirit* company on Sunday, March 12, 1944:

The "Blithe Spirit" Company
The Mendl household
Mr. and Mrs. Joseph Cotton
Miss Jennifer Jones
Mr. George Cukor
Mr. and Mrs. William Goetz
Mr. and Mrs. David Selznick
Mr. and Mrs. Lewis Milestone
Mr. Felix Ferri
Mr. and Mrs. Samuel Goldwyn
Miss Edith Gwynn

Mr. John Calvert
Mr. and Mrs. Basil Rathbone
Miss Hedda Hopper
Mr. and Mrs. Irving Berlin
Miss Louella Parsons and Dr. Martin
Miss Greer Garson
Mrs. Nina Garson
Miss Gladys Cooper
Dame May Whitty and Mr. Webster
Mr. William Eythe
Mr. and Mrs. Paul Lukas
Mr. Whitfield Cook
Mr. and Mrs. Lemuel Ayers
Private Gilbert de Goldschmidt-Rothschild
Miss Audrey Wood
Mr. and Mrs. Charles Brackett
Mr. Moss Hart
Mr. Oliver Thorndike
Baroness Katherine d'Erlanger
Mr. John Walsh
Mr. Cole Porter
Mr. Howard Sturges
Mr. and Mrs. Alex Beesley
Miss Anne Baxter
Miss Ethel Barrymore
Mr. and Mrs. Frank Sinatra
*Mr. and Mrs. Ralph Blum
Mr. and Mrs. Herbert Marshall
Mr. Edmond Goulding
Mr. Roland Leigh
Mr. Sholto Balie
Mr. and Mrs. Charles Feldman
Prince Thurn and Taxis
Miss Katharine Hepburn
Mr. and Mrs. Otto Preminger
Mr. and Mrs. John Loder (Hedy Lamarr)
Mr. and Mrs. William Powell
Mr. and Mrs. Charles Boyer
Miss Ingrid Bergman
Mr. E. Y. Harburg

Mr. Harold Arlen
Mr. and Mrs. Nat Goldstone
Miss Mary Pickford and Lieut. Charles Rogers
Miss Inez Wallace
Mr. Leland Hayward
Mr. and Mrs. Fred Astaire
Mrs. Fell
Miss Ginger Rogers
Mr. Raoul Pene du Bois
Mr. Eddie Stevenson
Mr. and Mrs. Gilbert Adrian
Mr. Michael Arlen
Mr. Ludwig Bemelmans
Colonel and Mrs. Jack Warner
Mr. and Mrs. Ray Milland
Miss Ann Sothern and husband
Mrs. Cobina Wright
Mr. Rex de St. Cyr
Mr. Atwater Kent
Miss Joan Crawford
Mr. and Mrs. Franchot Tone
Mr. and Mrs. Frank Ross (Jean Arthur)
Mr. and Mrs. Cary Grant
Mr. and Mrs. Martin Arrouge (Norma Shearer)
Miss Ida Koverman
Mr. and Mrs. Orson Welles (Rita Hayworth)
Mr. James Mitchell Leisen
Mr. Billy Daniels
Mr. and Mrs. Louis Verneuil
Mr. and Mrs. Nigel Bruce
Miss Jean Duprez
Mr. Charles Walters
Dr. and Mrs. Joel Pressman (Claudette Colbert)
Major Anatole Litvak
Mrs. William Paley
*Mr. Tonio Selwart
Miss Kay Francis
Mr. Michael Romanoff
Mr. and Mrs. Brian Aherne (Joan Fontaine)
Mr. and Mrs. Walter Pidgeon

*Mr. and Mrs. Darryl Zanuck
Mr. and Mrs. Frederick Brisson (Rosalind Russell)
Mr. and Mrs. Zachary Scott
Mr. and Mrs. Gregory Peck
Mr. Laird Cregar
Mr. Georges Metaxa
*Miss Anita Loos
Mr. and Mrs. Danny Kaye
*Miss Marlene Dietrich
Mr. and Mrs. J. Cheever Cowdin
Mr. and Mrs. Gary Cooper
Miss Fanny Brice
Miss Gypsy Rose Lee
Mr. Gregory Ratoff
Mr. Monty Woolley
Miss Susan Peters
Mr. and Mrs. Nat Wolff (Edna Best)
Mr. and Mrs. Arthur Schwartz
Mr. and Mrs. John Green
Mr. and Mrs. Reginald Gardiner
Mr. Harry Crocker
*Miss Ida Lupino
Mr. and Mrs. Arthur Rubinstein
Mr. and Mrs. Walt Disney
Mr. and Mrs. Charles Laughton
Mr. and Mrs. d'Abbadie d'Arrast (Eleanor Boardman)
Miss Heather Thatcher
Miss Signo Hasse
Mr. and Mrs. William Wessberg

APPENDIX C

~

Sample Entries from the Pebbles Guestbook

Among the items that survive from "Pebbles," Wilson's Connecticut estate, is a leather-bound guestbook containing the original signatures of visitors from 1934 to 1956. In addition to notable actors and collaborators from Wilson's shows, guests included leading figures of that time from the worlds of photography, fashion and jewelry design, and European high society. The following is a listing of some of the guests, along with the dates of their visit.

1934

January 27–28: David Herbert, Cecil Beaton, Lucia Davidova
May 19–21: Joyce Carey, Raymond and Adrianne Massey
May 30–31: Gladys Cooper
June 2–4: Alan Campbell, Dorothy Parker
June 5–6: James J. and May Chapman Wilson (Wilson's parents)
June 8–9: Peggy Wood
June 13–14: Hope Williams, Katherine Elisabeth Wilson
November 19–20: Beatrice Lillie, Gladys Calthrop
November 26–27: Alfred Lunt, Lynn Fontanne, Osgood and Janet Perkins
December 15–16: Hope Williams, Louis Hayward, Beatrice Kaufman

1935

January 26–28: Yvonne Printemps, Pierre Fresnay

February 16–17: Joyce Carey, Princess Natalie Paley, Raimund von Hofmannsthal

March 9–11: Leslie Howard, Merle Oberon, John Munroe

March 30–31: Cecil Beaton

April 13–15: Grand Duchess Maria Pavlovna, Cecil Beaton, Tonio Selwart

May 31–June 1: Robert Boothby

1936

February 21–24: Princess Natalie Paley, Grand Duchess Maria Pavlovna

February 29–March 2: Adrianne and Raymond Massey, Dorothy Wilson Cart

July 17–20: Niki de Gunzburg, Denise Bourdet, Fulco di Verdura

July 31–August 3: Vernon Duke

August 16–17: (Horst P.) Horst

October 17–18: Joyce Carey, Neysa McMein, Anthony Pelissier, Alan
Webb, Edward "Teddy" Underdown

October 23–24: Lucia Davidova, Horst, Gladys Calthrop, Niki de Gunzburg,
Fulco di Verdura

December 27–29: Princess Natalie Paley, Noel Coward, Joyce Carey, Alan
Webb

1937

January 1–4: Dickie Gordon, Misia Sert, Roussadana "Roussy" Sert, Niki de
Gunzburg, Fulco di Verdura

January 22–24: Gladys Calthrop

April 17–19: Ina Claire, George Cukor

July 19: Connie Gilchrist, Flora Campbell, Sylvia Leigh

September 8: Attending the wedding of John C. Wilson and Princess Paley
were Rev. Joseph H. Twichell, May C. Wilson, Theodore and Dorothy
Wilson Cart, James T. "Bus" and Jane Wilson, John and Dorothy Hamilton, Noel Coward (best man), Gertrude Bent, Niki de Gunzburg, Florence
J. Haskell

October 2–4: Irene Browne, Alan Webb, Niki de Gunzburg

1938

September 10–11: Horst

October 15–16: Niki de Gunzburg, Fulco di Verdura

October 22–28: Roger Stearns
November 19–21: Neysa (McMein) Baragwanath, Glen Byam Shaw
November 26–28: Richard Haydn, Glen Byam Shaw
December 8–9: Anthony Pelissier, Niki de Gunzburg

1939

February 3–5: Michael Duff, Kenneth Carten, Gladys Henson, Bea Lillie
April 21–23: Reed and Diana Vreeland, Niki de Gunzburg
May 6–8: Penelope Dudley-Ward, Angus Menzies, Kenneth Carten
May 14–15: Laurence Olivier, Dorothy Wilson Cart
May 20–21: Richard and Dorothy Rodgers, Adrianne Allen
June 23–25: Reed and Diana Vreeland, Niki de Gunzburg
July 9–10: Laurence Olivier, Vivian Leigh, Roger Stearns, John Williams

1940

May 5–6: Noel Coward, Alfred Lunt, Lynn Fontanne, Hope Williams
May 18–19: Horst, George Hoyningen-Huene, Reed and Diana Vreeland
June 18–20: Edwina d'Erlanger, Reed and Diana Vreeland, Fulco di Verdura
July 4–8: Grand Duchess Maria Pavlovna, Horst, George Hoyningen-Huene
July 12–14: Tyrone Power and Annabella (Suzanne Charpentier)
July 20–21: Rudolf K. Kommer
July 21–23: Laurence Olivier, Vivian Leigh
July 26–28: Raimund and Elizabeth von Hofmannsthal
August 11–13: Syrie Maugham, Jean Schlumberger
September 14–15: Elsa Schiaparelli, Gogo Schiaparelli, Jean Schlumberger,
    Liza Maugham Paravicini
September 21–23: Tyrone Power and Annabella
October 12–13: Jack and Neysa (McMein) Baragwanath
October 17–18: Karinska (Varvara Jmoudsky)
October 26–27: Whitfield Cook

1941

May 1–4: Alfred Lunt, Lynn Fontanne
May 26–28: Whitfield Cook
June 4–5: Rowland Leigh
June 10–12: Stewart Chaney
June 14–16: Fulco di Verdura, Syrie Maugham, Liza Maugham Paravicini,
    Jean Schlumberger

June 30–July 1: Valentina and George Schlee, Fulco di Verdura
July 7–8: Tilly (Losch) Carnavon, Stewart Chaney
July 19–20: Pauline Fairfax Potter, Niki de Gunzburg
July 22: Tyrone Power and Annabella
August 11–13: Leona Corbett, Whitfield Cook
August 17–18: Tyrone Power and Annabella
August 22–23: James Shelton
August 30–September 2: Elsa Schiaparelli, Roger Stearns, Fulco di Verdura
September 5–6: Martin and Katharine Manulis
September 11–12: Stewart Chaney
November 15–16: Mainbocher, Douglas Pollard, Neysa McMein

1942

May 9–10: Miles White, Thomas Farrar
May 16–17: Mainbocher, Douglas Pollard, Pauline Fairfax Potter
June 29–30: Norman Bel Geddes and Frances Waite, Thomas and Beatrice
   Farrar, Miles White
August 8–11: Annabella, Jean Schlumberger, Fulco di Verdura
August 16: Lemuel and Shirley Ayers, Miles White, Herbert Kingsley
September 4–5: David Herbert

1943

No entries

1944

May 4–7: Miles White, Jack Birchenall
July 21–24: Miles White
August 12–13: Cecil Beaton, Annabella
August 25–27: Erich Maria Remarque
September 20–22: Maria Holst
October 26–27: Miles White, Jack Birchenall

1945

May 11–12: Maria Holst
May 20–21: Alan Jay Lerner
June 29–July 2: Rene and Bronja Clair
July 13–16: Patricia Lopez-Willshaw, Bill Harris

1946

March 23–25: Martin and Katharine Manulis
March 29–30: Miles White, Maria Holst
May 18–19: Cecil Beaton
May 29–June 2: Janet Stewart, Erich Maria Remarque, Niki de Gunzburg, Antonio Castillo
July 9–12: Jean-Pierre Aumont, Roddy McDowall
July 13–16: Rene and Bronja Clair
July 18–19: Reed and Diana Vreeland, Henri Bernstein, Antonio Castillo
August 2–6: Clifton Webb, Olivia de Havilland, Phyllis Laughton, Albert Kornfeld
September 27–29: Fulco di Verdura, Jean Schlumberger
December 28–29: Helmut Dantine, Martin Manulis

1947

March 21–23: Oliver Smith, Maria Holst, Martin Manulis
March 29–31: Charlie de Beistegui, Patricia Lopez-Willshaw
April 4–6: McCrae Imbrie
April 10–11: Gant Gaither, Nicky Holden, Robert Kidde
May 29–31: Hugh Martin
June 5–6: Otis Bigelow, Stephen Cole
June 11–13: Cris Alexander
June 28–30: Roger Stearns, Adrianne Allen, Robert Flemyng
July 12–14: John Mills and Mary Hayley Bell, Janet Stewart, Mainbocher
July 25–27: Horst, Niki de Gunzburg
July 28–29: Richard Carlson
August 4–5: Noel Coward, Graham Payn, Robert Flemyng, Rene and Bronja Clair
August 5–7: Otis Bigelow
August 18–20: Noel Coward, Graham Payn, George Cukor, Margaret Case, May C. Wilson, Barbara Cart
September 5–8: Noel Coward, Graham Payn
September 19–21: Graham Payn, Niki de Gunzburg, Antonio Castillo
October 3–5: Noel Coward, Graham Payn
November 14–16: Mainbocher, Douglas Pollard
December 19–21: Cecil Everley

1948

February 2–3: Cris Alexander
February 7–9: Lorn Lorraine
March 29: Michael Duff, John Battles
May 2: Clifton Webb
June 1–2: Lemuel Ayers, Arnold Saint Subber
June 5–7: Noel Coward, Gladys Calthrop
June 8–9: Arnold Saint Subber
July 3–5: James S. Bush II, Janet Stewart, Arnold Saint Subber
July 8–10: Miles White, Maria Holst
July 16–19: Lemuel and Shirley Ayers, Arnold Saint Subber
July 31–August 2: Margaret Case
August 2–5: Lemuel and Shirley Ayers, Arnold Saint Subber
October 1–2: Jean Schlumberger, Christian Dior, Niki de Gunzburg
October 16–17: Terence Rattigan, Jean Schlumberger, Martin Manulis
December 26–27: Syrie Maugham, Fulco di Verdura, Jean Schlumberger

1949

January 29–30: Noel Coward, Graham Payn
March 25–27: Jean Schlumberger, Christian Dior, Niki de Gunzburg
April 8–10: Clifton Webb
April 11–12: Gertrude Bent
May 19–22: Oliver Smith, Miles White, Anita Loos, Jay Robinson
May 28–30: Noel Coward
July 21–26: Alfred Lunt, Anita Loos, Robert Ingham
August 1–2: Agnes de Mille
August 6–8: Herman Levin, Oliver Smith, Anita Loos, Margaret Case
August 19: Attending the fiftieth birthday of John C. Wilson were Cornel
    and Patricia Knight Wilde, John Baragrey and Louise Larabee, Martin and
    Katharine Manulis, Martha Louise Knill, Laurence Langner and Armina
    Marshall, Ralph Lycett, Dorothea Harding, Nancy Ryan, Elfi von Kant-
    zow, Dorothea Harding, Robert Ingham, Bob Kidde, Don Glenn, Bob
    Shaw
August 22–23: Anita Loos, Miles White
August 29–30: Carol Channing, Anita Loos, Oliver Smith
September 16–18: Valentina, Antonio Castillo, Horst
October 15–16: Anita Loos, Niki de Gunzburg
October 21–23: Christian Dior

October 30–31: Terence Rattigan, Irene Selznick, Binkie Beaumont, Fulco di Verdura

December 10–11: Noel Coward, Graham Payn, Joyce Carey, Frank L. Thompson

December 26–27: Anita Loos, Syrie Maugham

1950

April 2: Christian Dior, Patricia Lopez-Willshaw

May 27–29: John Sutro, Anita Loos

June 24–26: Valetin Parera

July 3–4: Gregory Ratoff, Tallulah Bankhead

July 5–6: Bruce MacCallister

July 8–9: Jane Bowles, Oliver Smith, Jimmy Welch, Frank L. Thompson

July 22–25: Jane Bowles, Oliver Smith, Robert Ingham

July 29–31: William Marchant, Margaret Case

September 2–4: Noel Coward

September 9–16: Noel Coward

September 10: Valentina and George Schlee

September 16–18: Anita Loos

October 28–29: Valetin Parera, Christian Dior

1951

April 27–30: Federico Pallavicini

May 25–27: Noel Coward, Niki de Gunzburg

May 30–June 1: Frank Thompson

June 11–13: Bob Tallman

June 23–25: Anita Loos, Oliver Smith

July 7–8: Claudette Colbert, Anita Loos, Alan Campbell

July 20–24: Margaret Case, Howard Sturges, Niki de Gunzburg

July 23: Chester (Chet) Stratton

August 11: Toby Rowland

August 12: Claudette Colbert

September 23: Mainbocher

October 5–8: Alfred Lunt, Lynn Fontanne, Valentina

November 4: Christian Dior, Valentina

November 17–18: Jean-Pierre Aumont, Lady Juliet Duff, Niki de Gunzburg

December 1–3: Anita Loos

1952

April 6: Federico Pallavicini, Anita Loos
April 13: Valetin and Anne Parera, Antonio Castillo
August 21–24: Bob Tallman
September 20–21: Terence Rattigan, Alan Webb
October 9: Margaret Case
October 12: Frith Banbury
November 9–10: Terence Rattigan, Frith Banbury

1953

March 20–23: Rolf Gerard, Mary Astor
April 27: Tyrone Power and Linda Christian
April 28–May 2: Frank Thompson, Stanley Simmons
June 18–19: Michael Abbott
July 3–6: Tyrone Power and Linda Christian
July 12–15: Richard de Menocal, Janet Stewart
July 20–21: Horst, Nicholas Lawford
July 25–27: Anita Loos
August 10–11: Michael Abbott
August 17–18: Howard Erskine
October 28–November 2: Gant Gaither, Lex Richards

1954

May 2–4: Richard Reardon
May 9–11: Richard de Menocal, Janet Stewart, Lex Richards
May 22–25: Edward Padula
May 28–30: Frank Thompson
June 11–13: Anita Loos, Federico Pallavicini
July 24–25: Anita Loos, Annabella, Niki de Gunzburg
August 14–16: Gordon Jenkins, Howard Hoyt, Lex Richards, Gant Gaither
September 11–12: David Brooks
October 19–20: Martin and Katharine Manulis

1955

June 27: Melissa Weston
July 7–8: Byron Mitchell

August 29: Henry Reid Wall, Oliver Smith
September 7: Madison Myers
September 25–26: Cecil Beaton, Anita Loos

1956

May 22–23: Madison Myers
June 1–3: Anita Loos, Gant Gaither
June 22–24: Gant Gaither, Madeleine (Hurlock) Sherwood
August 4–5: Frank Thompson, Madeline Sherwood
September 8–9: Noel Coward
September 21–23: Lex Richards
September 24–25: Madison Myers
October 27–28: Anita Loos, Gant Gaither

APPENDIX D

∼

Notable Photographers

During his career, a number of leading high-society and celebrity photographers were close friends with Wilson and his wife, Princess Natalie Paley, who modeled for *Vogue* and other publications. Studio portraits that are part of the John C. Wilson Archive include photographs by the following:

Cris Alexander (1920–2012)
Cecil Beaton (1904–1980)
Maurice Beck (1866–1960), with Helen Macgregor
Marcus Blechman (1922–2010)
Ira L. Hill (1877–1947)
Horst P. Horst (1906–1999)
George Platt Lynes (1907–1955)
Irving Penn (1917–2009)

APPENDIX E

~

List of Explanatory Boxes

The following people, places, and titles have individual boxes written by the editors. Listed in alphabetical order, they are followed by the page number on which they appear.

Bibliography

Atkinson, Brooks. *Broadway*, rev. ed. New York: Macmillan, 1974.

Banham, Martin, ed. *The Cambridge Guide to Theatre*. New York: Cambridge University Press, 1992.

Bankhead, Tallulah. *Tallulah: My Autobiography*. Jackson: University of Mississippi Press, 1951.

Bawden, Liz-Anne. *The Oxford Companion to Film*. New York: Oxford University Press, 1976.

Behrman, S. N. *People in a Diary: A Memoir*. New York: Little, Brown & Co., 1972.

The Best Plays. 89 editions. Editors: Garrison Sherwood and John Chapman (1894–1919); Burns Mantle (1919–1947); John Chapman (1947–1952); Louis Kronenberger (1952–1961); Henry Hewes (1961–1964); Otis Guernsey Jr. (1964–2000); Jeffrey Eric Jenkins (2000–2008). New York: Dodd, Mead & Co., 1894–1988; New York: Applause Theatre Book Publishers, 1988–1993; New York: Limelight Editions, 1994–2008.

Bloom, Ken. *Broadway: An Encyclopedic Guide to the History, People, and Places of Times Square*. New York: Facts on File, 1991.

Bloom, Ken, and Frank Vlastnik. *Broadway Musicals: The 101 Greatest Shows of All Time*. New York: Black Dog & Leventhal, 2004.

Bordman, Gerald, and Richard Norton. *American Musical Theatre: A Chronicle*, 4th ed. New York: Oxford University Press, 2010.

———. *American Theatre: A Chronicle of Comedy and Drama, 1914–1930*. New York: Oxford University Press, 1995.

———. *American Theatre: A Chronicle of Comedy and Drama, 1930–1969*. New York: Oxford University Press, 1996.

Bordman, Gerald, and Thomas S. Hischak. *The Oxford Companion to American Theatre*, 3rd ed. New York: Oxford University Press, 2004.

Brown, Jarod. *The Fabulous Lunts: A Biography of Alfred Lunt and Lynn Fontanne*. New York: Simon & Schuster, 1988.

Channing, Carol. *Just Lucky I Guess: A Memoir of Sorts*. New York: Simon & Schuster, 2002.

Citron, Stephen. *Noel and Cole: The Sophisticates*. New York: Hal Leonard, 2005.

Contemporary Theatre, Film, and Television: Who's Who. Vols. 1–60. Detroit, MI: Gale Research, 1978–2004.

Coward, Noel. *Future Indefinite*. 1954; reprint, London: Bloomsbury Methuen, 2004.

———. *Present Indicative.* 1937; reprint, London: Bloomsbury Methuen, 2014.

Day, Barry. *The Letters of Noel Coward*. New York: Alfred A. Knopf, 2007.

Edge, Deckle. *Design for Living: Alfred Lunt and Lynn Fontanne*. New York: Alfred A. Knopf, 2003.

Farley, Alan. *Speaking of Noel Coward: Interviews by Alan Farley*. Bloomington, IN: AuthorHouse, 2013.

Ganzl, Kurt. *Ganzl's Encyclopedia of the Musical Theatre*. New York: Schirmer, 1993.

Green, Stanley. *Broadway Musicals Show by Show*, 6th ed. Milwaukee, WI: Hal Leonard, 2008.

———. *Encyclopedia of the Musical Theatre*. New York: Dodd, Mead & Co., 1976.

———. *Hollywood Musicals Year by Year*, 2nd ed. Milwaukee, WI: Hal Leonard, 1999.

———. *The World of Musical Comedy*. New York: A. S. Barnes & Co., 1980.

Helburn, Theresa. *A Wayward Quest*. New York: Little, Brown, 1960.

Henderson, Mary C. *Theater in America*. New York: Harry N. Abrams, 1986.

Herbert, Ian, ed. *Who's Who in the Theatre*. 1912; reprint, London: Pitman, 1981.

Hischak, Thomas S. *Broadway Plays and Musicals*. 2009; reprint, Jefferson, NC: McFarland, 2015.

———. *Enter the Players: New York Stage Actors in the Twentieth Century*. Lanham, MD: Scarecrow Press, 2004.

———. *The Oxford Companion to the American Musical*. New York: Oxford University Press, 2008.

Hoare, Philip. *Noel Coward: A Biography*. New York: Simon & Schuster, 1995.

Kantor, Michael, and Laurence Maslon. *Broadway: The American Musical*. New York: Bullfinch Press, 2004.

Katz, Ephraim. *The Film Encyclopedia*, 3rd ed. New York: Harper Perennial, 1998.

Laffey, Bruce. *Beatrice Lillie: The Funniest Woman in the World*. London: Robson Books, 1989.

Langner, Lawrence. *The Magic Curtain*. New York: Dutton, 1951.

Lesley, Cole, Graham Payn, and Sheridan Morley. *Noel Coward and His Friends*. New York: William Morrow and Company, 1979.

———. *Remembered Laughter: The Life of Noel Coward*. New York: Random House, 1978.

Lillie, Beatrice, with John Philip and James Brough. *Every Other Inch a Lady: An Autobiography*. New York: Doubleday, 1972.

Lobenthal, Joel. *Tallulah! The Life and Times of a Leading Lady*. New York: Harper-Collins, 2008.

Loos, Anita. *Cast of Thousands*. New York: Grosset & Dunlap, 1977.

———. *A Girl Like I: An Autobiography*. New York: Viking, 1966.

Mander, Raymond, and Joe Mitchenson. *The Theatrical Companion to Coward*. London: Salisbury Square, 1957.

Mast, Gerald. *Can't Help Singin': The American Musical on Stage and Screen*. Woodstock, NY: Overlook Press, 1987.

McBrien, William. *Cole Porter*. New York: Vintage, 2000.

Mordden, Ethan. *Beautiful Mornin': The Broadway Musical in the 1940s*. New York: Oxford University Press, 1999.

———. *Sing for Your Supper: The Broadway Musical in the 1930s*. New York: Palgrave Macmillan, 2005.

Morella, Joe, and George Mazzei. *Genius and Lust: The Creativity and Sexuality of Cole Porter and Noel Coward*. New York: Carroll & Graf, 1995.

Morley, Sheridan. *Gertrude Lawrence: A Biography*. New York: McGraw-Hill, 1984.

Norton, Richard C. *A Chronology of American Musical Theatre*. New York: Oxford University Press, 2002.

Payn, Graham. *My Life with Noel Coward*. New York: Hall Leonard, 1996.

———, ed. *The Noel Coward Diaries*. New York: Little, Brown, 1982.

Schwartz, Charles. *Cole Porter: A Biography*. Cambridge, MA: DaCapo, 1979.

Smith, Cecil, and Glenn Litton. *Musical Comedy in America*, 2nd ed. New York: Theatre Arts Books, 1981.

Smith, David. *Sitting Pretty: The Life and Times of Clifton Webb*. Jackson: University of Mississippi Press, 2011.

Somerset-Ward, Richard. *An American Theatre: The Story of Westport Country Playhouse, 1931–2005*. New Haven, CT: Yale University Press, 2005.

Suskin, Steven. *Opening Night on Broadway: A Critical Quotebook of the Golden Era of the Musical Theatre*. New York: Schirmer, 1990.

Teichmann, Howard. *Smart Aleck: The Wit, World, and Life of Alexander Woollcott*. New York: Morrow, 1976.

Traubner, Richard. *Operetta: A Theatrical History*. Garden City, NY: Doubleday, 1983.

Wilmeth, Don. B., and Tice Miller, eds. *Cambridge Guide to American Theatre*. New York: Cambridge University Press, 1993.

Index

255

~

About the Author

John C. Wilson (1899–1961) was a prominent American theater producer and director during the golden age on Broadway and in London. His theatrical career began as business manager for Noel Coward, and he went on to produce and/or direct most of Coward's plays in the United States, including *Private Lives*, *Blithe Spirit*, *Present Laughter*, and *Tonight at 8:30*. Wilson was also long associated with famous acting couple Alfred Lunt and Lynn Fontanne, presenting several of their New York and London hits, including *The Pirate*, *There Shall Be No Night*, *The Taming of the Shrew*, and *Quadrille*. Among the other Broadway successes he produced were *The Winslow Boy*, *The Lady's Not for Burning*, and John Gielgud's *The Importance of Being Earnest*. Wilson was also an acclaimed director of musicals, staging such works as *Gentleman Prefer Blondes*, *Bloomer Girl*, the 1943 revival of *A Connecticut Yankee*, and *Kiss Me, Kate*. He was general manager of the Westport Country Playhouse in the 1940s and 1950s, bringing Hollywood stars to the Connecticut theater and making it one of the most famous summer stock playhouses in the nation. Wilson was married to Russian princess and *Vogue* model Natalie Paley, and the couple moved among high society in Europe and the United States with the likes of Noel Coward, Beatrice Lillie, Cole Porter and Linda Porter, Elsa Maxwell, Louis B. Mayer, Anita Loos, Gertrude Lawrence, and Tallulah Bankhead.

~

About the Editors

Thomas S. Hischak is an internationally recognized author and teacher in the performing arts and author of twenty-four nonfiction books about film, popular music, and theater, including *The Oxford Companion to the American Musical, The Encyclopedia of Film Composers, Through the Screen Door, Disney Voice Actors, American Plays and Musicals on Screen, The Tin Pan Alley Encyclopedia, Film It with Music, The Disney Song Encyclopedia, American Literature on Stage and Screen,* and *The Oxford Companion to American Theatre.* He is also the author of thirty-three published plays which are performed in the United States, Canada, Great Britain, and Australia. Hischak is Professor of Theatre at the State University of New York at Cortland and a Fulbright scholar who has taught and directed in Greece, Lithuania, and Turkey.

Jack Macauley is great nephew and godson of John C. Wilson and executor of the John C. Wilson Archive. He has worked extensively as a senior executive advisor in international corporate communications and corporate affairs strategy, representing individuals and companies in the United States, Western Europe, Latin America, Asia, and Australia. A graduate of the School of Journalism and Mass Communication at the University of North Carolina, Macauley spent the early part of his career in print, radio, and television news, as well as sports reporting, in Chapel Hill and Winston-Salem, North Carolina. He is a native of New Hope, Pennsylvania, and now resides with his wife Molly in Wilton, Connecticut.